STUCK
IN THE
MIDDLE

STUCK IN THE MIDDLE

Is Fiscal Policy Failing the Middle Class?

Antonio Estache
Danny Leipziger

editors

BROOKINGS INSTITUTION PRESS
Washington, D.C.

Copyright © 2009

THE BROOKINGS INSTITUTION
1775 Massachusetts Avenue, N.W., Washington, DC 20036.
www.brookings.edu

Library of Congress Cataloging-in-Publication data

Stuck in the middle: is fiscal policy failing the middle class? / edited by Antonio Estache and Danny Leipziger.
    p.   cm.
Includes bibliographical references and index.
Summary: "Examines both economic and social public policy initiatives in its assertion that enhancing the welfare of people in developed and developing nations requires an explicit focus on the middle class"—Provided by publisher.
  ISBN 978–0–8157–0284–9 (pbk. : alk. paper)
  1. Fiscal policy—Case studies. 2. Middle class—Government policy—Case studies.
I. Estache, Antonio. II. Leipziger, Danny M. III. Title.
HJ192.5.S78 2009
339.5'2—dc22   2009000818

9 8 7 6 5 4 3 2 1

The paper used in this publication meets minimum requirements of the American National Standard for Information Sciences—Permanence of Paper for Printed Library Materials: ANSI Z39.48-1992.

Typeset in Adobe Garamond

Composition by Circle Graphics, Inc.
Columbia, Maryland

Printed by R. R. Donnelley
Harrisonburg, Virginia.

Contents

Foreword

I t is well established that many more people consider themselves to be part of the middle class than actual income data would substantiate. And the economic success of the middle class is often seen as synonymous with welfare gains in societies in both developed and developing countries. Yet our ability to accurately tell how the plethora of public policy interventions affects the middle class is not at all well developed. The premise of this collection of papers is that for governments to sustain political support for cohesive national economic policies that are welfare enhancing, the interests of the middle of the income distribution need to be addressed, and the first step in this process is to document and analyze better the distributional consequences of fiscal policies.

The editors of this volume, Antonio Estache and Danny Leipziger, argue in their introductory chapter that how nations deal with the middle 50 to 60 percent of the income distribution has profound implications for development success in poor countries. Evidence supports the view that in the high-performing countries of East Asia, it has been the burgeoning middle class that has benefited most from development and contributed most to rising incomes. This is seen in South Korea, Singapore, and other rapidly advancing states and is increasingly seen nowadays in China, and perhaps soon in India and Vietnam as well. It is the nonrich, nonpoor part of society for which the bulk of new jobs needs to be created, and it is the consumption of that segment that drives economic growth beyond the initial export phase. These dynamics are well explored in the recent Commission on Growth and Development chaired by Michael Spence, and they underlie the efforts of institutions dedicated to poverty alleviation and economic development.

What makes this volume somewhat unique is the fact that the authors cover political and economic issues of distribution and that they look at developed and developing countries. This broad brush treatment highlights the importance of maintaining a middle-class focus for economic policies as the mainstay of sustainable political economy milieus necessary to promote reforms. In the absence of this, either elite capture or very narrowly focused and (in the view of authors) ultimately ineffective antipoverty programs emerge that do not have sufficient support to be sustained. The editors go one step further and argue that a failure to deal adequately with distributional aspects at home ultimately spills over into the international arena and threatens globalization. The tendency for those in the middle who are economically disadvantaged to blame free trade for job or income losses is pronounced. The view that protectionism of various sorts is in the national interest stems from the reality that governments are often unable to manage the grievances associated with economic losses of globalization even though the gains of economic openness far outweigh the losses.

The starting point from a public policy point of view is solid distributional analysis. The citizenry needs to know who benefits from individual economic programs, who pays for which taxes, and most importantly, how these public policies add up in terms of net benefits accruing to various income groups. This work was pioneered by Joseph Pechman and others at the Brookings Institution more than two decades ago. Pechman's *Who Paid the Taxes, 1966–85?* study published in 1985 is exactly the kind of analysis that Estache and Leipziger are advocating on a broader scale. The purpose of their volume is not to answer questions but rather to provoke a deeper questioning of the impacts of public expenditures and taxes on income groups in the hope that this will enrich policy debates and debunk poor policy choices that are adopted in the absence of broad popular support. Their underlying hypothesis is that those stuck in the middle can be useful allies for the less fortunate only if their own interests are adequately addressed.

JUSTIN YIFU LIN
Senior Vice President and Chief Economist
World Bank

1

Overview: Fiscal Policy, Distribution, and the Middle Class

ANTONIO ESTACHE AND DANNY LEIPZIGER

The economics of distribution has long dominated economic policy debates. The issue of income distribution in rich countries has centered on the question of who gains from public expenditures and who pays for them. In the United States, this discourse was aided analytically by the path-breaking work of Joseph Pechman more than thirty years ago.[1] His research at the Brookings Institution helped us understand not only who benefited from what kind of expenditure but also how they stacked up when aggregated across expenditure categories. Work on fiscal incidence has long been a central part of the economic policy debate as well, beginning long before, but aided by, Arnold Harberger and Richard Musgrave and others.[2] One of the outcomes of this analysis in the United States has been a recurring concern for the fairness of the system and, in particular, concern for the extent to which the middle class was being effectively disadvantaged by fiscal policies.

This concern for greater equity in fiscal policies has been a very high profile issue in Europe as well, where the advent of the European Union has placed a huge premium on the reduction of income disparities among members. It may be said that a large share of the significant gains of new entrants is attributable to the expenditure policies of the European Union. This income convergence

1. See, for instance, Pechman (1985).
2. See McClure (1975) for an overview.

within the EU has been mirrored by distributional changes within countries as well.

The incidence of tax and expenditure policies across income groups has had a profound effect on disposable incomes. The Luxembourg Income Study (LIS) reports very large differences between the ex ante and ex post income distributions for the full spectrum of the income distribution.[3] The net result is that while the pretax and transfer distribution of income in France is quite similar to that in the United States, for example, after government intervention, the distribution in France, like much of Europe, is seen to be much more egalitarian.

In a political economy sense, there is a strong argument that the validity of the underlying economic model requires broad public support in democratic societies and that wide disparities in income may give rise to questions about the course of economic policy. Populist policies and populist regimes emerge during periods when large portions of the public feel that they have little stake in the system because of basic unfairness of government policy and economic outcomes that dramatically favor the privileged.

This fundamental preoccupation with distribution has an even greater significance in developing countries, where the gap between the haves and the have-nots is larger and where many of the have-nots have tended to be below the poverty line or other measures of basic economic subsistence. The issue of how the quality and distribution of growth mattered for development was pioneered by Hollis Chenery and others and has remained a core feature of the development discourse ever since, although with some fluctuations of the intensity with which these concerns were recognized as important.[4]

There is currently an intensive discussion in policy circles on the inclusiveness of growth as seen in the cases of very rapid growers, like China or Vietnam, as well as in those countries stuck in low-growth traps, such as Bolivia or Nepal, as well as much of sub-Saharan Africa. Research on the theme of pro–poor growth, perhaps a misleading term, has shown that poverty reduction is clearly unattainable without high and sustained growth performance. However, it also shows that the degree of poverty reduction attainable per unit of growth depends very much on the underlying distribution of income.[5]

---

3. The Luxembourg Income Study (LIS), a research center and microdata archive, was founded in 1983 by Timothy Smeeding, Lee Rainwater, Gaston Schaber, and a team of multi-disciplinary researchers in Europe. With support from the Luxembourg government, LIS and its staff became an independent nonprofit institution in 2002. LIS now includes data from thirty countries from Europe, North America, Australasia, the Middle East, and Asia. The database contains over 150 datasets, organized into five time periods (known as waves) spanning the years 1968 to 2002. See (www.lisproject.org).

4. Chenery and others (1974); Thomas (2000).

5. Bourguignon (2004); Commission on Growth and Development (2008).

The inability of many countries to match the growth, poverty reduction performance, and consequent welfare gains of China has led to renewed discussion of the fairness of the rules of the game, as seen in the collapse of the Doha Round of trade negotiations, the failure to meet the Gleneagles development assistance targets, and the slow progress, particularly in Africa, in meeting many of the Millennium Development Goals (MDGs).

Global as Opposed to National Concerns for Income Disparities

Behind these debates is the central policy question of whether global income disparities are narrowing or not. The convergence hypothesis still has strong adherents; however, the evidence is not overwhelming when the megacase of China is excluded. On balance, researchers do find a case for some modified form of convergence between the rich and the poor nations; yet, the speed is uncomfortably slow. This reinforces the view that globalization is not working for many countries and that the global distribution of income and wealth is not only terribly skewed, but it is also leading to negative economic consequences, be it in the area of illegal migration stemming from Africa, abandonment of market economics in some parts of Latin America, or economic instability in areas of the Middle East and South Asia. This has led to a reexamination of some models of economic development and to a new debate on development orthodoxy.[6]

Recent evidence points to a dual phenomenon of slowly improving income distribution among countries, namely, some global convergence combined with increasing income disparities inside countries (that is, greater inequality among income groups within countries). A recent World Bank report makes a persuasive case that by 2030 global income disparity will increase unless specific global redistributive actions are taken.[7]

Ultimately, what these debates point to is a widespread failure to see the limits of market outcomes that are underregulated, undersupervised, or underscrutinized. Commentators like Joseph Stiglitz have pointed out glaring examples of government inaction, and events surrounding the subprime crisis and its aftermath bear this out in an unprecedented way.[8] It may well be argued that it is a basic function of government to decide whether increasing income inequality is a socially and politically desirable outcome and then to deploy various aspects of fiscal policy to deal with this economic reality. Yet there is a sense that, too

6. See Dani Rodrik's 2006 article "Goodbye Washington Consensus, Hello Washington Confusion? A Review of the World Bank's Economic Growth in the 1990s: Learning from a Decade of Reforms."

7. World Bank (2007a).

8. Stiglitz (2002).

often, governments only pay lip service to this function or deal with it only as crises emerge. New research by Ricardo Paes de Barros and others takes a look at economic opportunity in Latin America in the form of a human opportunity index, which reflects the view that economic disparities arise because of initially unequal, and some would say unfair, endowments (for example, access to education and basic health care) and because of unequal possibilities of the market.[9]

What makes this observation highly relevant today is the interrelationship, real or perceived, between global and national determinants of income distribution. In today's globalized world, many see international events as key drivers of domestic distributional outcomes. Indeed, globalization, according to opinion polls such as the 2007 47-Nation Pew Global Attitudes Survey, is seen by many as the cause of rising income inequality, leading to national opposition to free trade.[10] Additional spillover effects are emerging as opposition to foreign ownership of domestic assets, be they ports and utilities in the United States or national industrial champions in France. The emergence of new sovereign wealth funds adds to the debate.

Thus the link between rising inequality at home and attribution, rightly or wrongly, to international commerce is fueling a current of discontent with globalization that goes beyond the global inequities raised by Stiglitz and others.[11] This discontent threatens to put a brake on further globalization efforts that are positive in a net welfare sense.[12] The policy lever that is missing is the ability of national governments to deal effectively with the "losers" or those adversely affected not only by international forces, such as highly competitive exports, but more generally by firm destruction in a Schumpeterian sense that is essential for dynamic economic progress. If this process of industrial "churning" as termed by Paul Romer were to be slowed by the politics of the disaffected, global welfare gains would actually diminish, shrinking the overall pie and limiting the ability of governments to provide effective economic offsets to the dislocated.[13] Avoiding this outcome is a basic function of fiscal policy, broadly defined to encompass tax and expenditure policy and political economy concerns with distribution. In our view the important proposition is that those we loosely call the middle class are not only affected by economic policy but also are indispensible for any solution to these policy challenges.

---

9. The Human Opportunity Index (HOI) measures the percentage of available opportunities needed to ensure children's universal access to basic services and their equal allocation. The index ranges from 0 (absolute deprivation) to 100 (universality). See Paes de Barros and others (2009).

10. Pew Research Center (2007).

11. Stiglitz (2002).

12. Spence and Leipziger (2007a, 2007b).

13. See Romer (2007) for an overview of his views (www.stanford.edu/~promer/Economic Growth.pdf).

The Central Policy Role of the Middle Class

For our purposes, the middle class makes up the biggest proportion of the income distribution, those between the 4th and the 9th income deciles, that is the majority of the population, the largest segment of the working public, and the largest group of voters. How this 60 percent of the income distribution fares is central to society's political and social stability. It is also essential to the direction of economic policy. In the roughly fifty years between the end of World War II and the end of the Clinton administration in the United States, the gains of robust economic growth and increased international openness were dominant enough to deal effectively with the job losses in declining sectors. Job creation during the 1990s, for example, was spectacular in the United States, and the additional benefits of expansion reaped enormous welfare gains on EU members. The job of fiscal policy was to provide slight to moderately progressive taxation (for the United States and Europe, respectively) and to finance programs that aided poorer households in the United States and the poorer countries and regions in Europe.

Evidence since 2000, however, shows a disturbing trend, at least in the United States. The rich are getting richer, the poor have seen their circumstances improve, and the middle class has lost ground. In Europe this has not been the case because of large-scale redistribution. In developing countries, there is a large distinction between the rapid growers, where a new and burgeoning middle class has emerged, and those regions where growth has been slow and the distribution of income has either stagnated or worsened. In regions like East Asia and, more lately, South Asia, very rapid growth has created a dual phenomenon of increasing ex post inequality with rapidly declining poverty and movement inside the income distribution toward greater gains for the middle class. Gains are not equal as economic opportunity is unevenly seized—and a strong case can be made for leveling the ex ante playing field by investing more in education and access to economic assets such as land and credit that can provide for better income opportunities. In Africa, Latin America, and the Middle East, however, the overall economic gains have not been sufficient either to alter dramatically the plight of the poor or to offset the inherent advantages of ruling elites, which has led to uneven gains of income growth and distrust of market solutions, domestically as well as globally.

In a wide range of countries, it can be argued, government policy interventions need to be calibrated better to determine who gains and who loses. This is as true for tax incidence as it is for the benefit incidence of subsidies or the distribution of basic government education or health services. Such analysis is exceedingly important for the fate of the poor, the disadvantaged, or those affected negatively by economic change, so that policy design takes their circumstances duly into account. The main drivers of that economic change may well be domestic in origin, based on the advent of new technologies and changing preferences. But the perception of the majority of the population (and certainly the perception reported by the mass media) is different, namely, that globalization is to blame for negative economic impacts of almost any reform.

The competitive forces that destroy jobs are seen by the public to be driven by global supply chains; cheap, and in some cases subsidized, exports; and uncaring governments that allow this to happen. Rather than deal with issues in the context of unfair trade or suspicions of foreign investors, it would be far preferable for governments to deal with these dislocations through effective, well-designed, and distributionally sensitive fiscal policies. This is the basic thrust of this volume of essays.

Policy Choices

Although the theory of public economics tends to be quite clear on the ideal normative approach to the design of fiscal policies, the adaptation of these approaches to the real world may be one of the most underestimated challenges faced by policymakers and politicians. There is no off-the-shelf guide to address some of the basic questions of fiscal policy design, and the policy trade-offs can be daunting.

Should governments spend more on social expenditures or on infrastructure? Should they focus on expenditure and tax policies that support growth or on policies that create jobs or both? Should they make tax systems more progressive or focus on being efficient revenue generators? Should governments deliver public services, or should they privatize as many services as they can? These concerns continue to dominate the political discourse in any developed country. Increasingly, however, the issue of fiscal policy design is becoming a preoccupation in developing countries as well.[14]

One of the important and complex challenges facing fiscal policy is how to manage concerns for redistribution and the associated equity-efficiency trade-offs. How do the choices on the composition of public expenditure influence these trade-offs? The honest answer for now is: we do not really know. While we are able to assess trade-offs at the level of a specific electricity rate change or water regulatory revision or in the design of a specific education voucher program, we do not usually have a very good grasp of the sum of these actions for groups of the population. The cumulative impact of individual programs as they affect the overall distribution is posing a significant challenge to governments as the citizenry expects efficiency and equity.[15]

---

14. See Adam and Bevan (2005); Perotti (2007).

15. See the World Bank's *Global Monitoring Report* (2007b) and the International Monetary Fund's *World Economic Outlook* (2007).

In practice, much of the debate on fiscal policies boils down to the identification of the winners and the losers. The importance of this identification has significantly increased with the spread of democratic election processes around the world.[16] The democratization process is not the impetus to delve more strategically into fiscal policy choices; however, it does highlight the importance of greater policy transparency.[17] One major concern is the lack of independent studies that analyze the redistributive effects of a given policy, particularly in a world of sound bites, partisan lobbying, and frankly, considerable disinformation.

Political Accountability

From a policy perspective, a key challenge stems from the fact that the desire for stronger political accountability fostered by increasingly democratic processes is often impeded by short political cycles. Typically, these cycles are shorter than the time span needed to realize the payoffs to many fiscal policies.[18] These short cycles force politicians to pay much more attention to the voice of the short-term losers of policies than to the long-term winners. Moreover, because the choice of fiscal policies matters to their election or reelection chances, politicians have strong incentives to focus on individual economic interventions rather than on more comprehensive welfare outcomes. This implies that long-term public policies have to be built around short-term policies, which will get the support of the majority.

Consistency between short-term policies and the desirable long-run policies is essential. Consider the desire to reduce poverty and to redistribute, which is central to many of the political debates across country groups. Time-consistent policies imply that fiscal policies aimed at helping the poor in the short run also have to be helpful to them in the long run. If short-run policies give the wrong incentives to the poor, poverty will continue to prevail, notwithstanding any transitory arrangements that may be adopted by well-intentioned policymakers. Energy price subsidies, for example, tend to gather considerable public

16. Clearly, as pointed out by Haggard and Kaufman (2008), the dynamics of democratization are different across countries. The way democracies emerged in eastern Europe, Asia, Latin America, or even western Europe differ and are bound to influence policy preferences. But these questions are not new. Hirschman and Rothschild (1973), for instance, already were concerned with the political viability of policies under increased democracy and recognized the breadth of experiences that researchers had to account for.

17. See Iversen and Soskice (2006).

18. The election pressure does not come from the national elections only; it also comes from subnational elections. In some countries with a high degree of decentralization, an election at some point can take place almost every year. Brazil offers plenty of evidence of the consequences for policy choices of such a frequency.

appeal, although they are inefficient and, since normally universal in their application, not particularly beneficial to lower-income groups relative to other policy alternatives.

Although the importance of time consistency is generally well understood in policy circles, it is not often central to the decisions of politicians. For many, the decision to do the right economic thing often is driven largely by the political support for these policies. In practice, this means that the long-run viability of some key fiscal policies is likely to be driven by the political process.[19] Recognizing this reinforces the need to be able to analyze the distributional impact of tax and expenditure policies in a coherent and consistent fashion. Populists are able to do this rhetorically, while others face greater difficulties in countering claims with serious precision.

Recognizing the importance of the electoral process in this context, social scientists have started to look for a "representative voter" to assess the viability of specific policies. A standard result in that literature is the widely used "median voter theorem." It suggests that if voters can be ranked along a single dimension (for example, for or against redistribution), if they essentially have a choice between two parties (that is, left and right), and if they have single-peaked preferences in a majoritarian democracy, political preferences will converge toward programs favored by the median voter.[20] In a wide range of circumstances, the median voter represents the middle class. This middle class exists in a wide range of forms around the world, reflecting differences in the relative importance of income, status, or education across countries. With the changes in political regimes observed in the post–cold war period, including the increased power of emerging large majorities in the developing world, it is hard to ignore the important role of this middle class.[21] It is also important to focus on the extent to which the middle class often may own, collectively, the swing vote that will make desirable policies sustainable.

Despite its appeal, the median voter hypothesis is not without problems, particularly in the context of a developing country. In some settings, the decisive

19. See Moller and others (2003) for a discussion of the determinants of the relative poverty and related redistribution experiences in fourteen developed democracies. Their study shows a lot more variance in experiences than expected. See Haggard and Kaufman (2008) for a wide range of experiences of developing economies. See also Iversen and Soskice (2006) for an interesting model of redistribution that explains why some democratic governments are more prone to redistribute than others.

20. See Gruber (2007).

21. One lesson of the twentieth century is that there is a strong correlation between the development of a middle class and a country's economic success. The prospect of becoming middle class has been a major incentive for the poor in the United States since the New Deal, and for the poor in Europe since the Marshall Plan, was adopted. In developing countries, economic success has often been measured as the growth in the income level of the middle quintiles of the income distribution.

voter in developing countries indeed may often be in the richest quintile. In others, the masses of voters may be more unpredictable than assumed by the median voter model, allowing for the emergence of populist governments in which the preferences are not skewed in favor of the middle class. This divergence from the standard result does not imply that the middle of the income distribution is not relevant; rather, it argues for a broader definition of the average voter and a better understanding of the interests of the various actors and of the coalitions they may support. Simply looking at the data for developing countries, for instance, suggests that there could well be a natural coalition between the poor and at least the lower-middle class who together are likely to represent well more than 50 percent of the population and hence be a potent voice in new democracies.

This essential role of the middle class has been recognized by politicians in many regions.[22] It is a recurring theme in the United States or in Europe, but it is also an essential concern in many developing regions.[23] Moreover, it has emerged in a wide range of contexts such as trade, privatization, and pension reform as being critical to public acceptance of reforms. Indeed, many observers blame the recent policy reversals in Latin America on a shrinking middle class.[24] Research on the role of the middle class in East Asia in the context of the post-1997 crisis comes up with similar conclusions, and current estimates of 400 million Chinese joining the ranks of the middle class within a generation add to the topic's policy relevance.[25]

The Middle Class in Fiscal Policy

It is somewhat surprising that the role of the middle of the distribution has not yet been documented systematically in studies assessing the distributional implications of fiscal policy. In spite of a robust literature relying on general equilibrium models to assess the incidence of a wide range of policies, there is relatively little evidence on how the differential effects of various sectoral expenditure policies are shared among various income groups. At the aggregate level, which is relevant when considering the political support for policies, this gap in our knowledge is most pronounced.

22. Although there is a wide range of definitions of the middle class, from economic to sociological, we focus here on the most traditional economic definition that defines the middle class in terms of the income decile the population belongs to. As discussed later in this book, this is itself a subject of debate since there is no consensus on the specific deciles that define the middle class.

23. See Frank (2007) for the United States or Chauvel (2006) for France and Europe. In developing countries, there is a recurring concern for this class; Birdsall, Graham, and Pettinato (2000) provide a useful overview of the economic and political role of the middle class in developing countries for long-term, sustainable market-oriented growth and poverty reduction.

24. See Gaviria (2006) for a recent overview in the context of an assessment of social mobility.

25. Shiraishi and Phongpaichit (2008); Hattori, Funatsu, and Torii (2003), for instance.

Most of the research of the last fifteen years has improved our collective knowledge of the relation between the support for specific policies (in particular redistribution policies), the possible coalitions between the various classes, and the possible veto rights available to the richest income classes.[26] Some of this research has also provided excellent insights on the nature of the middle class, the determinants of its income level, and the other socioeconomic characteristics that define the middle class over time and across countries. However, there have been relatively few studies that have analyzed the interactions of these various strands of research and the design of key fiscal policies.

The expectations of the poor and the lower-income groups of their chances of climbing the economic and social ladders are particularly important. Roland Bénabou and Efe Ok have emphasized the empirical relevance of this idea by testing the prospect of upward mobility (the POUM hypothesis).[27] For the United States, they found that only one-fourth of the households had real incomes above the mean, yet two-thirds had expectations of earning above average incomes. Although the recent deterioration of income distribution in the United States may have altered these positive perceptions, the authors argued that this optimism about mobility should lower the demand for redistribution because individuals with expectations of upward mobility, even if currently poor, anticipate the losses (for themselves and for their descendants) of any future attempt to transfer income from rich to poor. This means that the demand for redistributive fiscal policies is more likely to dominate when the prospects for upward mobility are low for a large spectrum of the distribution. Although this scenario is more likely to happen in a developing country, it is also a clear concern in Organization for Economic Cooperation and Development (OECD) countries as suggested by Robert Frank for the United States, Louis Chauvel for Europe, or Carol Graham for Latin America.[28] All of these authors raise the need to account for distributional concerns of the potential middle class to ensure the support for key fiscal policies in the various countries they study.

The general point of the most recent research may be that while tolerance for inequality seems to be higher where there are perceived prospects for upward mobility, it is very low when there is a perceived risk of downward mobility. These worries about downward mobility are for many observers one of the main engines of the policy reversals observed in many parts of the world. This concern strengthens the argument for governments to invest in comprehensive assessments of how individual fiscal actions and programs collectively hurt or help prospects for the well-being of various income classes. Analysis of fiscal

26. See, for instance, Acemoglu and Robinson (2006); Bourguignon and Verdier (2000).
27. Bénabou and Ok (2001).
28. Frank (2007); Chauvel (2006); Graham (2005); Graham and Felton (2005).

incidence is at the core of a government's legitimacy in the eyes of the public; yet it is not currently a central feature of policy analysis, much less policy decisionmaking.

What Needs to Be Done, especially in Developing Countries?

As is well known, incomes and standards of living depend on individual household decisions, public investments and their distribution, the range of opportunities that society offers (frequently limited by class and caste discrimination, geographical disadvantages, or gender), and overall country prospects.[29] In attempting to raise standards of living, governments often favor segmented approaches, which more than likely are encouraged in the poorest countries that are aid dependent by donors wishing to measure the impacts of individual programs. Countries are pushed even more strongly to follow such an approach when they are guided by an ever increasing list of Millennium Development Goals, well-intentioned international efforts to raise economic and social indicators of well-being.[30] Although impact effectiveness is terribly important for program design, what frequently gets lost in the desire to measure inputs, outputs, and even outcomes is the overall impact on individuals and firms of a myriad of economic policies. The key to determining the overall impact of public policy is having an integrated view that can be provided by distributional analysis that integrates the influences of various interventions that are distributionally non-neutral. The essential first step, of course, is good distributional analysis at the microlevel.

There are many examples of distributional analysis that have served to inform policy decisionmaking. One such example is the reform of the fuel price subsidy program in Indonesia in 2005, in which a general national subsidy that was consuming an ever-increasing share of public expenditure was reduced and replaced by a household income transfer to poor families. After having conducted an extensive campaign to identify poorer households and monthly consumption estimates, the authorities were able to effectively target the income transfers. In other countries, governments have opted to help create wealth for the emerging middle class, a segment of society that might normally have to wait for many generations to generate household assets—Korea, Hong Kong (China), and Singapore have offered subsidized housing to the middle of the distribution, principally the emerging urban middle class. Furthermore, poverty mapping provides a good indicator of where to target essential public services

29. See, for instance, Lewis and Lockheed (2007) for a discussion of how this plays out in the context of girls' education—and overall country prospects.

30. For an unconventional view of MDGs and counter arguments, see Easterly (2007); Leipziger (2008).

and allows governments to avoid the salami approach to the provision of services that has been shown to be less effective than a combination of services in reducing poverty.[31]

There are also numerous examples of poorly targeted programs that have had disappointing results. In Chile, a promising and well-targeted program of education vouchers has failed to demonstrably affect educational outcomes among the lower deciles of the income distribution because of other sectoral and societal barriers that dominate education. Free social services that are not means tested often waste scarce public resources; others that are of poor quality or involve informal payments to ration free services have also failed.[32] Privatization that has not properly dealt with distributional concerns and has focused either on maximizing public revenue collection or even on improved overall efficiency without concern for tariff design has yielded poor outcomes and a harsh backlash to a promising policy idea.[33]

In attempting to integrate the distributional impacts of a variety of programs, methodological challenges arise; however, these can be overcome with the use of, for example, appropriate models (see MAMS [Maquette for MDG Simulations], a new generation of computable general equilibrium [CGE] models, and so on).[34] But a bigger constraint perhaps is the tendency to bifurcate the population into rich and poor. This misses the middle of the distribution that is key to economic success and political support. Hence our concern for those "stuck in the middle" of the income distribution. The middle of the distribution, called for convenience "the middle class" with the necessary caveats added, was key to the successful development experiences of Korea, China, Malaysia, and Vietnam, as well as other fast-growing economies.[35]

Successful politicians and technocrats have used multiple interventions to affect economic outcomes and also have focused on the emerging middle of the distribution. In the same way that economy-wide policy packages were adopted to yield success in international markets, the fast-growing economies of East Asia focused attention first on the middle of the distribution in terms of access to jobs, housing, and education, later moving to health, pensions, and other social goods.[36] Even if a formal integration of fiscal actions may have been lack-

31. See Chong, Hentschel, and Saavedra (2004); also Bedi, Coudouel, and Simler (2007).
32. See Lewis (2006) on informal payments in health.
33. See Estache, Gonzalez, and Tujillo (2007).
34. Bourguignon (2004) offers a very readable overview of these various methodologies. MDG is Millennium Development Goal.
35. Country case studies for the Commission on Growth and Development are available at (www.growthcommission.org), including Hoffman and Wu (2008) on China, Yusof and Bhattasali (2008) on Malaysia, and Rama (forthcoming) on Vietnam. See also Leipziger (1988, 1997).
36. See Rodrik and others (1994).

ing, there was implicit recognition of the role that expenditure policies, if properly targeted, would have on the standards of living of the bulk of the population. Much of this was dependent on robust tax collection efforts, which are a sine quo non for distributionally sensitive expenditure policy.[37]

The integration of tax and expenditure policies with distributional analysis is a challenge in developed and developing countries. In developed countries, the integration of policies with analysis is a main driver of political outcomes, as the most exposed populations expect to benefit from public expenditures and to be protected from economic shocks. That is only possible if redistribution from rich to middle-income groups and to the vulnerable exists. If the middle pays a lot in taxes and the rich benefit, as is the perception in the United States today, then one element of social cohesion, not to mention support for economic change, is eroded.[38] In developing countries, in which the main challenge is to lift the majority of the population to a higher standard of living while also directing special attention to the poor that are left behind in any sea change of economic fortunes, the support of the middle class oftentimes is unsought by the ruling elites. This is a grave error in the long run and can lead to serious political reversals. Smart fiscal design and implementation are key drivers, in our view, of successful economic policy formulation.

The Politics of the Paradox of Redistribution Once More

Because the prospects of the middle class appear to be so central to the sustainability of policies aimed at supporting the poorest, there is a need to document more systematically the extent to which governments respond to the concern of the middle class. It is important that public documentation focus on the overall effectiveness of fiscal policies in meeting the needs of the various income groups.

In analyzing developed Western economies, Walter Korpe and Joakim Palme argued that the risk is that the more government targets benefits at the poor and the more concerned the government is with creating equality through equal public transfers to all, the less likely government will, in the end, reduce poverty and inequality.[39] According to them, this paradox is the outcome of three basic circumstances: the size of the redistribution budgets tends to depend on the welfare state institutions rather than on the needs; there is often a trade-off between the extent of low-income targeting and the size of redistributive budgets; and when large shares of the population, in particular the poorest, do not want or do not have access to private insurance, market-dominated distribution tends to be even more unequal than that found in earnings-related social

---

37. See Moreno-Dodson and Wodon (2007).
38. See Frank (2007).
39. Korpe and Palme (1998).

insurance programs. So even if the intention is to help the poor, real-world institutions and incentives have been such that they have failed to deliver on their initial intentions to help the poor, and often possibly some of the middle class as well. Of course, the specifics will vary across countries since they have different budget constraints, different institutions, and different capacities. Nevertheless, we would argue that there is a risk that for those societies that need it most, because of their relatively high levels of inequality, adequate support for redistributive measures is lacking, particularly if the middle-class role in building the necessary political support is ignored.

This paradox of redistribution is to some extent a core concern of this book. A substantial body of research suggests that the standard policy recommendation to target social policies to low-income groups is not proving effective; at the same time, very little research looks at how policies aimed at protecting the poor and, at the same time, the most exposed middle class can be coordinated for the good of both groups. In fact, very little attention is given to the degree to which the demands from these two groups converge. Somehow, the analysis of the role of the state has been dominated by normative concerns and has ignored some of the most relevant positive evidence that tends to drive or should drive policy decisions. When accounting for fiscal constraints, politics, and institutions, how can governments respond to the widest range of needs in a sustainable way? One argument running through this volume is that expenditure incidence across the full spectrum of the income distribution needs to be explicitly undertaken, and the results need to feed directly into policy formulation.

As public assessments of policy performance become more widespread around the world, the vote of this forgotten middle is bound to become more important to the design of policies. In that case, policies that are good for long-term growth and long-term poverty reduction should, we argue, also be pro–middle class. This is one key assumption that underlies the analysis of much of the research in this field, including each of the chapters of this book.

The challenges in testing this assumption are not minor. The first concern is the absence of high-quality, comparable data. This impedes rigorous diagnostics and also encourages partial assessments of fiscal incidence policies. The second is the large disparity in initial economic conditions and economic potential across countries, both developed and developing, which sometimes forces simplifications in interpretation that are unfair to the local circumstances. The third challenge is the large heterogeneity of political preferences for either efficiency or equity, preferences that tend to drive the support for specific policies but that lack the sort of aggregation that we advocate in assessing real impacts on target income groups.

The final challenge may be the diversity of views among social scientists on the relative importance of the middle class. We believe that the economic and political importance of the middle class and its evolution is a central research area for economists, political scientists, and sociologists. We are of the view that the sustainability and effectiveness of fiscal policies will affect a broad class of national and global policy strategies. We believe that globalization trends and the future trends in trade, flows of ideas, and migration will revolve in large measure around the manner in which nations deal with domestic equity and economic opportunity. The role of the middle class in setting this course in developed and developing countries will strongly determine the future pace of globalization and indeed will often drive it.

Being able to leverage the global economy is one of the key findings of *The Growth Report,* recently released after a two-year study of an independent Commission on Growth and Development led by Professor Michael Spence. For the vision of sustainable and inclusive growth to take hold, societies must believe that their investments will pay off and that government will deliver a higher standard of income in the future. Thus government must be credible to the majority of the public, and a good deal of that credibility will come from broadly available social services, job creation for a new industrial sector, and visible symbols to underpin future income expectations. The key instruments involve fiscal policies, and these cannot in the view of the commission be divorced from growth dynamics. Indeed, this volume proceeds from the premise that fiscal incidence analysis is necessary to create the political and economic underpinning of viable growth strategies.

This Volume's Contribution to the Debate

The book starts with an overview of stylized facts on apparent winners and losers of fiscal policies based on a simple review of basic statistics on aggregate government expenditures. Unless governments develop some sense of how the individual fiscal programs collectively hurt or help the well-being and the prospects of various income classes, they will have a limited ability to generate the necessary support for long-run policies that are beneficial to the nonelites. This is simply because they will not be able to assess the risks of rejection by some income classes, pressure groups, or coalitions who, on average, do not benefit from fiscal programs.

Looking at aggregate programs can, however, be deceiving. Although there are commendable efforts underway to improve assessments of individual programs using impact evaluation techniques, the ability of societies to look at the big picture is not as coherent. As observed in many countries, governments design specific programs that provide support for specific populations on specific needs (for example, local jobs, education, or health vouchers). However, these necessarily do not improve overall well-being very much, since the interventions are partial in nature and do not take interaction effects sufficiently into account.

Consideration of the overall effectiveness of aggregate programs is needed, however. Increasingly, governments are indeed being held accountable for the success of their individual and collective fiscal programs as well as for the degree to which programs are fair, as perceived by their citizens. All this argues for a broader look at public policy impacts across programs and across income groups.

In chapter two, Andrés Solimano focuses on the main dimensions of the role of the middle class in the development process. The chapter analyzes simple correlations, but it generates a very powerful picture of the main empirical regularities of the behavior of the middle class across countries. It focuses on its size, its role in the labor market, and its role in determining the size of the government. Ignoring the complex issues associated with the definition of the middle class, he suggests, given the evidence reported, that the more recent evidence validates and reinforces previous statistical assessments of the role of the middle class.[40] The stylized facts reviewed by Solimano show that, overall, the middle class appears to be more than ever an essential feature of politically sustainable economic development. This assessment results in a strong case to argue for a central role for the design of fiscal policy—even if it is not clear whether the middle class *leads* the process of economic development or rather *follows* it (or whether both evolve jointly). However, Solimano also shows why it is easy to underestimate this role. For instance, simple correlations find only limited entrepreneurial power (in a Schumpeterian sense) of the middle class, particularly so in low-income nations, or only a limited association between it and the evolution of the labor market, which may explain why many policymakers may have ignored the middle class. They also fail to recognize, for instance, that the income–middle class relation with per capita income is stronger (higher coefficients of correlation) for the lower-middle class than for the upper-middle class.

That hints at the need for policymakers and politicians to better recognize the heterogeneity of the middle class and hence government's ability to work on a broad range of coalitions to raise well-targeted policy concerns. For many fiscal policies considered while in crisis and at lower stages of development, the coalition between the poor and the lower-middle class is often the most likely one among all possible coalitions. That is because in these situations their economic interests are relatively aligned. In practice, that coalition would range from the percentiles 1 to 60 and hence represents a significant potential voting majority.

But this political leverage cannot be managed simply through government spending in an effort to buy votes. Indeed, Solimano, as well as Evelyne Huber, Jennifer Pribble, and John Stephens in their chapter, also shows that the correlation between the share of the middle class and the overall size of government, in

40. See, for example, Birdsall, Graham, and Pettinato (2000).

general, is not very strong and varies across countries ordered by income per capita levels. Moreover, an analysis of the composition of public expenditures reveals that categories of social expenditures, such as education, health, and perhaps housing, are in general not as redistributive as often claimed. As discussed in Markus Goldstein and Antonio Estache's chapter, all too often, only small proportions of these expenditures reach the lower-middle class and the poor. The main policy instrument to support that broad coalition seems to be more encompassing social protection programs.

In chapter three, Maurizio Bussolo, Rafael De Hoyos, and Denis Medvedev offer an interesting twist on the debate of the importance of the middle class, focusing on its importance at the global level. The interest of this approach is that it recognizes that globalization has increased global awareness, which in turn makes people more aware of income disparities at the global rather than at the national level. This is bound to result in political pressures on government policies. With that concern in mind, the third chapter presents projections of the global income distribution likely to emerge under the most likely GDP and population growth scenarios. Their simulations validate the need to consider the political economy arguments in assessing the role of the middle class and its importance for targeting fiscal policies. They show that three-quarters of total world income is controlled by only one-quarter of the world's population, implying that three-quarters of the population are likely to be unhappy with their fate unless they see credible prospects for some upward mobility. These political concerns are all the more likely to matter if one believes that even in a fairly optimistic growth scenario for the next two decades, during which, as a result, global inequality will drop, *within*-country income disparities are very likely to widen. And this is likely unless specific policy actions are taken to avoid this deterioration in income distribution. The authors suggest that this result may point to the need to revisit the balance between global and country agendas and to emphasize the case for an increased recognition of the importance of the shrinking middle class at the country level at a time when the middle class seems to be growing at the global level.

The risks are high since specific groups of people within countries may not be able to adjust to the resulting new wave of globalization and may be left further behind. Worsening in-country inequality can increase the risk of social alienation of people at the wide bottom of the distribution and hence the rejection of policies desirable to promote sustained, shared, long-term growth.

The effort to stimulate or reinforce the emergence of the global middle class in the transition to this long-term goal may be an effective solution to mitigate the risk of rejections of otherwise desirable policies. Bussolo, De Hoyos, and Medvedev suggest that under current policies, the share of this class in the global population is likely to more than double in the next twenty years. Since they will move closer to the median voter in many of today's developing countries, they potentially will play a much more important role in fiscal and international policies.

Ultimately, the main message in their chapter may be that governments cannot afford to ignore the need to address equity concerns when designing efficiency-oriented policies. Although trade-offs will inevitably arise and often these will be country specific, the necessity of equity-enhancing policies is likely to increase with the increased global power of the middle class.

In chapter four, Goldstein and Estache offer an overview of how effective subsidies in general have been at dealing with these growing distributional concerns. The chapter also offers an overview of what subsidies are and how they are designed to work, in particular to help specific income groups, and concludes with some advice on how to pick subsidies under a wide range of informational and capacity constraints. The experience reviewed suggests that subsidies continue to be one of the most common instruments used to implement targeted support to specific social groups, as suggested by Bussolo and his coauthors.

However, Goldstein and Estache show that although clear rationales for subsidies as an essential fiscal policy instrument to address redistribution concerns exist in economic theory, the practice often does not deliver on the promises. Many of the subsidies in the developing world are indeed often regressive, and many in the developed world have an unclear incidence. They argue that political economy is the major driving force for this unclear or undesirable incidence.

Although many subsidies are indeed regressive in an absolute sense, when viewed from the point of view of the pocketbooks of poor and middle-class voters, they are, however, often a relatively important source of income as well. This is why these groups will continue to provide political support for these subsidies. Moreover, in spite of their regressivity, politicians seem to recognize that some amount of leakage to the middle class likely will continue to be necessary to sustain support for a subsidy that actually does target the poor disproportionately. Well-targeted subsidies that only favor the poor will not get the political support of the middle class unless they get some of the benefits as well. In other words, the political logic will often give a significant role to the middle class in ensuring that the poor get their fair share of the subsidies, even if this share is lower than the economic logic would have expected.

In chapter five, James Davies reviews the evidence on the global distribution of wealth and discusses whether there is potential for policies that will build household wealth for the poor and the middle class. He looks for policies that will win majority electoral support, recognizing that middle-income groups in low- and even most middle-income countries are not truly middle class. Davies's contribution is to show that although subsidies—in particular for health care and education—are essential, there are far better interventions to deal with the concerns of the middle class, and in particular to build up middle-class wealth, than subsidies. His review of the international experience suggests that fiscal policies and institutions that allow the middle class to build and maintain wealth are instrumental in coalescing support for policies and programs that in the end are effective in fighting poverty.

Although his survey is wide ranging and generally optimistic, he points to the challenges caused by deficiencies in land administration, underdeveloped financial institutions, and a lack of mortgage insurance and loans for home buying or building that allow people to acquire the quintessential middle-class assets such as private housing.

Davies also makes the case for further development of savings opportunities and mortgage finance. He argues that fostering competition among financial institutions and making certain that microfinance organizations are not impeded is very important, as is ensuring that tax-sheltered savings vehicles are available for the full range of saving purposes. To make housing finance effective, it is important to have effective land administration (and in many countries land reform), the possibility of mortgage foreclosures that are not too expensive to enforce or too long delayed, and a system of mortgage insurance to make possible low down payments without threatening the stability of the lending institutions.

In chapter six, Carol Graham offers some insights on the scope and limits of the recent research on "happiness economics" that is conducted to get a sense of the demand, and hence the support, for public services by the population. This innovative area of research offers unique new insights that have the potential to guide policy decisions. By understanding the preferences of voters, politicians may be directed into particular aspects of taxation and expenditures that are most highly valued by the public. Even if pure distributional analysis yields different rank orderings of interventions, actual societal preferences can explain why some European economies, for example, seem to attain greater social content.

Graham's contribution to this volume is to show that the limitations of happiness surveys—and economics—are stronger than their potential to guide fiscal choices. Happiness studies can provide critical insights into the determinants of human well-being, in areas ranging from income, poverty and inequality, public health, and fiscal policy. The studies thus provide a tool to assess the relative weights that particular populations—and socioeconomic cohorts, including the middle class—attach to various public expenditures, such as health, education, and social insurance, which can, indirectly, help inform the design of fiscal policy. They also highlight high levels of frustration, particularly about insecurity and inequality.

However, for a wide range of reasons reviewed in her chapter—data, techniques, and theory—caution is necessary before directly applying the results of happiness surveys to policy and, in particular, applying them as a basis for the design of fiscal policy. For instance, she shows that because people are loss averse, more expenditure on social insurance and safety nets may result in higher reported happiness. However, because of intertemporal problems, the same surveys cannot yet guide how much policymakers should *trade off* these kinds of expenditures for those with longer-term returns, such as children's education or retirement savings.

Although the previous chapters were written by economists, the main reason why the middle class should matter to the design of fiscal policies is their steadily growing political importance at the local and global levels. The need to recognize that politics should drive some of the choices of which economic instruments to use seems to be the main message so far. The last chapter is the only one written by political scientists.

In chapter seven, Huber, Pribble, and Stephens offer a political take on the design of fiscal policies. They first survey the literature comparing the political sustainability of welfare systems and then assess the viability of welfare policies that are targeted to the poor but that ignore the middle class.

In the Latin American context, they argue that an effective redistributive social policy regime that is politically sustainable and that would build up the right coalitions would consist of basic flat-rate family allowances paid to the lower 60 percent of income earners, which are then slowly faded out between the 60th and 80th percentiles. Thus they define the middle class as having a fairly wide range of income.

However, Huber, Pribble, and Stephens also argue that money transfers alone will not serve their intended purposes. They argue that allowances should be tied to compliance with other important social concerns. For instance, tying allowances to school attendance and medical checkups for the children or to job training for unemployed recipients and integration into public sector jobs would have desirable social payoffs. It would include basic flat-rate "citizenship pensions" for the same income categories, supplemented by a mandatory public earnings–related notional defined contribution system for the entire population. It would further include investment in public preschool and in free, high-quality public primary and secondary education, as well as a unified public health care system with free access for the lowest three quintiles and an income-related fee structure for the other two quintiles. If all of this is financed by proportional taxation, it will be massively redistributive, as demonstrated in the appendix. This is true even if the benefits accruing to the second and third quintile are somewhat higher than those for the first quintile, and even if benefits reach into the fourth quintile on a declining basis.

The key, then, is to build social programs that are effective at reaching the poor, but which do not become "poor people's programs" because they entail basic rights to transfers and quality social services for lower, working, and lower-middle classes. This is not an easy task. Moreover, factors such as campaign finance, the media, and interest groups strongly shape the behavior of politicians and parties as well and may threaten the sustainability of some reforms.

Challenges Ahead

This collection of papers makes a strong case for a return to past efforts to spend more time thinking about the composition of public expenditure rather than simply focusing on levels of expenditure. Recurring fiscal crises often tend to focus concerns on the need to cut aggregate expenditure levels. The research reported here suggests that the popular support for desirable efforts to cut aggregate expenditure levels will often require a much better awareness of the political importance of specific expenditure categories. This support is needed to ensure the long-run sustainability of fiscal reform packages covering a wider range of public sector activities. In particular, the authors in this book make a strong case for the political importance of social expenditure in that context.

Ultimately, what the various chapters show is that because politics will drive the sustainability of fiscal policies, fiscal policies need to recognize the politics of distribution up front. In particular, policies need to recognize the coalitions that currently drive and will increasingly drive the politics of distribution. All evidence points to an acceleration of the central role of the middle class as a driver of these coalitions in developed and developing countries. The economic importance of the middle class will be such that it will not only drive local politics and hence policies, but that it will also increasingly drive global politics and policies as well. The adage of thinking globally and acting locally may well require an additional reverse perspective, namely, that to act responsibly globally also requires responsible local actions as a prerequisite. If those who feel "stuck in the middle" are indeed underserved by public policies at home, their voice will carry a clarion antiglobalization cry that will diminish economic welfare for them and others. This is the outcome that needs to be avoided.

References

Acemoglu, D., and J. A. Robinson. 2006. "Persistence of Power, Elites and Institutions." Working Paper Series 06-05. MIT, Department of Economics.

Adam, C., and D. Bevan. 2005. "Fiscal Deficits and Growth in Developing Countries." *Journal of Public Economics* 89, no. 4 (April): 571–97.

Bedi, Tara, Aline Coudouel, and Kenneth Simler, eds. 2007. *More than a Pretty Picture: Using Poverty Maps to Design Better Policies and Interventions.* Washington: World Bank.

Bénabou, Roland, and Efe A. Ok. 2001. "Social Mobility and the Demand for Redistribution: The POUM Hypothesis." *Quarterly Journal of Economics* 116, no. 2: 447–87.

Birdsall, Nancy, Carol Graham, and Stefano Pettinato. 2000. "Stuck in the Tunnel: Is Globalization Muddling the Middle Class?" Working Paper 14. Brookings, Center on Social and Economic Dynamics.

Bourguignon, François. 2004. "The Poverty-Growth-Inequality Triangle." Paper presented at the Indian Council for Research in International Economic Relations, New Delhi, February.

Bourguignon, F., and T. Verdier. 2000. "Oligarchy, Democracy, Inequality and Growth." *Journal of Development Economics* 62, no. 2: 285–313.

Chauvel, Louis. 2006. *Les classes moyennes à la dérive.* Paris: Le Seuil.

Chenery, Hollis B., and others. 1974. *Redistribution with Growth: Policies to Improve Income Distribution in Developing Countries in the Context of Economic Growth.* Washington: World Bank.

Chong, Alberto, Jesko Hentschel, and Jaime Saavedra. 2004. "Bundling Services and Household Welfare in Developing Countries—The Case of Peru." Policy Research Working Paper Series 3310. Washington: World Bank.

Commission on Growth and Development. 2008. *The Growth Report: Strategies for Sustained Growth and Inclusive Development.* Washington: World Bank on behalf of the Commission on Growth and Development.

Easterly, William. 2007. "How the Millennium Development Goals Are Unfair to Africa." Working Paper 14. Brookings, Global Economy and Development.

Estache, Antonio, M. Gonzalez, and L. Tujillo. 2007. "Government Expenditures on Education, Health, and Infrastructure: A Naive Look at Levels, Outcomes, and Efficiency." Policy Research Working Paper 4219. Washington: World Bank.

Frank, Robert. 2007. *Falling Behind: How Rising Inequality Harms the Middle Class.* University of California Press.

Gaviria, A. 2006. "Movilidad social y preferencias por redistribución en América Latina." Bogotá: Universidad de los Andes-CEDE (Centro de Estudios sobre Desarrollo Económico).

Graham, Carol. 2005. "Some Insights on Development from the Economics of Happiness." *World Bank Research Observer* 20, no. 2: 201–31.

Graham, Carol, and A. Felton. 2005. "Does Inequality Matter to Individual Welfare: Some Evidence from Happiness Surveys for Latin America." Working Paper 38. Brookings, Center on Social and Economic Dynamics.

Gruber, J. 2007. *Public Finance and Public Policy.* New York: Worth Publishers.

Haggard, S., and R. Kaufman. 2008. *Development, Democracy, and Welfare States: Latin America, East Asia, and Eastern Europe.* Princeton University Press.

Hattori, T., T. Funatsu, and T. Torii. 2003. "Introduction: The Emergence of the Asian Middle Classes and their Characteristics." *Developing Economies* XLI, no. 2: 129–39.

Hirschman, A. O., and M. Rothschild. 1973. "The Changing Tolerance for Income Inequality in the Course of Economic Growth." *Quarterly Journal of Economics* 87, no. 4: 544–66.

Hofman, Bert, and Jingliang Wu. 2008. "Explaining China's Development and Reforms." Working Paper. Washington: World Bank, Commission on Growth and Development (www.growthcommission.org).

International Monetary Fund (IMF). 2007. *World Economic Outlook.* Washington.

Iversen, T., and D. Soskice. 2006. "Electoral Institutions and the Politics of Coalitions: Why Some Democracies Redistribute More than Others." *American Political Science Review* 100, no. 2 (May): 165–81.

Korpe, Walter, and Joakim Palme. 1998. "The Paradox of Redistribution and Strategies of Equality: Welfare State Institutions, Inequality, and Poverty in the Western Countries." *American Sociological Review* 63, no. 5: 661–87.

Leipziger, Danny, ed. 1988. *Korea: Transition to Maturity.* New York: Pergamon Press.

———. 1997. *Lessons from East Asia.* University of Michigan Press.

————. 2008. "MDGs and Africa: An Alternative View." *PREMnotes* 116 (February) (http://go.worldbank.org/6TQRA8WPP0).

Lewis, Maureen A. 2006. "Governance and Corruption in Public Health Care Systems." Working Paper 78. Washington: Center for Global Development.

Lewis, Maureen A., and Marlaine Lockheed. 2007. *Inexcusable Absence—Why 60 Million Girls Still Aren't in School and What to Do about It.* Washington: Center for Global Development.

McLure, Charles, Jr. 1975. "General Equilibrium Incidence Analysis: The Harberger Model after Ten Years." *Journal of Public Economics* 4, no. 2: 125–61.

Moller, S., and others. 2003. "Determinants of Relative Poverty in Advanced Capitalist Democracies." *American Sociological Review* 68, no. 1: 22–51.

Moreno-Dodson, B., and Q. Wodon. 2007. *Public Finance for Poverty Reduction: Concepts and Case Studies from Africa and Latin America: Directions in Development.* Washington: World Bank.

Paes de Barros, Ricardo, and others. 2009. *Measuring Inequality of Opportunities in Latin America and the Caribbean, Conference Edition.* Latin American Development Forum Series. Washington: World Bank.

Pechman, Joseph A. 1985. *Who Paid the Taxes, 1966–85?* Brookings.

Perotti, R. 2007. "Fiscal Policy in Developing Countries: A Framework and Some Questions." Policy Research Working Paper 4365. Washington: World Bank.

Pew Research Center. 2007. 47-Nation Pew Global Attitudes Survey. Washington: Pew Global Attitudes Project.

Rama, M. Forthcoming. "Making Difficult Choices: Vietnam in Transition." Working Paper. Washington: World Bank, Commission on Growth and Development (www.growthcommission.org).

Rodrik, D. 2006. "Goodbye Washington Consensus, Hello Washington Confusion? A Review of the World Bank's Lessons of the 1990s: Learning from a Decade of Reforms." *Journal of Economic Literature* 44, no. 4: 973–87.

Rodrik, D., and others. 1994. *Miracle or Design? Lessons from the East Asian Experience.* Washington: Overseas Development Council.

Romer, Paul. 2007. "Economic Growth." In *The Concise Encyclopedia of Economics,* edited by David R. Henderson. Indianapolis, Ind.: Liberty Fund (www.stanford.edu/~promer/EconomicGrowth.pdf).

Shiraishi, Takashi, and Pasuk Phongpaichit, eds. 2008. *The Rise of Middle Classes in Southeast Asia.* Kyoto Studies on Asia. Melbourne: Trans Pacific Press.

Spence, M., and Danny Leipziger. 2007a. "Globalization and Income Inequality." Working Paper. Washington: World Bank, Commission on Growth and Development.

————. 2007b. "Globalization's Losers Need Support." *Financial Times,* May 14.

Stiglitz, Joseph E. 2002. *Globalization and its Discontents.* New York: W. W. Norton.

Thomas, V. 2000. *The Quality of Growth.* Washington: World Bank.

World Bank. 2007a. *Global Economic Prospects: Managing the Next Wave of Globalization.* Washington.

————. 2007b. *Global Monitoring Report 2007:* Confronting the Challenges of Gender Equality and Fragile States. Washington.

Yusof, Z., and D. Bhattasali. 2008. "Economic Growth and Development in Malaysia: Policy Making and Leadership." Working Paper 27. Washington: World Bank, Commission on Growth and Development.

2

Stylized Facts on the Middle Class and the Development Process

ANDRÉS SOLIMANO

The traditional concern of economists working on development policy has been the poor. The analysis of broader social structures and social classes, such as the middle class and the rich, is more the staple of work of sociologists and political scientists. However, this is starting to change. Economists are looking at the middle class as a source of entrepreneurship, consumer power, and social stability. These propositions, of course, need empirical verification.

As income per capita increases, people leave poverty and enter the pool of what we call the middle class. In the last two decades or so, this process has been taking place in China, India, and some countries in Latin America. The middle class is typically identified with a large range of occupations and professions and includes people holding professional degrees, such as academics, lawyers, engineers, and doctors, as well as clergymen and lower-level occupations different from manual workers. The "lower-middle class" (people whose incomes are closer to the poverty line) can be a source of policy concern, since it is a segment closer to and more vulnerable to fall into poverty. At the same time, individuals in the upper ranges of the middle class can eventually become "rich," propelled by higher education levels, ambition, effort, and social connections. The prototype view of the middle class is that of a rather conservative, risk-averse group

I would like to thank Antonio Estache for useful conversations and Diego Avanzini for outstanding research assistance.

that seeks stable jobs and predictable economic fortunes. For that reason, the middle-class worker is the typical employee of the state (ministries, state bureaucracies, public enterprises, decentralized agencies, and so on). Also, small and medium-sized enterprises (SMEs) are often assumed to be a source of employment and income for the middle class. Thus the state and the market can originate a middle-class segment in society. In this chapter some of these intuitions are tested empirically.

The middle class has also some distinctive expenditure patterns and aspirations. Middle-class people increasingly demand better quality education, health care, more sophisticated tourist services, and new housing. Although neoclassical economic theory assumes that an individual's welfare is chiefly dependent on his personal income (and consumption), there is increasing evidence that people care also about relative income and that social context is important in forming people's aspirations and perceptions of their quality of life. Such authors as Robert Frank, Richard Layard, and Carol Graham underscore this point.[1] These ideas are not entirely new, however. Older generation economists such as Thorstein Veblen and James Duesenburry made similar points long ago. Similarly, in the popular imagination, people in the middle class are often characterized as being concerned with other people's standard of living and relative welfare ("close to the Joneses but far from the Smiths").[2]

The recent interest in the middle class comes also from political economy considerations. Policymakers and international organizations are interested in mobilizing and sustaining political support for certain economic policies and projects. In the 1990s, the dominant model in developing countries and former socialist economies was market-oriented economic reforms. We still know little about how these programs affected the middle class. The retrenchment of the state may have reduced public employment and thereby harmed the middle class. In contrast, liberal professions, such as finance and economics, may have received a boost with economic reforms; pro–private sector policies also may have encouraged entrepreneurship. These different possibilities underscore the limits of referring to "the" middle class as a homogeneous group. We need to break down the middle class into various segments, because lower-middle-class people may be more akin to the poor, while the upper-middle class resembles more the rich. This chapter considers a lower-middle class and an upper-middle class in the empirical analysis.

This new emphasis on the middle class arises from the observation that stable, higher-income democracies often have a strong middle class and relatively low levels of inequality. In contrast, countries with highly unequal patterns of

1. Frank (2007); Layard (2005); Graham (2007).
2. See Cashell (2007); Daly and Wilson (2006); Birdsall, Graham, and Pettinato (2000); Solimano (1998, 2005).

income distribution and stratified social structures often have a weak middle class that may be less influential in shaping political preferences. Polarized and unequal social structures often contribute to social conflict and populist politics.[3] Thus a stronger and more stable middle class is often considered as a stabilizing factor in politics and economics.[4] The empirical evidence is favorable to this hypothesis. In fact, William Easterly has shown, on the basis of cross-country and panel econometric regressions, that a higher share of income for the middle class (and lower ethnic polarization) is empirically associated with higher income, higher growth, more education, and other favorable development outcomes.[5] It is important to devise policies on education, health, housing, and social security that consider the demands and specificities of the middle class, such as its quest for upward mobility and its role as a stabilizing segment in society.

This chapter is organized into four sections. The second section that follows elaborates more on the reasons for a new interest in the middle class and takes up some issues of definition. The third section identifies the main economic and political economy variables that are correlated with the middle class, such as the level and inequality of per capita income and net wealth, the size of government, the size of small and medium-sized enterprises, and the degree of democracy in a country. The section then postulates the separate relation of each of these determinants with the size of the middle class. The fourth section assembles a database of these variables for a sample of 129 countries and studies the empirical correlations between the middle class and a set of determinants for a cross-section of countries grouped by income per capita levels and regions. The last section presents some conclusions from the analysis.

Roles of the Middle Class and Definition Issues

We can distinguish at least three roles performed by the middle class that can be of interest for development economics.

The middle class as a source of entrepreneurs. Since the time of the industrial revolution in England, the middle class has been seen as a source of entrepre-

3. See Solimano (2006) for the Latin American experience. During the first decade of this century, policy reversal toward policies of nationalization is already taking place in some Latin American countries (for example, Venezuela and Bolivia), and it is a serious possibility that this and other related policy moves will take hold in other countries as well. Neoliberal policies are often accompanied by the persistence of inequality and a relative neglect of the middle class as a potential beneficiary of economic reforms. Issues of social equity and distributive justice in policy design are examined in Solimano, Aninat, and Birdsall (2000).

4. The traditional mechanism for growth to become unstable is through private investment, which is very sensitive to instability and political polarization that occur in situations with weak middle classes and high inequality of income and wealth.

5. Easterly (2001).

neurial capabilities. Middle-class people were deemed to be more devoted to saving, accumulating capital, and taking productive risks in comparison with a landed aristocracy that preferred leisure more than hard work and entrepreneurship.[6] Recent evidence from low- to middle-income countries provided by Abhijit Banerjee and Esther Duflo tends to reject this view and emphasizes that middle-class individuals tend to be "entrepreneurs by necessity," for example, owners of small shops and firms that earn modest rates of return and provide an income for living.[7] In that sense they are more similar to the poor than to the successful Schumpeterian entrepreneur that makes big profits out of innovations. However, the generality of these findings may be at question, because the sample of the Banerjee and Duflo study consists mainly of poor countries rather than upper-middle-income and rich countries that have a more powerful middle class composed of a larger subcomponent with entrepreneurial inclinations.

The middle class as a source of consumer power. As income per capita rises, the size of the middle class, in absolute terms, is bound to increase and so does their purchasing power. This can be an important source of aggregate demand and thus the expansion of the consumer market in such areas as new services and housing, among others. For a sample of mainly low-income countries, Banerjee and Duflo found that as the share of household income devoted to food falls as income increases, middle-class people spend relatively more on entertainment, education, and health care and domestic in infrastructure than poor people.

The middle class as a stabilizing segment in society. Karl Marx saw the proletarians, that is, people whose only asset was their " labour-power," as a revolutionary class in capitalist society. A main argument for identifying the working class as the main engine for social change was its lack of assets—mainly capital. Marx held this view, probably because he was writing in the middle of the nineteenth century when the working class in advanced capitalist countries had yet little capacity to accumulate assets.[8] In contrast, he portrayed the *"petite bourgeoisie"*—our equivalent of the middle class—essentially as a class averse to social change because of its interest in protecting its assets and social position in society, in spite of the fact that they are not in the higher echelons of social hierarchy. In a sense this was an insightful perception. However, if the interest is to maintain social and political stability to promote economic growth and development, then having a large, stable, and powerful *"petite bourgeoisie"* may not be ultimately a bad thing. Of course, this opens a complex debate as to what extent the quest for stability may also serve to preserve social inequalities and injustices. Still, the "stability for growth" argument would favor having a large and stable middle class to ensure political stability in society. As political

---

6. Doepke and Zilibotti (2007).
7. Banerjee and Duflo (2008).
8. Nowadays, in many countries the "working class" owns property (mainly housing), holds savings accounts, and has other financial assets. See Moser (2007); Solimano (2007).

stability is important for private investment and growth, the size and stability of the middle class has potentially important economic implications.[9]

Definitions of the Middle Class

In the literature, various definitions of the middle class have been provided. Nancy Birdsall, Carol Graham, and Stefano Pettinato define the middle class as those who are between 75 and 125 percent of median per capita income.[10] Easterly uses the definition of per capita consumption that is between the 20th and 80th percentiles.[11] Banerjee and Duflo use households with per capita consumption that ranges between US$2 to US$4 and US$6 to US$9 in PPP (purchasing power parity) terms to define the groups as middle class for the sample of thirteen countries used in their empirical analysis.[12] In this chapter we use a relative-income definition that breaks down the middle class in two subcomponents besides an aggregate that overlaps with other definitions used in the literature:

—A broad middle class composed of individuals belonging to deciles 3 to 9 of the income distribution

—A lower-middle class, corresponding to deciles 3 to 6

—An upper-middle class, corresponding to deciles 7 to 9

In general the lower-middle class follows patterns similar to those of the poor and the behavior of the upper-middle class resembles more the behavior of the rich.

Economic Correlates of the Middle Class: Empirical Results

In this section empirical correlations among a set of variables are investigated, which are fundamentally of economic and political economy nature and which are postulated as having a relationship with the middle class:

—Development levels and per capita income

—Inequality of income and wealth

—Size of the state

—Share of small and medium-sized enterprises in employment and output

—Democracy

Development Levels and Income Per Capita

An empirical regularity of the development process is the expansion of the middle class. In that perspective, we can expect a positive correlation between the

9. Solimano (2007).

10. Birdsall, Graham, and Pettinato (2000).

11. Easterly (2001).

12. The countries are East Timor, Guatemala, India, Indonesia, Ivory Coast, Mexico, Nicaragua, Pakistan, Panama, Papua New Guinea, Peru, South Africa, and Tanzania; see Banerjee and Duflo (2008).

level of per capita income of a country and the relative size of its middle class. As mentioned before, economic growth that increases income per capita enables people to leave poverty and go into the middle class, with the ensuing roles discussed before (new entrepreneurship, consumer power, and political stabilization). This leads also to social mobility, with individuals moving up (or down) on the income and social status ladders, which is a healthy symptom of a dynamic economy. In addition, it is an empirical regularity—confirmed in this chapter—that middle and higher per capita income countries have, on average, a larger share of the middle class in real income than poor countries do. At this stage, it is best to avoid postulating a causality running from the middle class to growth and income per capita and rather propose a correlation.

Inequality

As previously discussed, it is to be expected that countries with lower *inequality* of income and wealth (that is, countries with less concentrated income and wealth distributions) have larger middle classes, as income is distributed more evenly across the population than it is in those countries with higher inequality. In general, inequality of income (and wealth) is characterized by a large share of income (and wealth) accruing to the rich and a lower share to the middle class and to the poor.[13] However, wealth and income concentrations are not the same concept, and often wealth is *more concentrated* than primary incomes (see figure 2-1, which compares Lorenz curves of income and wealth for a sample of 129 countries).[14] The important point is that a *negative* relationship is expected between the degree of concentration in income and wealth distribution and the relative size of the middle class in the economy.[15] Empirically, we will expect that countries with higher (lower) values of the income (and wealth) Gini coefficient have a lower (higher) share of the middle class in the personal distribution of income (and wealth). Again this hypothesis will be investigated empirically.

The Size of the State

In many countries a main employer of the middle class is the government (ministries, state agencies, public enterprises, among others). Thus one could expect that the middle class is larger in countries with larger governments. In addition,

---

13. See Atkinson (2006).

14. This analysis uses the dataset of James Davies (2008) consisting of the *net worth* (or *net wealth*) variable composed by the sum of physical (housing and shares of capital) and financial assets less debts.

15. Sometimes a high concentration of income and wealth at the top is referred to as *polarization,* and an inverse relationship between polarization and the relative size of the middle class is to be expected.

Figure 2-1. *Lorenz Curves for Income and Wealth Distributions*[a]

Cumulative proportion of GDP
per capita and net worth per capita

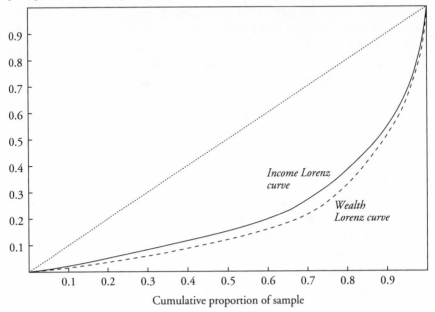

Income Lorenz curve

Wealth Lorenz curve

Cumulative proportion of sample

Source: Author's calculations.
a. Data are from a sample of 129 countries in 2000, the closest year available with information.

the middle class will be affected by the incidence of the government expenditure and the level and composition of taxes.[16] In this chapter the ratio of government expenditure to gross domestic product (GDP) is used as a proxy for the size of the government, but the correlations between the composition of public spending—particularly social expenditure—and the middle class (using the broad definition as well as the lower- and upper–middle-class segments) will also be analyzed.

Small and Medium-Sized Enterprises

SMEs are also a source of income and jobs for different groups of the population including the middle class. This class besides being identified as a typical employee of the government is also, in many countries, an owner (as well as

16. López and Torero (2007). Typically, public spending in tertiary education, pensions, public education, and health tends to benefit the (upper) middle class. Also, the level of taxes affects the disposable income of different groups in the population.

employee) of micro, small, and medium-sized enterprises. In this sense we can expect a positive relationship between the relative size of the small and medium-sized sector in the economy (measured in terms of output, employment, or both) and the relative importance of the middle class. Recent empirical evidence shows that, in relative terms, the SME sector is larger in higher-income countries than in middle- and lower-income countries.[17]

Democracy

Political scientists have always emphasized that stable and well-consolidated democracies have also larger middle classes. In addition, most stable democracies are located in high-income countries. Thus the level of economic development, democracy, and larger middle classes are all variables that seem to move together. The analysis in this chapter will focus on these patterns for a large sample, and a positive correlation is expected between democracy (using the dataset of the multicountry Polity IV project that orders countries by degrees of democracy) and the relative size of the middle class.

Empirical Results

In table 2-1, we present the average values of the variables used in this study. Our dataset covers 129 countries in which data on the following variables were collected: levels of per capita income, net wealth per person, and income distribution (income shares and Gini coefficients for income and wealth). Data on the ratio of public expenditure to GDP are available for 93 countries, the democracy index for 126 countries, and the shares of small and medium-sized enterprises of total employment (72 countries) and output (35 countries). Three social classes are identified in the data: the poor, the middle class, and the rich. The focus of the study is, however, on the middle class. Empirically, the income shares within countries for each class are as follows:

—The poor: bottom 1 and 2 deciles

—The middle class: deciles 3 to 9, following the definition of the broad middle class; the lower-middle class, deciles 3 to 6; and the upper-middle class, deciles 7 to 9

—The rich: approximated by the share of the 10th decile

It is apparent that the standard of living of a person classified as middle class depends on the average level of income of the country. So, in a low-income country a person considered to be middle class may correspond to the poor in a high-income economy. Overlaps across countries will occur. The focus of this

---

17. See Ayyagari, Beck, and Demirgüç-Kunt (2005). In turn, the SME sector has also lower productivity levels than medium-sized and large companies because the capital stock per worker is smaller for SMEs than for large firms. Accordingly, the real wages paid to the employees in SMEs tend to be lower than wages in larger firms, thereby affecting incomes of the poor and lower-middle-class individuals.

Table 2-1. *The Middle Class and Correlates*[a]

Cross correlations	Income groups[b]				
	Poor[c]	Middle-class[d]	Lower-middle class[e]	Upper-middle class[f]	Rich[g]
World Bank's income-based criterion					
Low-income economies	6.04	60.41	24.29	36.12	33.55
Lower-middle-income economies	5.54	59.94	23.62	36.32	34.51
Upper-middle-income economies	5.69	61.21	24.59	36.62	33.10
High-income economies	7.47	66.67	29.08	37.59	25.85
World Bank's regional criterion					
East Asia and Pacific	6.53	62.75	25.77	36.98	30.72
Europe, Central Asia, and North America	7.72	66.67	29.31	37.35	25.61
By OECD membership					
OECD countries	7.67	67.05	29.57	37.47	25.28
Non-OECD countries	7.75	66.43	29.15	37.28	25.81
By European Union membership					
EU members	7.91	67.34	29.98	37.36	24.75
Others	7.50	65.91	28.55	37.35	26.59
Latin America and the Caribbean	3.64	56.81	20.52	36.29	39.54
Middle East and North Africa	6.62	63.64	26.26	37.39	29.71
South Asia	7.70	60.21	25.67	34.54	32.12
Sub-Saharan Africa	5.10	57.60	21.96	35.63	37.31
All countries	6.17	61.88	25.27	36.61	31.95
No. of observations	129	129	129	129	129

Source: Author's calculations based on World Bank's *World Development Indicators* (2007b), Davies and others (2006) for data from the WIDER-UNU project on world wealth distribution, Marshall and Jaggers (2005) for data on the Polity IV Project, and Ayyagari and others (2005) for data from the SME database. See the appendix for details.

OECD = Organization for Economic Cooperation and Development; SMEs = small and medium-sized enterprises.

a. Selected indicators for 129 countries in 2000, the closest year available with information.

b. Percentage of GDP.

c. Poor = deciles 1–2.

Income and wealth				Other indicators			
GDP per capita[h]	Income Gini index	Net worth per capita[h]	Net worth Gini index	Govern-ment expenses[b]	Democ-racy index[i]	SMEs' employment[j]	SMEs' output[b]
1,349.10	0.422	3,960.17	0.709	20.00	0.97	36.19	24.00
3,982.84	0.438	11,162.62	0.709	21.63	0.65	38.76	29.41
7,999.65	0.423	20,232.75	0.705	27.22	7.83	51.14	40.79
23,769.67	0.330	89,192.45	0.665	33.49	9.46	63.93	48.77
10,006.21	0.391	45,237.73	0.676	21.25	5.87	67.45	35.97
15,177.41	0.325	48,801.64	0.668	30.70	5.91	49.98	42.91
27,461.19	0.320	96,685.34	0.676	36.02	9.94	67.40	53.63
6,988.23	0.328	19,080.73	0.664	26.72	3.55	35.06	31.21
19,773.78	0.313	65,127.29	0.657	36.23	9.46	59.22	48.69
9,431.95	0.338	30,249.77	0.682	23.34	2.05	35.21	26.52
5,627.84	0.510	16,457.70	0.743	20.72	3.45	55.94	45.34
6,441.90	0.379	19,250.69	0.676	29.49	2.38	..	..
2,239.84	0.381	7,275.13	0.682	16.76	4.60	..	..
1,882.42	0.470	4,615.79	0.729	24.01	0.93	32.66	..
8,596.30	0.405	28,874.90	0.698	26.26	4.02	51.08	42.14
127	129	129	129	93	126	72	35

d. Middle class = broad definition, deciles 3–9.

e. Lower-middle class = deciles 3–6.

f. Upper-middle class = deciles 7–9.

g. Rich = top decile.

h. PPP (purchasing power parity) adjusted 2000 international US dollars.

i. Democracy index is from the Polity IV Project and is based on a Polity score that captures this regime authority spectrum on a twenty-one-point scale ranging from −10 (hereditary monarchy) to +10 (consolidated monarchy).

j. Percentage of total employment.

chapter is on the middle class *within countries* rather than on the *world* (or *global*) middle class.[18]

Economies are grouped according to their level of per capita income using the definitions of the World Bank (low-income, lower-middle-income, upper-middle-income, and high-income) and also by regional groupings of the World Bank.

The average income share of the middle class (broad definition, hereafter referred to as MC) in the world economy (129 countries) is close to 62 percent (data circa 2000). This relative size of the middle class increases with the level of per capita income: the MC share for low-income countries (say, countries with a per capita income of less than US$905 in PPP) is 60.4 percent, while the share of the middle class in high-income countries (those countries with GDP per capita above US$11,000) is much higher, at 66.6 percent. In turn, we find that the shares of the upper-middle class have a narrower range of variation across countries, ranging from 36.1 in low-income countries to 37.5 percent in high-income economies, than the shares of the lower-middle class, which varies from 24.2 percent in low-income countries to 29.1 percent for high-income countries; see table 2-1.

An interesting empirical finding is that the increase in the income share of the middle class in higher-income countries is accompanied by a *decline* in the average share of the rich. So it is a progressive or redistributive shift away from higher-income people (defined as the top 10 percent). In fact, the income share of the rich is smaller in high-income economies (on average 25.8 percent) than the corresponding share in low-income economies (33.5 percent). This confirms the basic hypothesis that high-income countries have a smaller share of income going to the rich (top 10 percent) and a larger share of income going to the middle classes (deciles 3 to 9) than is the case in poor and middle-income countries. A similar conclusion can be drawn using the Gini coefficients of income (calculated by the World Bank) and the Gini coefficient of wealth

---

18. The global income distribution intends to reflect the distribution of income among all citizens of the world. The World Bank's *Global Development Prospects* (2007a) defines the global middle class as having per capita income ranging from US$4,000 to US$17,000, which corresponds roughly to the per capita income of Brazil and Italy, respectively, according to the World Bank. It is clear for many countries, particularly low-income and middle-income countries, that the average income of a person belonging to the national middle class is well below the average income of the citizen of the global middle class. In fact, upper-income people in lower-income economies are bound to be only middle-income people according to the global middle class definition. It is estimated that growth of the global middle class in coming years will be concentrated mainly in developing countries and is associated with global economy-wide growth, increases in education levels, shifts in income distribution, and other factors. This is expected to have effects on international trade in goods and services as well as on domestic demand. See Milanovic (2006); World Bank (2007a).

(computed by UNU-WIDER).[19] In fact, the average (income) Gini for high-income economies is 0.33 compared with that of 0.42 for low-income economies (and close to 0.44 for lower-middle-income economies) (table 2-1). A higher Gini, in the range (0, 1), of course, means higher inequality.

We verify also that the degree of concentration of wealth is often higher than that for income. In fact, the average Gini coefficient for wealth (net worth) is 0.66 for high-income economies and 0.71 for low-income economies. Figure 2-1 displays Lorenz curves for income and for wealth, and the former lies closer to the 45 degree (line of full equality) than the Lorenz curve for wealth, showing that inequality of incomes is less than inequality for wealth using cross-country data.

When we consider the regional country groupings, we find some interesting contrasts: the region of Latin America and the Caribbean has the lowest average share of the middle class in income (and the highest share of the top 10 percent), followed by Africa. Also, Latin America has the highest inequality indicators measured by both Gini of income and Gini of wealth. This confirms for regions that inequality and the relative importance of the middle class are inversely correlated. The regions with higher shares of the middle class are Europe, Central Asia, and North America, followed by the Middle East and North Africa and East Asia and Pacific.

Regarding other variables, the analysis shows that the size of government expenditure increases with the level of per capita income. Low-income and lower-middle-income countries have a ratio of public spending to GDP ranging between 20 to 21.6 percent, respectively, whereas the same ratio fluctuates between 27.2 and 33.4 percent in upper-middle-income and high-income economies, respectively. Again the higher ratio of public expenditure is associated with larger middle classes in high-income economies. Also, we find a substantially higher share of SMEs in employment in high-income economies (close to 64 percent) compared with the share of SMEs of around 36 percent for low-income countries. Upper-middle-income countries have a corresponding share of SMEs in employment of 51 percent, and for lower-middle-income countries, it is nearly 39 percent. The differences are smaller for the shares of SMEs in output, but still the positive correlation with income per capita levels holds.

Analysis of Correlations

In this section we present the results of the correlation analysis for the different determinants of the relative size of the middle class.

19. UNU-WIDER, World Institute for Development Economics Research of the United Nations University.

Levels of Per Capita Income and Per Capita Wealth

The coefficient of correlation between the share of the middle class (broad definition) and the levels of per capita income in PPP for a sample of 127 countries is 0.411 (see table 2-2). In turn, the correlation of the share of the (broad) middle class with per capita net worth is lower (a coefficient of 0.346). Figure 2-2 presents a scatter diagram of the income shares of the middle class (broad definition) at different levels of per capita income. It is apparent that there is a lower average share of the middle class and a greater variability for low-income and middle-income economies than there is for high-income economies. The relationship between the relative size of the middle class and per capita income levels really "stabilizes" for countries with per capita income levels above US$11,000 (which are high-income economies as defined by the World Bank).

If per capita net wealth is used, the shares of the middle class become more stable at a threshold of around US$50,000; see figure 2-3. Again the dispersion of MC shares is greater for lower- and middle-income economies.

When the middle class (in the full country sample) is broken down into lower-middle and upper-middle classes, the corresponding relation with per capita income is stronger (higher coefficients of correlation) for the lower-middle class (a correlation of 0.42) than for the upper-middle class (a correlation of 0.23; see table 2-2). This suggests that economic growth should benefit more people whose incomes are closer to poverty than those whose incomes are closer to the rich. Growth is, in a sense, pro–lower-middle class.[20] From a political economy perspective, one may think of a broader coalition between the poor and the lower-middle class (covering a group that ranges from percentiles 1 to 60) since their interests are relatively aligned. In terms of number of votes, this coalition between the poor and the lower-middle class is likely to be a majority of the population; however, in terms of economic power (say income per person) each individual is less empowered because most income distributions are asymmetric and tend to be concentrated toward high-income levels.

Inequality

Let us turn now to the relationship between the middle class and inequality of income and wealth. The coefficients of correlation between the share of the middle class and the Gini coefficients for income and the Gini of net wealth are negative for the whole sample and for all income groups (see tables 2-1 and 2-2 for descriptive statistics of the middle class and correlation coefficients). Furthermore, this negative correlation is higher for the income Gini (a coefficient of –0.94) than for the net wealth Gini (a coefficient of –0.67), suggesting

---

20. The coefficient of correlation between the broad definition of the middle class and the lower-middle class is higher than the corresponding correlation with the upper-middle class; see table 2-2.

a tighter inverse relationship between shares of the middle class and the degree of inequality of income than between the share of the middle class and the degree of net wealth inequality.[21] In turn, the latter relationship (between the share of the middle class and wealth inequality) has a larger dispersion than does the relationship between the share of the middle class and income inequality (compare the dispersion of both dot clouds in figure 2-4). It is also interesting to note that the negative correlation with both Ginis is stronger for the lower-middle class than for the upper-middle class (see table 2-2).

These results confirm our presumption that more unequal societies (those with higher Gini for income and net wealth) have smaller middle classes (relatively speaking) than more equal economies (those economies with lower Ginis) have.[22]

Unlike the relation between the share of middle class and the level of per capita income, the relation between the MC share and the Gini holds robust across all per capita income groups, although the correlation between the MC shares and the income and wealth Ginis decline for the high-income group.[23]

The Middle Class and Government Expenditure

For a sample of 93 countries, table 2-2 shows a correlation of 0.36 between the share of the middle class (broad definition) and the ratio of the level of total public spending (government expenses) to GDP, as a proxy for the size of the state. This suggests a not-too-strong correlation between both variables. Moreover, this correlation is weaker and more unstable for various country groups, even for high-income countries. This may reflect our imperfect measure of size of government or simply that both variables are not strongly correlated or a combination of both factors. Further testing of the relationship could be conducted using data on public employment (as a share of total employment) and the share of the middle class. When the middle class is disaggregated into lower-middle and upper-middle, there is a stronger correlation with the public spending to GDP ratio for the lower-middle class than for the upper-middle class (see table 2-2 and figure 2-5).

The analysis explores the effects of the *composition* of public expenditure using data compiled by the IMF for its *Government Finance Statistics Yearbook*. The results reveal that for the whole sample, in general, social expenditure is not very progressive (table 2-3). In fact, government spending in education, for example, has a positive correlation only with the top decile. This is probably influenced by the expenditure in tertiary education that is known not to reach middle- and lower-income groups in a significant way. Also, public expenditure

---

21. There is also a negative correlation between the income share of the rich (top 10 percent) and the level of per capita income of the country for the overall sample (−0.40).

22. These countries happen to be those with higher per capita income levels.

23. Tables are available on request from the author.

Table 2-2. *Matrix of Correlations of Income Groups, Income and Wealth, and Selected Indicators*[a]

	Cross correlations	Poor[b]	Middle class[c]	Lower middle class[d]	Upper middle class[e]	Rich[f]
				Income groups		
Income groups	Poor[b]	1.000 (129)				
	Middle class[c]	0.807 (129)	1.000 (129)			
	Lower middle class[d]	0.927 (129)	0.956 (129)	1.000 (129)		
	Upper middle class[e]	0.217 (129)	0.723 (129)	0.489 (129)	1.000 (129)	
	Rich[f]	−0.891 (129)	−0.987 (129)	0.986 (129)	−0.615 (129)	1.000 (129)
Income and wealth	GDP per capita[g]	0.328 (127)	0.411 (127)	0.421 (127)	0.231 (127)	−0.405 (127)
	Income Gini index	−0.954 (129)	−0.940 (129)	−0.992 (129)	−0.460 (129)	0.981 (129)
	Net worth per capita[g]	0.236 (129)	0.346 (129)	0.333 (129)	0.243 (129)	−0.330 (129)
	Net worth Gini index	−0.655 (129)	−0.676 (129)	−0.697 (129)	−0.368 (129)	0.697 (129)
Other indicators	Government expenses[h]	0.295 (93)	0.359 (93)	0.355 (93)	0.217 (93)	−0.354 (93)
	Democracy index[i]	0.054 (126)	0.025 (126)	0.043 (126)	−0.025 (126)	−0.034 (126)
	SMEs' employment[j]	−0.006 (72)	−0.019 (72)	−0.017 (72)	−0.018 (72)	0.016 (72)
	SMEs' output[h]	−0.031 (35)	0.073 (35)	0.033 (35)	0.187 (35)	−0.043 (35)

Source: Author's calculations based on World Bank's *World Development Indicators* (2007b), Davies and others (2006) for data from the WIDER-UNU project on world wealth distribution, Marshall and Jaggers (2005) for data from the Polity IV project, and Ayyagari and others (2005) for data from the SME database]. See the appendix for details.

SMEs = small and medium-sized enterprises.

a. Selected indicators for 129 countries in 2000, the closest year available with information. Numbers in parentheses indicate the number of observations available for estimating each correlation.

b. Poor: deciles 1–2.

c. Middle class: broad definition, deciles 3–9.

Income and wealth				Other indicators			
GDP per capital[g]	Income Gini index	Net worth per capita[g]	Net worth Gini index	Government expenses[h]	Democracy index[i]	SMEs' employment[j]	SMEs' output[h]
1.000							
(127)							
−0.402	1.000						
(127)	(129)						
0.912	−0.316	1.000					
(127)	(129)	(129)					
−0.265	0.688	−0.196	1.000				
(127)	(129)	(129)	(129)				
0.505	−0.351	0.405	−0.272	1.000			
(93)	(93)	(93)	(93)	(93)			
0.253	−0.045	0.212	−0.020	0.211	1.000		
(124)	(126)	(126)	(126)	(92)	(126)		
0.479	0.007	0.420	−0.029	0.222	0.160	1.000	
(72)	(72)	(72)	(72)	(60)	(70)	(72)	
0.565	−0.028	0.546	−0.004	0.188	−0.076	0.698	1.000
(35)	(35)	(35)	(35)	(31)	(34)	(35)	(35)

d. Lower-middle class: deciles 3–6.

e. Upper-middle class: deciles 7–9.

f. Rich: top decile.

g. PPP (purchasing power parity) adjusted 2000 international US dollars.

h. Percentage of GDP.

i. The democracy index is from the Polity IV Project and is based on a Polity score that captures this regime authority spectrum on a twenty-one-point scale ranging from −10 (hereditary monarchy) to +10 (consolidated democracy).

j. Percentage of total employment.

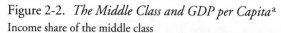

Figure 2-2. *The Middle Class and GDP per Capita*[a]
Income share of the middle class

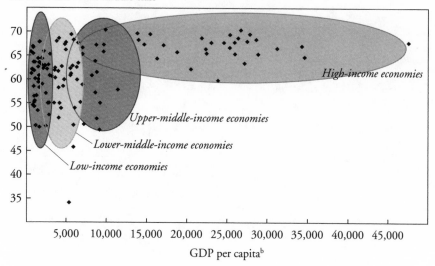

GDP per capita[b]

Source: Author's calculations.

Low-income economies: GNIpc ≤ US$905; mean, 60.41 percent; variance, 0.0022.

Lower-middle-income economies: US$905 ≤ GDPpc ≤ US$3,595; mean, 59.94 percent; variance, 0.0045.

Upper-middle-income economies: US$3,596 ≤ GDPpc ≤ US$11,115; mean, 61.21 percent; variance, 0.0050.

High-income economies: GNIpc ≥ US$11,116; mean, 66.67 percent; variance 0.0006.

GNIpc: gross national income per capita.

a. Data are from a sample of 127 selected countries in 2000, the closest year available with information. The broad definition (deciles 3–9) of "middle class" is used.

b. GDP per capita is measured by purchasing power parity (PPP) adjusted 2000 international US dollars.

in health has some correlation with the upper-middle class and the rich (defined as the top decile). The only item that has more significant correlation with the non-rich is the category of social protection.

When the same calculations are done for country groupings according to income levels and regional groupings, the incidence does not change in a significant way. On the whole the incidence of social expenditure in education, health, and housing is not redistributive either to the poor or to the lower-middle class.

The Small and Medium-Sized Enterprises and the Middle Class

The results show a weak correlation and an unexpected sign between the shares of small and medium-sized enterprises in employment and output and the share of the middle class using the broad and upper- and lower-middle-class

Figure 2-3. *The Middle Class and Net Worth per Capita*[a]
Income share of the middle class

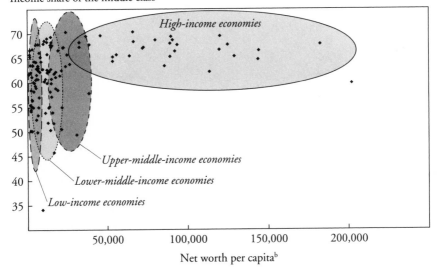

Net worth per capita[b]

Source: Author's calculations.
Low-income economies: GNIpc ≤ US$905; mean, 60.41 percent; variance, 0.0022.
Lower-middle-income economies: US$906 ≤ GNIpc ≤ US$3,595; mean, 59.94 percent; variance, 0.0045.
Upper-middle-income economies: US$3,596 ≤ GNIpc ≤ US$11,115; mean, 61.21 percent; variance, 0.0050.
High-income economies: GNIpc ≥ US$11,116; mean, 66.67 percent; variance 0.0006.
GNIpc: gross national income per capita.
a. Data are from a sample of 129 selected countries in 2000, the closest year available with information. The broad definition (deciles 3–9) of "middle class" is used.
b. Net worth per capita is measured by purchasing power parity (PPP) adjusted 2000 international US dollars.

classifications. This may reflect also our smaller country sample for which SME data are available and other factors at work that would require additional research (figures 2-6a, 2-6b).

Democracy

To test the relationship between democracy and the share of the middle class, we use a democracy index produced by the Polity IV project.[24] This index, which is based on a spectrum that ranges from 0 to 10 (the higher the index, the more democratic the society), comprises three dimensions: competitiveness of political participation, the openness and competitiveness of executive recruit-

24. See Marshall and Jaggers (2005).

Figure 2-4. *The Middle Class and Income and Net Worth Gini Indexes*[a]

Income share of the middle class

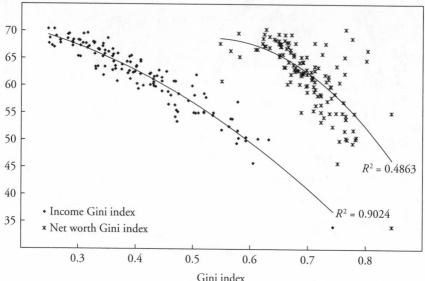

Source: Author's calculations.

a. Data are from a sample of 129 selected countries in 2000, the closest year available with information. The broad definition (deciles 3–9) of "middle class" is used.

ment, and constraints on the chief executive and guarantees on civil liberties for all citizens. Here, democracy is considered as a variable that encompasses several degrees of democratic (or undemocratic) rule rather than as a simple dichotomy of democracy versus autocracy. The average score of the democracy index is low for low-income and lower-middle-income countries (an average value that is less than 1) and much higher for upper-middle-income countries (an average value of 7.8) and higher-income countries (an average of 9.5). For the overall sample, the correlation with the share of the middle class (broad definition) is almost nonexistent (0.025; see table 2-2). However, for the group of high-income countries, there is a positive and relatively high correlation between the share of the middle class and the democracy index. Figure 2-7 displays the relation between the share of the middle class and the country grouping according to democratic rule. In general, for low- to middle-income countries, there is a wide dispersion in the degree of democratic rule for similar shares of the middle class (the low correlation between the two variables mentioned before); it is only for high-income countries that a positive and more stable relation is observed between high shares of the middle class in income and high degrees of democratic rule.

Figure 2-5. *The Middle Class and Government Expenses*[a]

Income share of the middle class

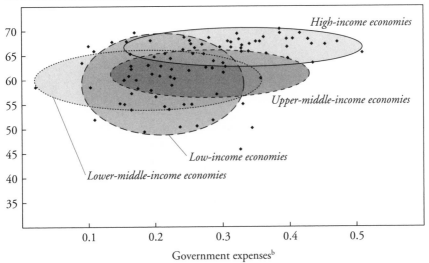

Source: Author's calculations.

Low-income economies: GNIpc ≤ US$905; mean, 60.41 percent; variance, 0.0022.

Lower-middle-income economies: US$906 ≤ GNIpc ≤ US$3,595; mean, 59.94 percent; variance, 0.0045.

Upper-middle-income economies: US$3,596 ≤ GNIpc ≤ US$11,115; mean, 61.21 percent; variance, 0.0050.

High-income economies: GNIpc ≥ US$11,116; mean, 66.67 percent; variance 0.0006.

GNIpc: gross national income per capita.

a. Data are from a sample of 93 selected countries in 2000, the closest year available with information. The broad definition (deciles 3–9) of "middle class" is used.

b. Government expenses are measured as a percentage of GDP.

Concluding Remarks

The middle class is a topic of growing interest in the field of development economics. The alleged positive effects of a stable and solid middle class on the rate of economic growth and development are linked to the middle class as a source of entrepreneurship, consumer power, and social and political stability. This chapter has investigated some of the main empirical regularities of behavior of the middle class across countries. The potential for entrepreneurship and productivity of the middle class is mixed, and almost no correlation is found, in this chapter, between the relative size of the middle class and the relative importance of the small and medium-sized sector in output and employment using cross-sectional data. Other studies based on household surveys also find limited entrepreneurial power (in a Schumpeterian sense) of the middle class in low-income nations. Middle-class members that run small firms in these countries seem to

Table 2-3. *Matrix of Correlations of Mean Income per Income Groups and Public Expenditures*[a]

| Cross correlations | Mean income per income group | | | | |
	Poor[b]	Middle class[c]	Lower-middle class[d]	Upper-middle class[e]	Rich[f]
Poor[b]	1.000				
	(129)				
Middle class[c]	0.807	1.000			
	(129)	(129)			
Lower-middle class[d]	0.927	0.956	1.000		
	(129)	(129)	(129)		
Upper-middle class[e]	0.217	0.723	0.489	1.000	
	(129)	(129)	(129)	(129)	
Rich[f]	−0.891	−0.987	−0.986	−0.615	1.000
	(129)	(129)	(129)	(129)	(129)
Total government outlays	0.137	0.028	0.087	−0.117	−0.059
	(84)	(84)	(84)	(84)	(84)
Social expenditure					
Housing and	−0.069	−0.266	−0.181	−0.352	0.22
community	(70)	(70)	(70)	(70)	(70)
Health	−0.143	−0.064	−0.102	0.064	0.09
	(70)	(70)	(70)	(70)	(70)
Education	−0.114	−0.093	−0.101	−0.026	0.102
	(70)	(70)	(70)	(70)	(70)
Social protection	0.364	0.425	0.424	0.222	−0.424
	(70)	(70)	(70)	(70)	(70)
Nonsocial expenditure					
Public order and safety	0.15	0.058	0.121	−0.150	−0.088
	(42)	(42)	(42)	(42)	(42)
Economic affairs	0.127	0	0.074	−0.187	−0.038
	(70)	(70)	(70)	(70)	(70)
Environmental	0.151	0.051	0.035	0.086	−0.073
protection	(6)	(6)	(6)	(6)	(6)
Recreation, culture,	0.29	0.204	0.26	−0.036	−0.238
and religion	(69)	(69)	(69)	(69)	(69)
Other expenditure					
General public	0.115	0.061	0.087	−0.037	−0.079
services	(70)	(70)	(70)	(70)	(70)
Defense	0.08	0.057	0.083	−0.036	−0.066
	(70)	(70)	(70)	(70)	(70)

Source: Author's calculations based on World Bank's *World Development Indicators* (2007b) and IMF's *Government Finance Statistics Yearbook, 2002* (2003). See the appendix for details.

a. Selected indicators for 129 countries in 2000, the closest year available with information. Numbers in parentheses indicate the number of observations available for estimating each correlation.

b. Poor: deciles 1–2.

c. Middle class: broad definition, deciles 3–9.

d. Lower-middle class: deciles 3–6.

e. Upper-middle class: deciles 7–9.

f. Rich: top decile.

Figure 2-6. *Small and Medium-Sized Enterprises and the Middle Class*[a]

a. SMEs' employment[b]

Income share of the middle class

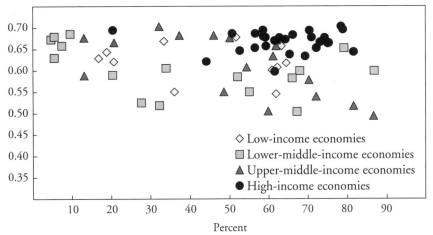

Percent

b. SMEs' output[c]

Income share of the middle class

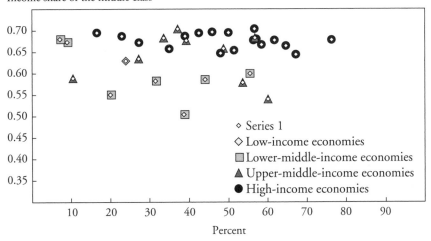

Percent

Source: Author's calculations.

Low-income economies: GNIpc ≤ US$905; mean, 60.41 percent; variance, 0.0022.

Lower-middle-income economies: US$906 ≤ GNIpc ≤ US$3,595; mean, 59.94 percent; variance, 0.0045.

Upper-middle-income economies: US$3,596 ≤ GNIpc ≤ US$11,115; mean, 61.21 percent; variance, 0.0050.

High-income economies: GNIpc ≥ US$11,116; mean, 66.67 percent; variance, 0.0006.

GNIpc: gross national income per capita.

a. Data are from a sample of 72 selected countries in 2000, the closest year available with information. The broad definition (deciles 3–9) of "middle class" is used.

b. SMEs' employment is measured as a percentage of total employment.

c. SMEs' output is measured as a percentage of GDP.

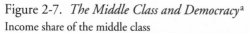

Figure 2-7. *The Middle Class and Democracy*[a]

Income share of the middle class

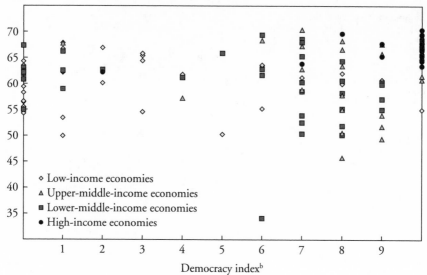

Democracy index[b]

Source: Author's calculations.

Low-income economies: GNIpc ≤ US$905.

Lower-middle-income economies: US$906 ≤ GNIpc ≤ US$3,595.

Upper-middle-income economies: US$3,596 ≤ GNIpc ≤ US$11,115.

High-income economies: GNIpc ≥ US$11,116.

a. Data are from a sample of 123 selected countries in 2000, the closest year available with information. The broad definition (deciles 3–9) of "middle class" is used.

b. The democracy index corresponds to the Institutionalized Democracy Indicator from the Polity IV Project. See appendix for details.

be more "entrepreneurs by necessity." This chapter suggests that as income per capita levels increase and countries enter into a higher level of development, they tend to have also a larger middle class, measured as a proportion of national income. In turn, the consumer power of the middle class expands as income per capita increases, leading to a larger internal market. On the sociopolitical stabilization role of the middle class, the evidence is indirect in the sense that high-income countries with stable democracies and mature economies have also relatively larger middle classes than middle- and lower-income countries do. In fact, these results show that in high-income economies the relative share of the middle class (using a broad definition of deciles 3 to 9) is close to *6 percentage points higher* than the share of the middle class in low-income countries, suggesting a *positive* relationship between the level of economic development measured by per capita income levels and the share of the middle class.

In turn, the relationship between the share in income of the middle class and the level of per capita income is nonlinear and shows more dispersion for low-

and middle-income countries with per capita incomes below US$11,000 than it does for rich countries. The relationship between the share of the middle class and per capita net wealth is also positive but displays more dispersion than the relationship between the share of the middle class and income per capita.

It is interesting that the income–middle class relation with per capita income is stronger (higher coefficients of correlation) for the lower-middle class than for the upper-middle class. From a political economy perspective, one may think in terms of a broader coalition between the poor and the lower-middle class as their economic interests are relatively aligned between them. That coalition could include a sizeable part of the population, including individuals with income shares from the percentiles 1 to 60.

The results in this chapter also show that countries with more unequal income and wealth distribution have smaller middle classes in relative terms, suggesting a *negative* relationship between the degree of inequality of income and wealth and the (relative) size of the middle class. In fact, the correlation between the share of the middle class and the coefficient of income Gini is negative and close to 95 percent, and the correlation of the relative size of the middle class with the coefficient of wealth Gini is around 67 percent (in the full sample of 129 countries). The relation between the share of the middle class and the Ginis holds strong across all per capita income groups, although this relation is lower for high-income economies with per capita incomes above US$11,000, reflecting the fact that rich countries have lower levels of income inequality than lower-income nations.

The chapter also shows that the correlation between the share of the middle class and the overall size of government, in general, is not very strong and varies across countries ordered by income per capita levels. Moreover, the data on the composition of public expenditures reveal that categories of social expenditure such as education, health, and perhaps housing are generally not very redistributive, reaching just relatively small proportions of the lower-middle class and the poor. The component whose incidence is more progressive is social protection. Likewise, no significant correlation was detected between the relative size of the small and medium-sized enterprises, measured both as shares of total employment and total output, and the shares of the middle class in real income. Finally, when an index of democracy was correlated with the middle class shares, little or no correlation was found between both variables except for the group of high-income economies.

Our analysis is cast in terms of correlation rather than causality because of the apparent two-way interaction between social structures and income distribution on the one hand and economic and political economy variables, such as income and wealth per capita levels, inequality, size of government, the SME sector, and degree of democracy, on the other. To what extent the middle class *leads* the process of economic development or *follows* with economic development (or whether they both evolve jointly) is still an open question for further research in this emerging field of the determinants of middle-class behavior.

References

Atkinson, A. B. 2006. "Concentration among the Rich." Research Paper 2006/151. Helsinki, Finland: UNU-WIDER (World Institute for Development Economics Research of the United Nations University).

Ayyagari, Meghana, Thorsten Beck, and Asli Demirgüç-Kunt. 2005. "Small and Medium Enterprises across the Globe." Draft (March). Washington: World Bank.

Banerjee, Abhijit V., and Esther Duflo. 2008. "What is Middle Class about the Middle Class around the World?" *Journal of Economic Perspectives* 22, no. 2 (Spring): 3–28.

Birdsall, Nancy, Carol Graham, and Stefano Pettinato. 2000. "Stuck in the Tunnel: Is Globalization Muddling the Middle Class?" Working Paper 14. Brookings, Center on Social and Economic Dynamics (August).

Cashell, B. 2007. "Who Are the 'Middle Class'?" RS22627. Washington: Congressional Research Service.

Daly, M., and D. Wilson. 2006. "Keeping Up with Joneses and Staying Ahead of the Smiths: Evidence from Suicide Data." Working Paper 2006-12. Federal Reserve Bank of San Francisco (April).

Davies, James, ed. 2008. *Personal Wealth from a Global Perspective.* Oxford University Press.

Davies, James, and others. 2006. "The World Distribution of Household Wealth." Helsinki, Finland: UNU-WIDER (World Institute for Development Economics Research of the United Nations University).

Doepke, M., and F. Zilibotti. 2007. "Occupational Choice and the Spirit of Capitalism." Working Paper 12971. Cambridge, Mass.: National Bureau of Economic Research (February).

Easterly, William. 2001. "The Middle Class Consensus and Economic Development." *Journal of Economic Growth* 6, no. 4: 317–35.

Frank, Robert H. 2007. *Falling Behind: How Rising Inequality Harms the Middle Class.* The Aaron Wildavsky Forum for Public Policy. University of California Press.

International Monetary Fund. 2003. *Government Finance Statistics Yearbook, 2002.* Volume 26. Washington: IMF, Statistics Department (yearbook and CD-ROM).

Graham, Carol. 2007. "What Happiness Research Can (and Cannot) Contribute to Policy Reforms: Lessons from Research on Latin America and Beyond." Draft presented at the World Bank Workshop "Fiscal Incidence and the Middle Class: Implications for Policy." June 5.

Layard, Richard. 2005. *Happiness: Lessons from a New Science.* New York: Penguin Press.

López, Ramón, and Máximo Torero. 2007. "Economic Growth, the Fiscal Sector and Income Distribution." Draft presented at the World Bank Workshop "Fiscal Incidence and the Middle Class: Implications for Policy." Washington, June 5.

Marshall, Monty G., and Keith Jaggers. 2005. "Political Regime Characteristics and Transitions, 1800–2004." Severn, Md.: Center for Systemic Peace, Polity IV Project. (Data User's Manual and Database.)

Milanovic, Branko. 2006. "Global Income Inequality: What It Is and Why It Matters." Policy Research Working Paper Series 3865. Washington: World Bank.

Moser, Caroline O. N., ed. 2007. *Reducing Global Poverty: The Case for Asset Accumulation.* Brookings.

Solimano, Andrés, ed. 1998. *Social Inequality.* University of Michigan Press.

———. 2005. "Towards New Social Policies in Latin America: Growth, the Middle Class and Social Rights." *ECLAC Review* 87 (December).

———, ed. 2006. *Vanishing Growth in Latin America: The Late Twentieth Century Experience.* Northampton, Mass.: Edward Elgar Publishers.

———. 2007. "Social Protection and Asset Accumulation by the Middle Class and the Poor in Latin America." In *Reducing Global Poverty: The Case for Asset Accumulation,* edited by Caroline O. N. Moser, pp. 122–33. Brookings.

Solimano, Andrés, Eduardo Aninat, and Nancy Birdsall, eds. 2000. *Distributive Justice and Economic Development: The Case of Chile and Developing Countries.* University of Michigan Press.

World Bank. 2007a. *Global Development Prospects: Managing the Next Wave of Globalization.* Washington.

———. 2007b. *World Development Indicators.* Washington (selected series, countries, and years).

Description of Variables and Country Classifications

Data on income distribution are collected from 2000, the closest year available with information.

Description of Variables

Data for the first seven variables come from the World Bank's *World Development Indicators* (WDI), version 2007:

—Poor: deciles 1 and 2
—Middle class (broad definition): deciles 3 to 9
—Lower-middle class: deciles 3 to 6
—Upper-middle class: deciles 7 to 9
—Rich: top decile
—GDP per capita (PPP adjusted): gross domestic product per capita adjusted by the purchasing power parity (PPP) for international 2000 US dollars
—Income GINI index: the numerator is the area between the Lorenz curve of the distribution and the uniform distribution line; the denominator is the area under the uniform distribution line.

Data for the next two variables come from the World Institute for Development Economics Research of the United Nations University (UNU-WIDER) study "The World Distribution of Household Wealth" (see Davies and others 2006):

—Net worth per capita (PPP adjusted): wealth per capita adjusted by the purchasing power parity (PPP) for international 2000 US dollars; here wealth is defined as net worth, that is, the value of physical and financial assets less liabilities.

—Net worth Gini index: a measure of wealth inequality. It is defined as a ratio with values between 0 and 1: the numerator is the area between the Lorenz curve of the net worth distribution and the uniform distribution line; the denominator is the area under the uniform distribution line.

Data for government expenses come from the World Bank's *World Development Indicators* (WDI), version 2007, for selected years:

—Government expenses (percentage of GDP): cash payments to provide the government's goods and services. These expenditures include compensation of employees (such as wages and salaries), interest and subsidies, grants, social benefits, and other expenses, such as rent and dividends.

Data for the democracy index come from the Polity IV project of the Center for Systemic Peace (see Marshall and Jaggers 2005):

—Democracy index: corresponds to the Institutionalized Democracy Indicator from the Polity IV project. The indicator of democracy is an additive eleven-point scale (0–10), derived from coding the competitiveness of political participation, the openness and competitiveness of executive recruitment, and constraints on the chief executive.

Data for the following two variables come from the study by Ayyagari, Beck, and Demirgüç-Kunt (2005):

—SMEs' employment (percentage of total employment): small and medium-sized enterprise sector's share of formal employment using the official country definition of SME. Values are averages for each country during the period 1990–99.

—SMEs' output (percentage of GDP): SME sector's contribution to GDP using the official country definition of SME. Values are averages for each country during the period 1990–99.

Country Classification

Income grouping of countries: countries are grouped according to their gross national income per capita (GNIpc) using the World Bank's criterion.

Low-Income Economies: GNIpc ≤ US$905

Bangladesh, Benin, Burkina Faso, Burundi, Cambodia, Central African Republic, Côte d'Ivoire, Ethiopia, The Gambia, Ghana, Guinea, Guinea-Bissau, Haiti, India, Kenya, Kyrgyz Republic, Lao PDR, Madagascar, Malawi, Mali, Mauritania, Mongolia, Mozambique, Nepal, Niger, Nigeria, Pakistan, Papua New Guinea, Rwanda, Senegal, Tajikistan, Tanzania, Uganda, Uzbekistan, Vietnam, Republic of Yemen, Zambia, Zimbabwe.

Lower-Middle-Income Economies: US$906 ≤ GNIpc ≤ US$3,595

Albania, Algeria, Armenia, Azerbaijan, Belarus, Bolivia, Bosnia and Herzegovina, Cameroon, China, Colombia, Dominican Republic, Ecuador, Arab Republic of Egypt, El Salvador, Georgia, Guatemala, Guyana, Honduras, Indonesia, Islamic Republic of Iran, Jamaica, Jordan, Lesotho, Macedonia (FYR), Moldova, Morocco, Namibia, Nicaragua, Paraguay, Peru, Philippines, Sri Lanka, Swaziland, Thailand, Tunisia, Turkmenistan, Ukraine.

Upper-Middle-Income Economies: US$3,596 ≤ GNIpc ≤ US$11,115

Argentina, Botswana, Brazil, Bulgaria, Chile, Costa Rica, Croatia, Hungary, Kazakhstan, Latvia, Lithuania, Malaysia, Mexico, Panama, Poland, Romania, Russian Federation, Serbia and Montenegro, Slovak Republic, South Africa, St. Lucia, Turkey, Uruguay, Venezuela (RB).

High-Income Economies: GNIpc ≥ US$11,116

Australia, Austria, Belgium, Canada, Czech Republic, Denmark, Estonia, Finland, France, Germany, Greece, Hong Kong (China), Ireland, Israel, Italy, Japan, Republic of Korea, Luxembourg, Netherlands, New Zealand, Norway, Portugal, Singapore, Slovenia, Spain, Sweden, Switzerland, Trinidad and Tobago, United Kingdom, United States.

Regional grouping: countries are grouped according to the World Bank's criterion. Europe and Central Asia are regrouped together with North America because of the similarities in organization and economies. This new region (called Europe, Central Asia, and North America) is disaggregated further by two different criteria: on the basis of OECD (Organization for Economic Cooperation and Development) membership and European Union membership. The countries included in each region are the following.

East Asia and Pacific

Australia, Cambodia, China, Hong Kong, China, Indonesia, Japan, Republic of Korea, Lao PDR, Malaysia, Mongolia, New Zealand, Papua New Guinea, Philippines, Singapore, Thailand, Vietnam.

Europe, Central Asia, and North America: by OECD Membership

OECD countries: Austria, Belgium, Denmark, Finland, France, Germany, Greece, Ireland, Italy, Luxembourg, Netherlands, Norway, Portugal, Spain, Sweden, Switzerland, United Kingdom, United States.

Non-OECD countries: Albania, Armenia, Azerbaijan, Belarus, Bosnia and Herzegovina, Bulgaria, Canada, Croatia, Czech Republic, Estonia, Georgia, Hungary, Kazakhstan, Kyrgyz Republic, Latvia, Lithuania, Macedonia (FYR), Moldova, Poland, Romania, Russian Federation, Serbia and Montenegro, Slovak Republic, Slovenia, Tajikistan, Turkey, Turkmenistan, Ukraine, Uzbekistan.

Europe, Central Asia, and North America: by European Union Membership

EU Members: Austria, Belgium, Bulgaria, Czech Republic, Denmark, Estonia, Finland, France, Germany, Greece, Hungary, Ireland, Italy, Latvia, Lithuania, Luxembourg, Netherlands, Poland, Portugal, Romania, Slovak Republic, Slovenia, Spain, Sweden, United Kingdom.

Others: Albania, Armenia, Azerbaijan, Belarus, Bosnia and Herzegovina, Canada, Croatia, Georgia, Kazakhstan, Kyrgyz Republic, Macedonia (FYR), Moldova, Norway, Russian Federation, Serbia and Montenegro, Switzerland, Tajikistan, Turkey, Turkmenistan, Ukraine, United States, Uzbekistan.

Latin America and the Caribbean

Argentina, Bolivia, Brazil, Chile, Colombia, Costa Rica, Dominican Republic, Ecuador, El Salvador, Guatemala, Guyana, Haiti, Honduras, Jamaica, Mexico, Nicaragua, Panama, Paraguay, Peru, St. Lucia, Trinidad and Tobago, Uruguay, Venezuela (RB).

Middle East and North Africa

Algeria, Arab Republic of Egypt, Islamic Republic of Iran, Israel, Jordan, Morocco, Tunisia, Republic of Yemen.

South Asia

Bangladesh, India, Nepal, Pakistan, Sri Lanka.

Sub-Saharan Africa

Benin, Botswana, Burkina Faso, Burundi, Cameroon, Central African Republic, Côte d'Ivoire, Ethiopia, The Gambia, Ghana, Guinea, Guinea-Bissau, Kenya, Lesotho, Madagascar, Malawi, Mali, Mauritania, Mozambique, Namibia, Niger, Nigeria, Rwanda, Senegal, South Africa, Swaziland, Tanzania, Uganda, Zambia, Zimbabwe.

3

The Future of Global Income Inequality

MAURIZIO BUSSOLO, RAFAEL E. DE HOYOS,
AND DENIS MEDVEDEV

With the increasing pace at which domestic markets are becoming integrated into the global economy, the debate on income disparities around the world has intensified. An interesting side effect of globalization has been the change of the benchmark against which people measure their own well-being. Increased international trade flows, greater exposure to international travel, and improved and cheaper communication all have made it easier to assess one's well-being within an international context. These phenomena are giving more relevance to the concept of global income distribution.[1] The common understanding is that the recent globalization process has exacerbated inequalities between rich and poor *countries* and between poor and rich *individuals* within the countries. The literature, nevertheless, does not provide an unambiguous support for this statement. Among others, François Bourguignon and Christian Morrisson showed that during the last thirty years there was very little change in the global income distribution, Xavier Sala-i Martin argued that global disparities have decreased, and in a diametrically opposing view, Branko Milanovic suggested that the global distribution deteriorated between 1988 and 1993.[2]

1. Milanovic (2006).
2. Bourguignon and Morrison (2002); Sala-i Martin (2006); Milanovic 2002. Most of the discrepancies in the trends in global income distribution arise from differences in data sources, country and year coverage, and the way in which different studies impute missing data. Bourguignon and Morrison (2002) and Sala-i Martin (2006) used GDP per capita as the measure of average incomes across countries, whereas Milanovic (2002) used the mean income reported in household survey data.

All of the literature on the global income distribution is concerned with ex post assessments of its changes, and a large proportion of this literature is focused on testing whether globalization has increased or decreased global inequality. The present study is quite different from this earlier work by focusing on the ex ante prospects for global income distribution. We develop a novel analytical framework—the Global Income Distribution Dynamics (GIDD)—which combines a computable general equilibrium (CGE) model with a micro-simulation system at the global level.[3] The GIDD generates a counterfactual global income distribution by taking into account expected changes in the age and education structure of the population, worker migration from farm to non-farm activities, changes in skilled-to-unskilled and farm-to-nonfarm wage premiums, and differential income growth rates across countries. The latter give rise to the *convergence* component of changes in global inequality, that is, changes in global distribution due to changes in average incomes between countries while keeping within-country inequality constant. Other changes—demographic transition, internal migration, and the evolution of wage gaps—generate the *dispersion* component, that is, the expected changes in the income distribution within countries. Thus GIDD-based analysis allows us to understand how changes in global income distribution are accounted for by changes in growth rates across countries and changes in income distributions within national states. By estimating a global macro-micro model, this study represents a big leap in the understanding of global income inequality.

The forward-looking scenario in this study draws attention to several important developments that are likely to shape the evolution of the global income distribution between now and 2030. Convergence of average incomes in developing countries to high-income levels is likely to offset worsening within-country distributions in many nations and lead to a significant decline in global inequality. Furthermore, inequalities around the world are likely to converge as countries with high initial inequality experience a narrowing of income gaps, while countries with low initial inequality are likely to see their distributions widen. Finally, these trends are likely to result in the emergence of a large global middle class, composed mostly of developing country nationals. The rising share of the global middle class in many of today's low- and middle-income countries is likely to have numerous political economy implications, such as providing continued support for further globalization.

This chapter is organized in the following way. The next section discusses the contributions in the literature on global income distribution, identifying the sources behind the debate about its recent trends. The third section develops a model for Global Income Distribution Dynamics that is then used to perform

---

3. See Bussolo, De Hoyos, and Medvedev (2008) for the full methodological details of the GIDD.

ex ante simulations of global inequality. A brief description of the data and the results are presented in the fourth section. In this section we use the GIDD to project the global income distribution for 2030; we decompose the total change in inequality into the effects due to changes in between-country average incomes and changes explained by shifts in within-country inequality. The final section concludes.

Are Incomes around the World Becoming More Unequal?

Assessing what has happened to global income distribution in the last two decades, and what could happen in the next twenty-plus years, presents a number of challenges. Part of the difficulty lies with choosing an appropriate measure of inequality to capture income disparities around the world. The literature identifies three main approaches to measuring income inequality around the world, all of which have strengths, but each of which measures a slightly different thing.[4]

Intercountry inequality is a concept favored by macroeconomists. It measures relative movements across countries and gives each country an equal weight in the world distribution (that is, population size does not matter). This literature tends to conclude that in the last two decades income distribution has become more unequal.

International inequality takes into account the relative sizes of countries (that is, results are population weighted). Its proponents (such as Henri Theil and James Seale in 1994) have pointed out that failing to use population weights will cause, for example, the fast growth of China to be offset exactly by the anemic growth rates of countries like Malawi or Honduras, even though the number of Chinese citizens who experienced improvements in their incomes far exceeds the populations of either of the other two countries.[5] The broad consensus in this literature is that income inequality has decreased, although this finding is mostly driven by the fast growth in China and India.[6]

Global inequality, which compares individual incomes regardless of country of citizenship, is a fairly recent concept.[7] Global inequality takes into account

4. In this discussion the authors have adopted the naming conventions of the World Bank (2005). Milanovic (2005) referred to the different measurements discussed as inequality concepts 1, 2, and 3.

5. Theil and Seale (1994). Bourguignon, Levin, and Rosenblatt (2004) pointed out that using the intercountry concept may represent an implicit welfare judgment, whereby the rising incomes of more populous countries cannot offset the losses of smaller countries when their incomes are falling.

6. The influence of China and India is so large that omitting these two countries would reverse this conclusion. International inequality excluding China and India has increased in the past two decades.

7. Milanovic (2002).

within-country inequality, which is ignored by the international inequality approach, in which each individual is deemed to earn the country's average income. To a large extent, fast growth in the large, emerging economies tends to offset the increases in inequality within countries; therefore, by this measure, global inequality has remained roughly constant since the late 1980s.[8] Even though these three methodologies can yield quite different pictures of past and future trends, and none is clearly preferable to the others, it is worth elaborating on some general trends.[9]

Intercountry measurements of inequality suggest that the last five decades of development have done little to bring the average incomes of developing countries closer to those of the countries of the Organization for Economic Cooperation and Development (OECD). For example, Danny Quah finds "emerging twin peaks" in the global distribution, supporting the argument that the relative distance between the top and the bottom of the global income distribution has increased since the 1950s.[10] More generally, Pritchett has concluded that a "big time" divergence in incomes occurred between 1870 and 1990, evidenced by a doubling of the gap between the per capita incomes of the rich and poor countries.[11] Underlying this general pattern is a large degree of variation in individual country performance, with growth peaks and valleys across various regional groupings and time periods. However, the overall trend is one of increasing distance between countries in different income brackets, although Pritchett also showed evidence of convergence at the top of the distribution (that is, among the group of today's high-income countries).

Once different weights are assigned to countries on the basis of their population (using the international inequality approach), the global income distribution appears to have improved. For example, Bourguignon, Victoria Levin, and David Rosenblatt demonstrated a decrease in world income inequality between 1980 and 2002, as long as the relevant inequality measures are not too sensitive to the distance of mean income from the bottom.[12] Using the Gini index, the Theil index, and mean logarithmic deviation, Atkinson and Brandolini observed a similar decrease in global income inequality between 1970 and 2000.[13]

The extent of changes in these conclusions once a within-country inequality dimension is added has been a hotly debated subject. Milanovic suggested that

8. See Bussolo and others (2007).

9. Ravallion (2004). It should also be noted that measurement of inequality is sensitive to both the precise indicators used to measure it and the time horizon chosen.

10. Quah (1996, 1997).

11. Pritchett (1997). The ratio of per capita incomes of the richest and poorest countries in the sample has grown by a factor of more than five.

12. Bourguignon, Levin, and Rosenblatt (2004) showed that it is possible to produce rising inequality statistics if, for example, the sensitivity of the Atkinson inequality index to deviations from mean income at the bottom of the distribution is set sufficiently high (over five).

13. Atkinson and Brandolini (2004).

ignoring intracountry income inequality may lead to a completely different understanding about the levels and trends of global inequality.[14] On the other hand, Bourguignon and Morrison argued that inequality between countries has been responsible for most of the time-series variation in global inequality. Thus, despite the finding of the World Bank that within-country inequality has been steadily increasing since the late 1980s, the overall direction of change in global inequality since the 1980s is not clear.[15]

Methodology: Global Income Distribution Dynamics

The GIDD framework is based on CGE-microsimulation methodologies developed in the recent literature.[16] The starting point is the global income distribution in 2000, assembled using microdata from various sources as follows: for seventy-three low- and middle-income countries, household surveys are available, which account for 1.2 million households and more than 5.1 million individuals; for twenty-five high-income and twenty-two developing countries, only grouped income data (usually vintiles) are available. These 120 countries cover more than 90 percent of the global population.[17] The hypothetical 2030 distribution is then obtained by applying three main exogenous changes to the initial distribution:

—Demographic changes, including aging and shifts in the skill composition of the population

—Shifts in the sectoral composition of employment

—Economic growth, including changes in relative wages across skills and sectors

The GIDD's framework is depicted in figure 3-1.[18] Our simulations include the expected changes in the shares of population by groups formed by age and education characteristics (the top two boxes in figure 3-1). The future changes in population shares by age (upper left part of the figure) are taken as exogenous from the population projections provided by the World Bank's Development Data Group. Therefore, we assume that fertility decisions and mortality rates are determined outside the model. The change in shares of the population by education groups incorporates the expected demographic changes (linking arrow from top left box to top right box in figure 3-1). Next, new sets of

14. Milanovic (2002).

15. World Bank (2005). Some of the studies examining global inequality have relied on parameterized Lorenz curves to add the within-country dimension to the analysis. See, for example, Sala-i-Martin (2002a, 2002b); Bhalla (2002). Others, such as Milanovic (2002) and the World Bank (2005), have built up the global distribution from household surveys.

16. See Bourguignon, Bussolo, and Pereira da Silva (2008); Chen and Ravallion (2003); Bussolo, Lay, and van der Mensbrugghe (2006).

17. Throughout the chapter, when we talk about the global distribution, we are indeed referring to the GIDD sample covering 90 percent of the world's population.

18. A full technical documentation of the GIDD's microsimulation model is available in the companion paper by Bussolo, De Hoyos, Medvedev (2008).

Figure 3-1. *Empirical Framework*

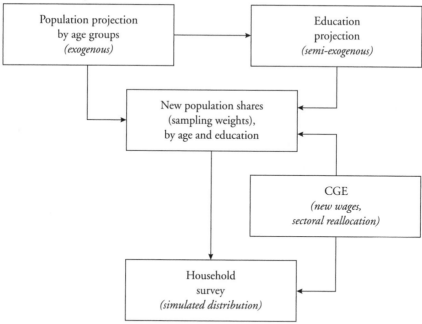

CGE = computable general equilibrium.

population shares by age and education subgroups are computed, and household sampling weights are rescaled according to the demographic and educational changes above (box in the middle of figure 3-1). In a second step, the demographic changes will have an impact on labor supply growth by age and skill groups. These changes are incorporated into the computable general equilibrium model to simulate overall economic growth, growth in relative incomes by education groups, and sector reallocation of labor (in the figure, the direct link between the middle and bottom rectangles). Finally, the results of the CGE are passed on to the reweighted household survey (the bottom link in figure 3-1).

In reality these changes take place simultaneously, but in the GIDD's simplified framework they are accommodated in a sequential fashion. In the first step, total population in each country is expanded until it reaches the World Bank's projections for 2030. The structure of the population is also changed; for example, as fertility rates decrease and life expectancy increases, older age cohorts will become larger in many countries. To accommodate these changes in the survey data, larger weights have been assigned to older people than to younger individuals. In the next step, workers move from traditional agricultural sectors to more dynamic industrial and service sectors, and new incomes are estimated for these movers. Finally, consistent with an overall growth rate of real income per capita, changes in labor remuneration by skill level and sector are applied to each worker in the sample depending on the worker's education and sector of employment. The number of workers changing sector of occupation and the growth differential in labor remuneration, which are used to "shock" the micro-data, are consistent with the results of the global CGE model.[19]

The sequential changes described above reshape national income distribution under a set of strong assumptions. In particular, income inequality within population subgroups formed by age, skills, and sector of employment is assumed to be constant during the period of study. Moreover, data limitations affect estimates of the initial inequality and its evolution. Although consumption expenditure is a more reliable welfare measure than income, and its distribution is normally more equal than the distribution of income, consumption data are not available for all countries' surveys. To get a global picture, the present study had to include countries for which only income data were available.

Finally, measurement errors implicit in purchasing power parity exchange rates, which have been used to convert local currency units, also affect comparability across countries. The resulting income distribution should thus not be seen as a forecast of what the future distribution might look like. Instead it should be interpreted as the result of an exercise that captures the ceteris paribus distributional effect of demographic, sectoral, and economic changes. Although the results of this exercise provide a good starting point for debating potential policy trade-offs, they should not be used as the basis for detailed policy blueprints.

Notice that within the GIDD, the convergence component of the global income distribution, that is, the growth in average incomes, and the dispersion component, that is, the within-country distributional effect, will be determined in a simultaneously consistent way. In other words, if the exogenous changes in a country's demographic structure are associated with higher growth in per capita incomes but also with higher inequality, these two effects will be captured by our model. The impact of the convergence and dispersion components of global inequality will be determined by the country's initial position in the global distribution. Thence, the global distributional effect of higher-than-average growth rates in poor countries (those in the lower part of the global distribution) will be to reduce global inequality; the global distributional effect of changes in within-country dispersion will also depend on the country's initial position in the global distribution.

---

19. Note that the outcomes of the CGE model are also influenced by the same demographic changes described above.

Figure 3-2. *Lorenz Curves*

Cumulative income share (percent)

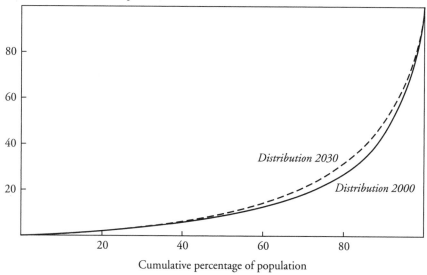

Cumulative percentage of population

The Global Income Distribution in 2030

We use the methods developed in the previous section to "roll" the global economy to 2030. The macroeconomic assumptions underlying this exercise as well as the prospects for global growth have been discussed by the World Bank and Bussolo and others.[20] In this study we concentrate on the global distributional effects behind the expected changes in per capita incomes and its distribution within countries.

In figure 3-2 we plot Lorenz curves for the global income distribution in 2000 and 2030. From the figure, it appears that the largest changes in income distribution between 2000 and 2030 are found around the middle of the distribution rather than toward the upper or lower tails of the distribution. In fact, because the two Lorenz curves intersect in these tails, it is not possible to say that the 2030 distribution Lorenz dominates that of 2000, that is, that inequality is lower in 2030 in relation to 2000, regardless of the inequality measure being used. However, using standard inequality statistics such as the Gini index, the Theil index, and the mean logarithmic deviation, which are indicators that do not give too much weight to the extreme parts of the distribution, a marked reduction of inequality, as shown in table 3-1, is recorded during the period considered here.

The remainder of this section analyzes the drivers of these expected distributional changes by means of two complementary approaches. First, we conduct

20. See World Bank (2006, chapter 3); Bussolo and others (2007).

Table 3-1. *Global Income Inequality*

Index	2000	2030	Dispersion only	Convergence only
Gini	0.672	0.626	0.673	0.625
Theil	0.905	0.749	0.904	0.749
Mean log deviation	0.884	0.764	0.893	0.759

Source: Authors' calculations using data from Global Income Distribution Dynamics (GIDD).

the analysis in terms of the convergence and dispersion components, that is, changes in income disparities between and within countries. This is discussed in the next two subsections, which show that the reduction in global income inequality between 2000 and 2030 is the outcome of two opposing forces: the inequality-reducing convergence effect and the inequality-enhancing dispersion effect (table 3-1). Second, we develop an alternative way of analyzing the evolution of the global income distribution by focusing on the global middle class. The third subsection shows that the combination of the convergence and divergence components drives the dramatic increase in the size of the global middle class and its profound compositional change in favor of developing country nationals. In particular, developing country members of the global middle class are likely to become an increasingly important group within their own countries, raising their political influence and providing continued momentum for policies favoring global integration.

Dispersion Component: Intracountry Inequality on the Rise

Within countries, income distribution will be altered by demographic changes, changes in skilled-to-unskilled wage premiums, and rural-urban migration. In figure 3-3 we plot nonparametric kernel densities of the global income distribution in 2000, together with a hypothetical distribution capturing only the changes in within-country inequality between 2000 and 2030. The hypothetical distribution was created by dividing household incomes in 2030 by the country-specific growth rate of the average incomes between 2000 and 2030. In other words, the dispersion component is the outcome of all the changes outlined in the methodology section, keeping average incomes in each country constant.

Overall, distributional changes within countries have a slight inequality-enhancing effect, with the global income distribution widening by one-tenth of a Gini point (see table 3-1). Within-country income distribution is affected by two sets of factors: shifts in the demographic structure of the population, in terms of aging and education attainment, and changes in rewards for individuals' characteristics, such as education level, experience, sector of employment, and so on. Therefore, the changes in income distribution within each country

Figure 3-3. *Dispersion Component, 2000–30*

Density

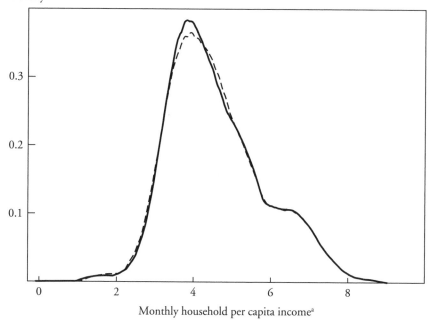

Monthly household per capita income[a]

a. PPP adjusted; log.

can be further decomposed into changes due to shifts in the demographic structure of the labor force and changes due to adjustments in the rewards to personal characteristics. In creating a hypothetical global income distribution for which the only changes occurring between 2000 and 2030 are the shifts in the demographic structure within each country, we can show that the global Gini coefficient would have remained constant. Hence the dispersion component is explained basically by changes in rewards to individuals' characteristics.

The rather modest impact brought about by the dispersion component can be hiding important country-specific changes that at the global level end up canceling each other out. To explore this possibility, figure 3-4 shows the change in the Gini coefficient for each country between 2000 and 2030. More than two-thirds of low- and middle-income countries in the study sample, composing 86 percent of the population in the developing world, are projected to experience a rise in inequality by 2030. For some countries the increase is quite significant. The pure demographic component is depicted by the vertical bars in figure 3-4. Notice that there is very little correlation between the distributional effects of demographic changes and the total change in within-country inequality. Therefore, the general positive shifts in country-specific Gini coefficients

Figure 3-4. *Variation of Gini Coefficient between Base Year and 2030*

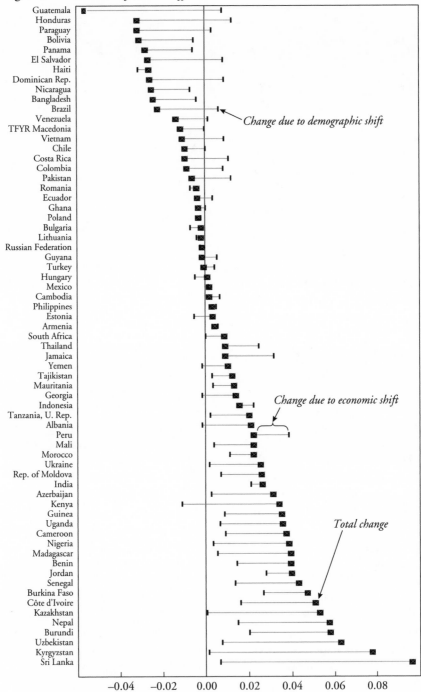

can be attributable to increases in the skilled and urban wage premiums (the difference between the solid squares and the vertical bars in figure 3-4).

Almost all the countries expecting a reduction in inequality are highly unequal Latin America economies. However, inequality-increasing changes take place in African and Asian countries that have relatively low initial inequality. As discussed earlier, widening gaps in factor rewards, and particularly in the premium paid for higher skills, tend to produce larger changes in inequality and generally determine the overall direction of the effect. The results therefore illustrate a convergence of income distributions across countries, which can be interpreted as a manifestation of the Kuznets hypothesis or as a consequence of the globalization-induced equalization of factor prices.

Convergence Component: The Poor World Is Catching Up

There are three aspects determining the existence, sign, and magnitude of each country's contribution to the convergence component: a particular country will have a global distributional impact if its rate of growth differs from the global average; given that the first condition is satisfied, the sign of the distributional effect will depend on the country's initial position in the global distribution; and the magnitude of the impact is determined by the size of the growth rate differentials (with respect to the global average) and the country's share in the global population. Hence, initial poor countries with higher-than-average growth rates will have an inequality-reducing effect with a magnitude determined by the size of the country's population.

Figure 3-5 shows the change of the global income distribution that is due to differences in growth rates between countries when global average income is kept constant. Had the convergence effect been the only change taking place between 2000 and 2030, global inequality would have been reduced by about 5 Gini points (see table 3-1). This means that the improvement in the global distribution reported in the simulation is entirely explained by growth rate differentials across countries, with poor countries catching up with middle- and high-income countries.

The Middle of the Distribution: Is a Global Middle Class Emerging?

The previous sections focused on explaining changes of global income inequality by using a standard decomposition analysis. Three main results have emerged. First, even with significant changes of within-country inequality levels, all the potential reduction of global inequality can be accounted for by the projected convergence in growth rates of average incomes across countries. Second, the aggregate impact of the changes of the within-countries component of inequality appears to be minor; however, specific countries, and specific household types within countries, may experience large distributional shifts. Third, a main cause of local inequality changes is the adjustments of factor rewards. To

Figure 3-5. *Convergence Component, 2000–30*

Density

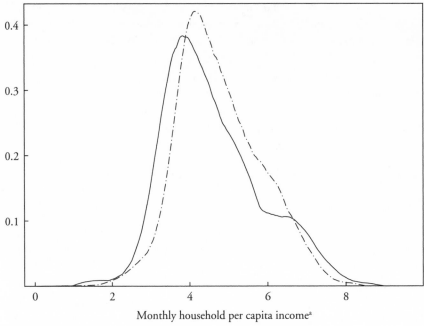

Monthly household per capita income[a]

a. 1993 PPP; log.

translate these results into a more practical and policy-relevant perspective, this section considers what happens to a specific income group during the 2000–30 time period. The group under consideration is labeled the global middle class (GMC) and is composed of people whose income levels are between the average incomes of Brazil and Italy, in purchasing power parity terms.[21]

The idea of focusing on this group is that it should allow analysis to reveal more clearly—or at least under a different light when compared with the previous decomposition analysis—the links between growth, inequality, globalization, and policy. More explicitly, in GMC terms, the growth convergence discussed above means that citizens from developing countries should account for a larger share of this middle class income group and also that the overall size of this group should increase. This should have implications for international policies, such as multilateral trade liberalization, that, in turn, have boosted

21. In 1993 PPP prices, the lower threshold is US$303 per person per month, while the upper threshold is US$611 per person per month. This means that per capita earnings of members of the global middle class are 10 to 20 times above the international poverty line of US$1 a day. These income thresholds are due to the global middle class definition proposed by Milanovic and Yitzhaki (2002).

Table 3-2. *Composition of the Global Middle Class, 2000 and 2030*
Percent

Component	2000		2030	
	Population	Income	Population	Income
Poor[a]	81.5	28.7	61.4	15.8
Middle class[b]	7.9	14.1	16.4	14.3
Nationals from high-income countries	3.5	6.9	1.2	0.5
Nationals from low- and middle-income countries— the proportion of which comes from	4.4	7.3	15.2	4.9
East Asia and Pacific	1.4	2.2	7.8	1.6
Eastern Europe and Central Asia	1.1	1.8	2.5	0.9
Latin America and the Caribbean	1.3	2.3	2.3	1.3
Middle East and North Africa	0.4	0.7	0.7	0.3
South Asia	0.1	0.0	1.6	0.7
Sub-Saharan Africa	0.1	0.3	0.3	0.1
Rich[c]	10.6	57.2	22.2	69.9
Total	100	100	100	100

Source: Authors' calculations.

a. Poor: per capita income is below the average of per capita income of Brazil.

b. Middle class: per capita income is between that of Brazil and of Italy.

c. Rich: per capita income is at or above the average of per capita income of Italy.

globalization in recent decades. And depending of what happens to the middle class within each country, domestic policies may change as well. Even with increasing within-country inequality, as shown above, developing country members of the GMC are likely to become a much stronger force in domestic politics as they increasingly would be considered middle class in their own countries. Mayda and Rodrik confirmed these hypotheses while showing that individuals' relative economic and social status is highly correlated with proglobalization preferences.[22] The literature on the political economy of trade policy proposes that the direction of policy is determined by the preferences of the median voter.[23] At the beginning of this century, the median voter in most developing countries is unlikely to be a member of the middle class, which may help explain why some studies find a negative relationship between promarket policies of the incumbent party and its performance at the ballot box; however, this situation, as shown in table 3-2 and figure 3-6, may be quite different by 2030.[24]

22. Mayda and Rodrik (2005).

23. Mayer (1984).

24. Olivera and Lora (2005).

Figure 3-6. *Changes in the Proportion of the Population Belonging to the Global Middle Class*

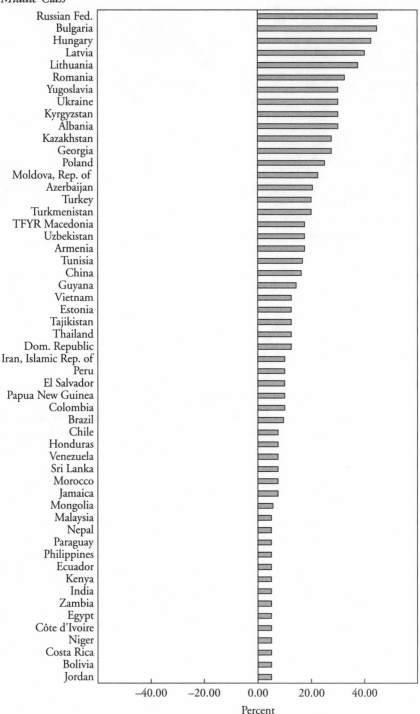

Figure 3-6. *Changes in the Proportion of the Population Belonging to the Global Middle Class (continued)*

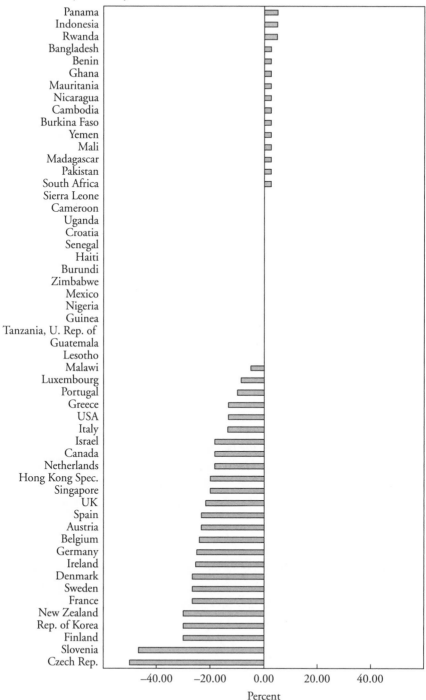

Percent

Our estimates show that the GMC is likely to grow from 430 million in 2000 to 1,147 million in 2030, more than doubling its share in the global population (table 3-2). Furthermore, the composition of this group of consumers is likely to change radically. In 2000, developing country nationals accounted for 56 percent of the GMC; by 2030 they are likely to represent nearly 93 percent of its population (table 3-2). The biggest contributors to the increase in the GMC members are the Asian countries led by China and India. These two countries alone are responsible for nearly two-thirds of the entire increase in the GMC, with China accounting for 52 percent of the rise in the GMC population and India adding another 12 percent. At the same time, the reorientation of the global middle class toward citizens of low- and middle-income countries is very broad based, with all six World Bank developing regions contributing to the growth in the GMC. As shown in figure 3-6, nearly all developing countries in our sample see an increase in the proportion of GMC members in their populations. There are only six exceptions to this observation, and five of them—the Czech Republic, Slovakia, Slovenia, Hong Kong, and Singapore—are today's upper-middle-class countries transitioning to high-income status.

There are several reasons behind the dramatic increase projected in the size of the GMC and the major shift in composition in favor of the low- and middle-income countries. Faster population growth in the developing world is responsible for some of the change in the composition. Thus regions with population growth above the world average (for example, South Asia and sub-Saharan Africa) will increase their share in the global middle class. The main determinant of joining the middle-class ranks, however, is not population growth but income growth. Although East Asia's population grows more slowly than the world average, this region is projected to increase its share of residents in the global middle class by a factor of almost six, compared with a doubling for Africa. The difference is due to the fact that annual per capita income growth in Asia is forecast to be more than twice the growth in sub-Saharan Africa, easily offsetting the decline in the former's population share.

Another determinant of the changing composition of the middle class is the (unequal) shape of the initial income distribution by region. South Asia, which could see a dramatic increase (thirty-one-fold) in the share of its residents in the global middle class, is currently the least unequal region in the world. This means that the benefits of its projected per capita growth of 3.9 percent per year (roughly equal to that of East Asia) are distributed across the population much more equally than in other regions. Sub-Saharan Africa, by contrast, has an initial inequality level that is nearly twice as high. Therefore the same amount of growth would be much less effective at moving large numbers of people up the ladder of income distribution.

Most developing country members of today's (as of 2000) global middle class earn incomes far above the averages of their own countries of residence. In other words, being classified as middle class at the global level is equivalent to being at the top of the distribution in many low-income countries. For example, in our sample, as of 2000, 183 million (out of the total 240 million) developing country citizens in the global middle class are in the top 20 percent of earners within their own countries. By contrast, only 15 percent of members of the global middle class occupy the lower seven deciles of their national income distributions. Thus, for many nations, the correspondence between the global middle class and the within-country middle class is quite low. The situation will change quite dramatically by 2030. A full 63 percent of developing country members of the global middle class will be earning incomes in the seventh decile or lower at the national level. Consider the example of China, where 56 million people belonged to the global middle class in 2000—each of them earning more than 90 percent of all Chinese citizens. By 2030 there will be 429 million Chinese in the global middle class, and their earnings will range from the sixth to the ninth decile of the Chinese national income distribution. They will no longer be among the richest Chinese citizens but will probably be considered upper-middle class. Another example is Brazil, a country that grows one-third as fast as China in per capita terms. Even with slower growth, the number of Brazilians in the GMC will rise from 28 million in 2000 to 55 million by 2030. The compositional change is also important. In 2000 the Brazilians in the global middle class were split evenly across the eighth and ninth income deciles of their national distribution. By 2030, 75 percent of the members of the global middle class will earn the incomes of the sixth and seventh deciles in Brazil, and no member of that class will earn more than 80 percent of the country's population.

Consistent with these data, by 2030 the middle class, together with the rich, will account for a larger share of the population in a greater number of countries. In 2000 the middle class and the rich exceeded 40 percent of the population in just six developing countries, and these countries were home to 0.8 percent of the population of the developing world. By 2030 the middle class and the rich will exceed 40 percent of the population in 34 countries, and these countries will account for 39 percent of the world's developing country population. Therefore, although the ability of the global middle class (together with the rich) to influence policy in many low- and middle-income countries is initially limited by its small size, this group is likely to become a much stronger political force at the global and national levels by 2030.

Conclusions and Future Research

In measuring social welfare, economists have struggled to provide simple statistics that reflect changes in average income and its distribution. This chapter has used a new tool for assessing changes in global income distribution—the

GIDD—to illustrate the trends in these two variables in an ex ante framework. According to the data underlying the GIDD, three-quarters of total world income is controlled by only one-quarter of the world population.[25] More important, we showed that even in a fairly optimistic scenario—where recent trends of strong growth rates for developing countries continue for the next two decades and, as a result, global inequality is in decline—*within*-country income disparities may widen.

This important finding is relevant for policymaking for several reasons. First, the friction between improved convergence of average incomes across countries and widening disparities within them suggests the need to revisit the balance between global and country agendas. Additional multilateral trade liberalization is likely to sustain growth for many developing countries. However, specific groups of people within countries may not be able to adjust to the resulting new wave of globalization and may be left further behind. Worsening inequality can also mute the positive effects of growth on poverty reduction and increase the risk of social alienation of people at the bottom of the distribution. In the end, it may cause counterproductive backlashes against the global liberalization that started the whole process.

One trend that may counterbalance the potential antiglobalization sentiment is the emergence of the global middle class: a group of consumers who demand access to, and have the means to purchase, international goods and services. Our results have shown that the share of these consumers in the global population is likely to more than double by 2030. Even more important, the members of the global middle class will move closer to the median voter in many of today's developing countries, potentially playing a much more important role in domestic policies and supporting further global integration.

At the same time, the emergence of the global middle class will not attenuate rising income inequality, and counterbalancing within-country distributional tensions is likely to require specific domestic policies. Governments should be able to design equity-enhancing policies that can also increase efficiency, but at times they may face trade-offs. For instance, raising direct taxes to excessive levels to finance social services, such as education, targeted to the poor may create disincentives and even curb investment. However, in the long run, once access to education has become more equitable, a larger share of the population will be educated; therefore, growth should also be higher. These long-term benefits of redistribution should be considered when assessing trade-offs between equity

25. This statistic is obtained by ordering all countries according to their per capita incomes, from the richest country to the poorest, and then adding up their populations until the resulting group accounts for 75 percent of world income. In this way, poor and rich individuals within rich countries are added together to form the final group. When all individuals in the world are ordered according to their incomes and irrespective of their nationality, the threshold of three-quarters of global income is reached by a group that is composed of just 20 percent of the world population.

and efficiency. The design and successful implementation of a development strategy that positively reinforces growth and equity objectives is highly country specific. It will depend, among other things, on countries' initial conditions in terms of equity, institutions, and economic structures. By simulating different scenarios and policies, the data and model framework of this chapter represent a first step toward designing these successful development strategies.

References

Atkinson, A. B., and A. Brandolini. 2004. "Global World Inequality: Absolute, Relative or Intermediate." Paper prepared for the 28th conference of the International Association for Research in Income and Wealth (IARIW). Cork, Ireland, August 22–28.

Bhalla, S. 2002. "Imagine There's No Country: Poverty, Inequality, and Growth in the Era of Globalization." Washington: Institute for International Economics.

Bourguignon, François, Victoria Levin, and David Rosenblatt. 2004. "Declining International Inequality and Economic Divergence: Reviewing the Evidence through Different Lenses." *Économie Internationale* (4th Q): 13–26.

Bourguignon, François, and Christian Morrisson. 2002. "Inequality among World Citizens: 1820–1992." *American Economic Review* 92, no. 4: 727–44.

Bourguignon, François, Maurizio Bussolo, and L. Pereira da Silva, eds. 2008. *The Impact of Macroeconomic Policies on Poverty and Income Distribution: Macro-Micro Evaluation Techniques and Tools.* Washington: World Bank and New York: Palgrave Macmillan.

Bussolo, Maurizio, Rafael De Hoyos, and Denis Medvedev. 2008. "Economic Growth and Income Distribution: Linking Macroeconomic Models with Household Survey Data at the Global Level." Paper presented at the 30th conference of the International Association for Research in Income and Wealth (IARIW). Portoroz, Slovenia, August 24–30.

Bussolo, Maurizio, Rafael De Hoyos, Denis Medvedev, and Dominique van der Mensbrugghe. 2007. "Global Growth and Distribution: Are China and India Reshaping the World?" Policy Research Working Papers Series 4392. Washington: World Bank.

Bussolo, Maurizio, J. Lay, and Dominique van der Mensbrugghe. 2006. "Structural Change and Poverty Reduction in Brazil: The Impact of the Doha Round." Policy Research Working Paper Series 3833. Washington: World Bank.

Chen, S., and Marten Ravallion. 2003. "Household Welfare Impacts of China's Accession to the World Trade Organization." Policy Research Working Paper Series 3040. Washington: World Bank.

Mayda, A. M., and Dani Rodrik. 2005. "Why Are Some People (and Countries) More Protectionist than Others?" *European Economic Review* 49, no. 6 (August): 1393–430.

Mayer, W. 1984. "Endogenous Tariff Formation." *American Economic Review* 74: 970–85.

Milanovic, Branko. 2002: "True World Income Distribution, 1988 and 1993: First Calculation Based on Household Surveys Alone." *Economic Journal* 112, no. 476: 51–92.

———. 2005. *Worlds Apart: Measuring International and Global Inequality.* Princeton University Press.

———. 2006. "Global Income Inequality: What It Is and Why It Matters." Policy Research Working Paper Series 3865. Washington: World Bank.

Milanovic, Branko, and S. Yitzhaki. 2002. "Decomposing World Income Distribution: Does the World Have a Middle Class?" *Review of Income and Wealth* 48, no. 2 (June): 155–78.

Olivera, M., and M. Lora. 2005. "The Electoral Consequences of the Washington Consensus." Working Paper 530. Washington: Inter-American Development Bank.

Pritchett, Lant. 1997. "Divergence, Big Time." *Journal of Economic Perspectives* 11, no. 3 (Summer): 3–17.

Quah, Danny T. 1996. "Twin Peaks: Growth and Convergence in Models of Distribution Dynamics." *Economic Journal* 106, no. 437: 1045–055.

———. 1997. "Empirics for Growth and Distribution: Polarization, Stratification, and Convergence Clubs." *Journal of Economic Growth* 2, no. 1: 27–59.

Ravallion, Martin. 2004. "Competing Concepts of Inequality in the Globalization Debate." In *Brookings Trade Forum 2004*, edited by Susan M. Collins and Carol Graham, pp. 1–38. Brookings.

Sala-i-Martin, Xavier. 2002a. "The Disturbing 'Rise' of Global Income Inequality." NBER Working Paper 8904. Cambridge, Mass.: National Bureau of Economic Research (April).

———. 2002b. "The World Distribution of Income (Estimated from Individual Country Distributions)." NBER Working Paper 8933. Cambridge, Mass.: National Bureau of Economic Research (May).

———. 2006. "The World Distribution of Income: Falling Poverty and . . . Convergence, Period." *Quarterly Journal of Economics* 121, no. 2: 351–97.

Theil, Henri, and James L. Seale Jr. 1994. "The Geographic Distribution of World Income, 1950–1990." *De Economist* 142, no. 4: 387–419.

World Bank. 2005. *World Development Report 2006: Equity and Development.* Oxford University Press for the World Bank.

———. 2006. *Global Economic Prospects 2007: Managing the Next Wave of Globalization.* Washington.

4

The Scope and Limits of Subsidies

MARKUS GOLDSTEIN AND ANTONIO ESTACHE

Subsidies are a potentially powerful tool to address concerns about income redistribution when the design of tax systems is ineffective and politically too difficult to alter to achieve fairness. The ability to target subsidies also makes them a potentially effective instrument to correct market failures. Because they are relatively low-cost instruments that can be used to support a wide range of targeted political objectives, subsidies pervade almost all dimensions of our lives. The obvious subsidies are the ones that make the newspapers and generate large public protests such as agriculture, fuel, transport, but there are many more than those making the headlines. At all stages of development, subsidies are everywhere.

Although the monitoring of the fiscal costs of these subsidies tends to be quite imperfect, looking at the information available from international databases easily hints at their high costs. A recent survey conducted by the World Trade Organization (WTO) for its 2006 report on world trade suggests that trade-related subsidies represent at least 1.6 percent of GDP in developed economies, 1.7 percent in transition economies, and 0.6 percent in developing economies.[1] These figures are lower bounds, because they ignore all forms of indirect subsidies, such as tax or financing concessions, which are not accounted

The authors thank Tara Bedi and Angeli Kirk for excellent research assistance.

1. WTO (2006).

for by standardized international reporting of national data. Even as lower bounds, these figures are a significant fiscal burden for any country.

This high cost certainly contributes to the bad reputation of subsidies in many policy and academic circles. But there are additional reasons for the concern with the omnipresence of this instrument. When used poorly, they reduce the efficiency of investment, production, and consumption decisions without delivering much of the fairness or the correction of externalities they are supposed to deliver. Subsidies indeed have the reputation of often being ineffective and mistargeted, in addition to being unduly costly.

This situation raises the central question: why are subsidies still so popular if they are such an unreliable instrument? This is where the middle class enters the discussion. Indeed, if subsidies are intended to be redistributive but are not, and yet they continue to enjoy political support, could it simply mean that their ultimate incidence is on such a broad and powerful basis that it generates enough support for their long-term survival? The source of this broad base could easily be the middle class. It represents 30 to 60 percent of the overall population, in terms of income levels. In the poorest countries, the middle class will see little benefit in a coalition with the poor if reforms designed to pass on more to the poor imply that the rich and the middle class will have to lose some of their benefits. In higher-income countries, the middle class sees itself as close enough to the upper-income classes, so it would not vote to reduce a benefit that it could soon realize.

But the evidence could also be consistent with a number of alternative explanations. The first of these is an Olsonian one: the small group that currently benefits from subsidies has a much stronger incentive to fight for their maintenance or to block any efforts to reform them as opposed to the diffuse, much larger group that would benefit if the subsidies were to be removed. In the case of agriculture in the United States or in Europe, for instance, the current beneficiaries represent a narrow group that is enjoying payoffs so high that it has a stronger motivation to fight for maintenance of these subsidies than anyone else in society has to fight for their improvement or elimination. These types of subsidies are often regressive. In the case of agriculture again, a large share of the landowners are actually not small farmers but investors, which include the rich but also part of the middle class that has enough political clout to maintain the subsidy. So in many instances, there is a natural coalition to leverage fiscal decisions and block changes. Once more, there is a potential role for the middle class in explaining the survival of subsidies or the unhappiness with their elimination in spite of their ineffectiveness in contributing to poverty alleviation or to the internalization of externalities.

A second alternative explanation would leave only a marginal role to the middle class. The facts are also consistent with the possibility that the diversity of subsidies is such that there are enough types of subsidies in existence to meet the needs of everyone and give everyone, or at least a strong majority, a sense that they have an incentive to collude with other subsidy beneficiaries to keep their respective share of the total subsidy pie. This implies that the political support does not really come solely from a coalition based on income levels but from a coalition of different segments of society that are happy to share in the atomized benefits that the individual mistargeting of fiscal instruments allows. Farmers, teachers, industrial producers, workers, or unions, all get a share of the pie and collectively decide to support the overall design of policies, even if they appear to be penalized by the design of specific instruments. This is one case in which the parts look better to voters, taxpayers, producers, and consumers than the sum of the parts. Indeed, an extension to this argument is that subsidies that are badly targeted could do better to increase support for their continuance and thus ensure their political survival—leakage beyond the targeted group can help secure needed votes.

A final possible explanation is that researchers are barking up the wrong tree by using the wrong notion of regressivity. Instead of looking at the percentage of total benefits captured by an income group, the focus should be on the benefits received as a percentage of household income by income group, which would explain better the lasting political support and may highlight an underappreciated role of the middle class in a coalition with either the upper- or lower-income classes.

There is thus a wide range of reasons why the middle class is important in this context, but there are just as many why this class only plays a modest role in maintaining regressive subsidies. Ultimately, the answer is empirical and depends on a wide range of circumstances.

To assess the importance of the incidence of the middle class on the support or rejection of subsidies, the chapter is organized as follows. First, we review the basic economic arguments for subsidies, emphasizing the difficulty of assessing their effectiveness in practice. We then turn to evidence of the fact that these economic reasons are subject to fiscal and political realities. Although we can attempt to lay out the economic arguments for subsidies, this calculus quickly runs aground on the shoals of political considerations and fiscal constraints, so we lay out a simple framework for thinking about these. In the third section, some political economy arguments are discussed, which are needed so that one can appreciate some of the drivers of the viability of subsidies. In the fourth section, we examine the evidence on the redistributional impact of this high-profile fiscal instrument by reviewing the empirical evidence on subsidies in a wide range of countries. This evidence indicates that most subsidies in the developing world are regressive, so the subsequent section develops the arguments for why such regressive subsidies might be expected to persist over time and why they may enjoy the support of the middle class on average. The last section concludes.

On the Complexity of Subsidy Assessments

While everybody seems to have a view on how good or a bad subsidies are, the evidence suggests that the assessment of their incidence is often not a straight-forward exercise. For a given policy goal, policymakers may have to contend with a multitude of often contradictory subsidies that are already in place.

Consider the role of subsidies in the context of climate change, for instance. Given the increased awareness of the risks associated with climate change, it is useful to assess how past and current subsidies are contributing to the current situation and how these policy interventions often intended to protect the poor ended up having very different impacts on the various income classes than the one intended by policymakers.

It could be argued that the quality of the air we are breathing is an out-come of the subsidies that have been enacted with the intent to cut transport costs. Indeed, one ingredient that affects the quality of the air we breathe is automobile emissions, and the fuel that creates these emissions is subsidized. This is because many governments charge below-market rates for the extrac-tion of oil while others may subsidize the cost to consumers. Who actually gains from those subsidies, and hence who supports them?

On the one hand, in most developing countries, subsidies targeted to oil consumption by cars are likely to be highly regressive since ownership of vehi-cles tends to be concentrated in the upper-income brackets. In developed countries, the situation is less clear since older, less fuel-efficient generations of cars tend to belong to the poorest segments of the population, and high-gasoline-consuming new vehicles tend to belong to the rich, leaving the mid-dle class relatively worse off.

On the other hand, governments may subsidize the reduction of auto emis-sions and the use of public transportation. For example, New Delhi recently switched to natural gas as the fuel for public transport, and as part of this switch, the government subsidized the conversion of engines of motorized rickshaws. In Europe, in addition to the subsidies to public transportation modes, such as subways, government subsidies for the purchase of clean cars run as high as 20 percent of the cost of the clean vehicles. In many large cities, the incidence of public transportation tends to be spread across all income classes, while the subsidies to private vehicles tend to benefit the middle- and upper-income classes that can afford vehicles with cleaner technologies.

The fact that any given subsidy program can be associated with so many dif-ferent, sometimes contradictory, outcomes explains our collective poor grasp of the incidence of subsidies. It is all the more problematic that these widely spread subsidies have significant fiscal implications, however one chooses the denomi-nator. For example, according to the British minister for European affairs in

Table 4-1. *Fiscal Costs of Subsidies as a Share of GDP*

Country grouping	Share of GDP (percent)
Africa	0.58
Asia	0.79
India	2.60
China	1.10
Asia without China and India	0.49
Central and Latin America	0.48
Middle East	0.56
Transition economies	1.71
Developing economies	0.60
Developed (OECD) economies	1.56

Source: Authors' calculations based on data from World Trade Organization (WTO) (2006).

2005, the European Union was spending 2 euros in subsidies per cow per day.[2] These subsidies can add up to a large fraction of national budgets. Egypt, for example, spent an estimated 6.9 percent of GDP on fuel subsidies and 1.6 percent of GDP on food subsidies in 2005–06.[3] Furthermore, changes to the levels of these subsidies can have large policy implications: when Malawi removed primary school fees in the 1990s, enrollment went up by 1 million children over six years, and the enrollment gap between the rich and the poor closed.[4]

Table 4-1 summarizes the information available across regions on the lower bound of the fiscal costs of subsidies as a share of GDP—approximated by trade-related subsidies. In general, excluding India and China, subsidies represent about 0.5 percent of GDP in developing economies. The Asian giants are outliers in the sample of forty-two countries covered by the 2006 WTO survey: India spends about 2.6 percent of its GDP on subsidies and China spends about 1.1 percent. In transition economies the share is also high with about 1.7 percent of GDP spent on subsidies. It is interesting to note that in almost all of the countries in the developed OECD economies group, the share is above 1 percent, with the notable exception of the United States, where it is 0.5 percent.

The contrast between the high political visibility of subsidies and their high cost and uncertain effectiveness explains the differences in perspectives on subsidies between economists and politicians. Although in view of the potentially significant redistributive payoff of subsidies as well as their potential role in

2. Daniel Wortmann, "The EU's Agricultural Dilemma," *Deutsche Welle,* June 22, 2005 (www.dw-world.de/dw/article/0,2144,1625243,00.html).

3. IMF (2006).

4. Al-Samarrai and Zaman (2007).

correcting market failure, they should be as popular among economists as they are among policymakers; in practice they are not. It turns out that economists tend to dislike them because the justification presented for subsidies by policymakers is often muddled, leading to outcomes that end up achieving neither redistribution nor improved functioning of markets. For many, subsidies are thus undesirable because they distort decisions and do not reach those they should. It turns out that the evidence reviewed here suggests that, on the equity front, this view is frequently right—subsidies are often regressive. However, the bad reputation of subsidies is hard to reconcile with the long-lasting effective support they enjoy from politicians that perpetuates their existence. The pervasiveness of this instrument is an indication of its broad support beyond politicians. But this support for an apparently ineffective and possibly regressive instrument is puzzling.

Why Do Many Economists Still Support Subsidies?

The tendency in public discourse and the press is to think of subsidies as payments to producers. However, as some of the examples above show, subsidies apply to producers and consumers. Simply put, the definition of a subsidy is when the price (or what would be the market-determined price) is lower than the cost, and the government provides the funds to fill this gap.

Clearly this can lead to confusion in the appreciation of what is a subsidy and how effective it is. The core source of this confusion stems once more from the competing rationales used to justify subsidies. Consider the case of primary health care. One often hears a wide range of arguments as to why governments should subsidize it. One group argues that primary health care is a basic right, so access to it must be an equity issue. The hard-headed economist says no, lack of access to primary health care is a market failure due to incomplete information on the part of the clients, or maybe a discount rate issue leading to an underinvestment in preventive health. The not-so-hard-headed economist says no, access to primary health care is an externality—healthier people will be better able to participate in society—a concept that people do not take into account when making individual, private health care choices.

All of these arguments might be valid reasons for a subsidy. However, they can have different implications as to whom the government subsidizes, how much of a subsidy is offered, how the subsidy is offered, and the like. If there is no clear consensus or discussion on why the subsidy is justified (at least the main reason why), then the success or failure of a subsidy cannot be measured. Thus it will be hard to have a constructive or meaningful policy debate about how to allocate scarce financial resources.

In economics literature, there are two main justifications for subsidies. The first justification is based on equity, and here subsidies are viewed as a tool for redistribution. The second is an efficiency argument: Markets are not working correctly, and a subsidy is needed to help correct the market failure. In the realm of policymaking, these two justifications face two central constraints: fiscal limitations and political feasibility. Before discussing these constraints in greater depth, it is worth briefly revisiting the theoretical arguments that provide the justification for subsidies.

Subsidies to Improve Equity

When the goal is equity (and not market failures) government wants to redistribute income. From a strict welfare point of view, the best way to do this is to just give the poor a lump sum transfer. But this may involve prohibitive administrative costs (for identification, delivery, leakage, and the like), and also there may be political obstacles (for example, it is possibly a lot more difficult politically to transfer a chunk of money to the poor than it is to lower the price they pay for a given good). Given these issues, government may want to turn to subsidies as a tool for redistribution.

Now that government has decided to subsidize, the first question (which incidentally also applies to the lump sum case) is what is meant by equity: who gets how much? Ultimately this comes down to the social welfare function that will determine the weights that different types of individuals in society will receive (for example, everyone, poor or not, could be weighted equally, or more weight might be given to the poor). Equity is a broad and politically charged concept and the subject for another, longer discussion.[5] In the end, weights in society will be determined by the institutions and the process by which these institutions make decisions. The specific distribution of benefits aside, equity is the most commonly cited reason by politicians as a justification for subsidies.

Subsidies to Improve Efficiency

Economic theory provides a clear role for government intervention when markets are not working properly. When the discussion is on whether to apply subsidies or taxes, there are two main manifestations of market failure that would justify intervention. The first case is that of externalities. Recall that the definition of an externality is when the action of an agent affects at least one other through mechanism(s) other than price. An important point to note about externalities is that they create a difference between marginal social cost (benefit) and private cost (benefit)—and this may be a gap that needs a subsidy. One clear example of a case in which the government may want to fund this gap is the provision of treatment for tuberculosis. Tuberculosis is spread fairly easily; for example, when an infected individual coughs in a public place, he or she poses a significant risk to those around. Many indi-

5. See, for example, World Bank (2006b).

viduals will not take this infectiousness (and their effect on others) into account when deciding to purchase treatment. As a result, governments may wish to fill the gap between the social and private returns to treatment by subsidizing care (and many in fact do).

A special case of externalities is public goods. Public goods are an externality because individuals do not take into account the marginal benefit (or cost) to other individuals when deciding how much of a public good to purchase. By definition, public goods are goods that are nonrivalrous (one person's consumption does not affect another's) and nonexcludable. These are hard criteria to meet, and in reality there are few pure examples (national defense and the BBC are two). The arguments for why things may initially seem like public goods break down on closer examination. For example, roads are often called a public good, but technically they are not: when enough individuals start to use a road, they become rivalrous (or traffic by another name). There is a large set of goods that have *some* aspects of public goods (they are either nonrivalrous or nonexcludable). Here, the simple logic for government provision or funding breaks down (witness the debate over toll roads).

In addition to externalities, another source of market failure that may justify initiating a subsidy is problems of information. The most straightforward examples of these are information-related market failures in insurance and credit markets. For example, part of the logic for microfinance is that the information costs for very small borrowers are often prohibitive for standard institutions, and thus some form of subsidy is needed. In many cases, when technical assistance and the cost of funds are included, subsidies continue to play an important role in many microfinance institutions.

Merit Goods?

Having looked at equity and efficiency as logic for subsidies, we can turn to a sometimes used third reason—merit goods. The basic reasoning behind merit goods is that government should subsidize certain goods because government has determined that they are good for people, irrespective of what the people themselves think. The merit goods argument is used not only to argue for public support for goods such as museums but sometimes to justify a host of basic social services—primary education, clean water, and the like. It is worth trying to dissect this definition a bit to understand what this justification could include. A broader definition breaks merit goods into three parts:

—"individuals cannot correctly perceive their own welfare," which basically is paternalism: the state knows best

—"society may wish for an equitable distribution of these goods," which is equity

—"consumption of certain goods contributes to the formation of values upon which society is based," which is an externality (for example, in education one of the justifications is that better educated people make better citizens and better voters, which is something that is not taken into account very much when individuals choose their level of education)

In the end, one may decide that this is a good reason to justify a government subsidy (for example, most every country has government-subsidized museums), but one needs to be explicit about it and to clearly separate it from equity and efficiency arguments. Too often merit goods are used as a sort of catchall explanation or as a mislabelled argument for efficiency or equity.

Equity and Efficiency Trade-Offs: Sometimes, but Not Always

Often there may be an efficiency and equity trade-off in the government's choice to subsidize. An easy example of this is that a subsidy formulated for equity reasons may generate inefficiencies in markets as well (for example, bread is subsidized, which in turn generates inefficiencies in agricultural markets). However, a subsidy for efficiency reasons can have negative equity implications (for example, a subsidy for the provision of court services will be regressive in a country in which the poor have little access to the formal court system). On another level, these trade-offs can also manifest when a broader view is adopted that takes into account the way in which the subsidy will be funded. The incidence and efficiency cost of the tax or another revenue source have to be considered so that a complete picture of trade-offs is presented. We discuss this broader view below in the context of examining incidence.

While common, such trade-offs are not always the case, and there are some cases in which there may not be an equity and efficiency trade-off. One such case is when the correction of the market failure is not possible or is too costly. In this case, some redistribution can improve efficiency. Take the case of primary education. George Psacharopoulos estimated that the returns to primary education were 24 percent in Africa and 20 percent in Asia.[6] The obvious efficiency-enhancing solution would be to create sufficient credit markets so that the poor could borrow and take advantage of these high returns (in much the same way that there are student loan markets for tertiary education in the United States). However, this is not practical for a host of practical and political reasons. Hence, an equity-enhancing subsidy (making primary education free) would in this case also serve an efficiency goal. Another case in which there is no clear equity and efficiency trade-off is in the removal of certain subsidies that are regressive and that contribute to inefficiency. For example, in Japan, the average farm household income is 110 percent of the average household income, yet from 2000 to 2002, producers received $47.5 billion in subsidies.[7] Such examples are not confined to developed countries, as we shall see later. For now we

6. Psacharopoulos (1994).
7. Aksoy and Beghin (2004).

turn to an examination of the constraints that affect how the theoretical justifications are actually implemented in practice.

Political Considerations in the Formulation of Subsidies

In the assessment of the political factors that will influence the practical feasibility of either an equity- or efficiency-enhancing subsidy, there are three central questions that help to demarcate the analysis. First, who will be the winners and losers because of this policy, and whom will they vote for (if they vote)? Second, who are the interest groups around this issue, and how much power do they have? Third, what is the time horizon of policymakers? In the end, when political considerations and constraints are added to the policy mix, the outcome does not have to be either fair or efficient, as we saw in the examples above for farm subsidies.

The primary set of constraints to formulating subsidy policy consists of the political configurations in which subsidy policy is made; coalitions between the middle class and either the rich or the poor can prove critical to the ultimate outcomes. In some countries, the middle class will prove to be a significant voting block. In addition, in many countries, the middle class will have a strong role in shaping the position of important interest groups (for example, unions and producer associations). We will return to these two cases below when we examine possible explanations for the persistence of regressive subsidies.

The second set of constraints in making subsidy policy centers on where the money is going to come from. There are three possible options, starting with taxation for redistribution. One important thing to keep in mind is that when tax and redistribution are discussed in relation to subsidies, taxes themselves entail some efficiency cost. In some contexts in which tax systems are not functioning well and much economic activity is informal, the efficiency cost of taxes can be quite high.

The government subsidization of health care in Finland provides a good example of using taxes to finance subsidies. In Finland, the national health insurance is funded mostly through payroll deductions—a progressive tax, but it also has some other sources (returns on assets, for example). Patients pay only 24 percent of their health care costs; the remainder is financed by local (43 percent) and national governments (18 percent) and national health insurance (15 percent). National health insurance contributes to a large fraction of the economy: health is a significant part of government spending, accounting for 25 percent of municipal budgets, while welfare and social security account for about 20 percent of national government expenditure. This money seems to be spent to good effect. According to a survey published by the European Commission in 2000, Finland has the highest number of people satisfied with their health care system in the EU. More than 80 percent of

Finnish respondents were satisfied compared with the EU average of 41.3 percent of respondents.

A second way to finance subsidies is to use cross subsidization. This can be within a given sector. For example, in Gabon, users of urban electricity subsidize water and electricity for residents of rural areas and small towns. Cross subsidization can also occur across sectors. For example, in Ecuador, a surcharge on telecommunications provides some of the financing for water services. A final mode for the finance of subsidies, at least in the developing world, is through grants from donors. Grants obviously are not sustainable indefinitely, but when properly designed and planned for phaseout, they can provide an important boost on the capital investment side, for example, by building power generation capacity and connecting new users to the grid.

The political and fiscal constraints can often interact to have a powerful effect on subsidy policy. One example comes from the provision of food subsidies in Sri Lanka (a case which we discuss in more detail below). At independence, Sri Lanka established a universal food subsidy. In the early 1950s, inflationary pressure rose as the price of rice increased (the main subsidized good). The government then engaged in "overenthusiastic" adherence to an International Monetary Fund (IMF) program that resulted in a significant cut in subsidies. The cut was met with heavy protests and riots, in which labor (including the middle class) was heavily involved. This, in turn, led to a partial policy reversal and the resignation of the prime minister. The government ultimately fell, and the new government restored the level of subsidies (helped in part by a fall in the price of rice). This is just one example from a point in time, but throughout the history of this program in Sri Lanka, there have been a number of cases of fiscal constraint that led to political turmoil around this subsidy.

Do Subsidies Help the Poor in Practice? The Evidence on Equity

Given the frequent justification of subsidies on equity grounds by politicians, it is worth looking at the incidence of a range of subsidies. According to a recent review of utility subsidies, "in high-income countries, only 50 percent of water utilities charge tariffs high enough to cover more than operation and maintenance cost. In low-income countries, barely 3 percent of water utilities were able to achieve this level."[8] Since access to water is roughly universal in high-income countries, depending on the specific tariff structure, the odds are that the subsidies are likely, at the least, to benefit all income classes somewhat and possibly the poorest more. In developing countries, since coverage is much less widespread, people with access to water services tend to be from the richest income classes. In Africa, for instance, while the subsidy may be designed as a progressive

8. Komives and others (2005, p. 22).

instrument for people with access to the service, for any given tariff structure, the subsidy may be supporting mostly the upper-middle-income classes, which represent the poorest part of the segment of the population that does have access to water service. When the people without access are considered, the water subsidies in developing countries are likely to be regressive since the poor and the lower-middle classes are often excluded from the subsidized services. Thus it is important to try to come up with a concept of incidence that recognizes all income classes.

In what follows, we use the concept of *absolute incidence,* which is defined as the share of total spending on a subsidy that goes to an income group. When the upper-income levels capture a larger share of the subsidy in proportion to the population, we classify the subsidy as *regressive.* When the middle class (middle-income groups) captures a disproportionate share of subsidy spending, we classify the subsidy as a *bell curve.* In the cases when the poor capture a disproportionate share—that is, when the subsidy is actually redistributing wealth—it is classified as *progressive.*

Table 4-2 provides the evidence on education spending gleaned from a number of recent World Bank public expenditure reviews (PERs).[9] In this table, we can see that in two-thirds of the cases, spending on primary education is progressive. There is no strong reason for the middle class to be a major actor in the rejection or support of subsidies aimed at the primary education sector.

The table also shows that in 40 percent of the primary education cases of this relatively small sample, the public sector is not delivering on its equity objectives. In three countries, spending is effectively neutral; in one case, the middle class captures disproportionate benefits; and in four cases, spending is actually regressive, favoring the rich and the middle class. This very simple review of a key social sector already hints at a problem with the effectiveness of subsidies. The review also suggests that in 20 percent of the cases, the beneficiaries of the ineffectiveness of the expenditure include the middle class and all of its political power.

The story emerging for secondary and tertiary education provides an even stronger sense that there may be a good case for the middle- and upper-income classes to object to significant reforms of the financing of education. In almost all cases, public expenditures in secondary and tertiary education are regressive. The exception to this is secondary expenditure in Dominica, which is progressive. The other exceptions are Ecuador and Jamaica, where the middle quintiles capture a disproportionate share of the spending relative to the poor and the rich (and hence the distribution has a bell curve shape).

---

9. Note that the years in parentheses after a specific country are not necessarily the year of the PER but rather the year that the data used are from.

Table 4-2. *The Incidence of Government Spending on Education*

Country	Primary	Secondary	Tertiary	Overall
Argentina (1999)			Regressive	Regressive
Bolivia (2002)	Progressive	Regressive	Regressive	
Cambodia (1997)	Neutral	Regressive	Regressive	
Cambodia (2002)	Progressive	Regressive	Regressive	Neutral
Djibouti (2002)	Regressive	Regressive	Regressive	Regressive
Dominica (2002)	Progressive	Progressive	Regressive	
Dominican Republic (1998)	Progressive	Regressive	Regressive	Progressive
Dominican Republic (2004)	Progressive	Urban: regressive Rural: progressive	Regressive	
Ecuador (1999)	Progressive	Bell curve	Regressive	
El Salvador (2002)	Progressive	Regressive	Regressive	Progressive
Ethiopia (2002)	Regressive	Regressive		Regressive
Jamaica (2000)	Progressive	Bell curve	Regressive	Neutral
Indonesia (2005)	Progressive	Regressive	Regressive	Regressive
Lesotho (2002)	Neutral		Regressive	Regressive
Madagascar (2001)	Regressive	Regressive		
Mexico (2002)	Progressive	Regressive	Regressive	Neutral
Mozambique (1997)	Regressive	Regressive	Regressive	Regressive
Pakistan (1999)	Progressive	Regressive		
Swaziland (2001)	Bell curve	Regressive	Regressive	Regressive
Tajikistan (2003)	Neutral	Regressive	Regressive	Regressive
Vietnam (1998)	Progressive	Regressive		
Vietnam (2002)	Progressive	Regressive		

Source: World Bank public expenditure reviews (PERs), various years.

Table 4-3 also uses data from public expenditure reviews to examine another sector that the government often subsidizes in an attempt to reduce poverty and inequality, which is health. The health sector is more heterogeneous across countries, and hence this incidence analysis is less comparable across countries than is the incidence analysis for education. Nonetheless, the majority of cases examined in table 4-3 show regressive patterns of the distribution of government largesse, sometimes in ways that might not be expected.

Take the three rows that show data from Jamaica. The table shows that outpatient care and hospital care are progressive, while primary care is regressive. In contrast, in Indonesia, there is a pattern similar to that for education in which the higher level of care is regressive. The case of Mexico is interesting because there is a fund that is financed by contributions by formal sector employees and their employers. If we net this out, the net distribution is neutral, but more on Mexico below.

It is also worth looking at incidence in infrastructure. Figure 4-1 draws on data from Kristin Komives and colleagues to show some results for electricity

Table 4-3. *The Incidence of Government Spending on Health*

Country	Type	Distribution
Bolivia (1999)	Social insurance	Regressive
	Public expenditure	Progressive
Bolivia (2002)	Overall (excluding health insurance)	Progressive
Cambodia (2002)	All health care	Bell curve, Regressive
	Primary health care	Relatively neutral
Djibouti (1996)	Hospital care	Regressive
Dominican Republic (2004)	Overall	Regressive
Ecuador (1999)	Health care IESS	Regressive
	Health care MSP	Relatively neutral
	Health care SSC	Progressive
El Salvador (2002)	Hospital care	Relatively neutral
	Primary health care	Progressive
Ethiopia (2002)	Primary health care	Progressive
	Immunizations	Regressive
	Overall	Regressive
Jamaica (1991–2002)	Average ratio of poorest to richest quintile for public hospital use (Q1/Q5)	1.83; Progressive
	Average ratio of poorest to richest quintile for primary care use (Q1/Q5)	0.82; Regressive
	Average ratio of poorest to richest quintile for outpatient care (Q1/Q5)	1.76; Progressive
Indonesia (2005)	Hospital care	Regressive
	Health cards	Progressive
	Primary health care	Relatively neutral
	Overall	Regressive
Mexico (2002)	All public health expenditure	Regressive[a]
Mozambique (1997)	Immunizations	Relatively neutral
	Antenatal	Relatively neutral
	Hospital care	Regressive
	Overall	Regressive
Uzbekistan (2003)	Hospital care	Regressive
	Overall	Regressive

Source: World Bank public expenditure reviews (PERs), various years.

IESS = Instituto Ecuatoriano de Seguridad Social (Ecuadorian Social Security Institute); MSP = Ministerio de Salud Pública (Ecuadorian Ministry of Public Health); SSC = Seguro Social Campesino (Ecuadorian rural social security).

a. This is the distribution of all public expenditure in health. But private contributions to Instituto Mexicano del Seguro Social (IMSS, Mexican Social Security Institute, serving formal sector workers) are not netted out of total public expenditure. If private contributions to IMSS are netted out, then it becomes neutral.

Figure 4-1. *Performance Indicators for Benefit Targeting*
Incidence

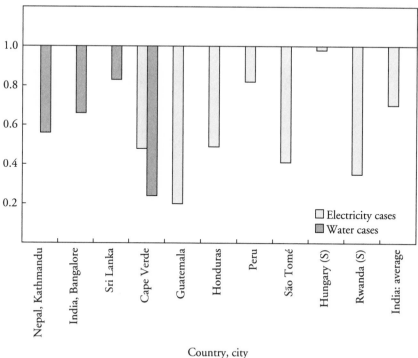

Source: Komives and others (2005).

and water. This figure is for quantity-based infrastructure subsidies.[10] The targeted performance indicator is the share of subsidies that go to the poor by the population share of the poor. So 1 is a neutral subsidy (that is, all groups benefit equally), greater than 1 is progressive, and less than 1 regressive. In figure 4-1, all of these (quantity-based) utility subsidies are regressive.[11]

Keep in mind that most of these types of subsidies are increasing block tariffs (IBTs)—by which the subsidy decreases as volume increases—and hence by design, these are supposed to be progressive. Note that once administrative targeting is added (for example, geographic targeting) these can break the line into progressive, and there are indeed examples of this.[12] For example, in Bogota, where IBTs are combined with geographically designed tariffs, the incidence is 1.09. Of course, means-tested programs are also more progressive—the

10. Komives and others (2005).
11. The exception is Gujrat, which is neutral, and is not shown here as we have used the India average to save space.
12. See Komives and others (2005, pp. 92–94).

Figure 4-2. *Mexico: Benefits and Taxes*

Percent

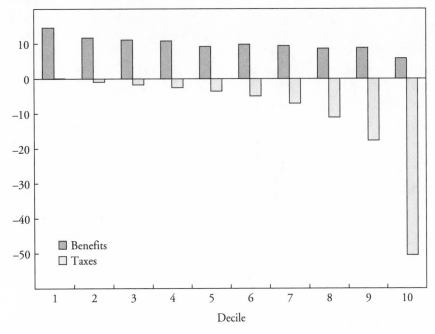

Source: World Bank (2004).

Georgian Winter Heating Assistance Program, which uses proxy means test-ing (among others), has an incidence indicator of 1.2, despite the fact that it excludes a large fraction of poor households (75 percent). Another example is the means-tested water supply in Paraguay that has an incidence indicator of 1.64.

Nonetheless, based on the accumulated evidence above, it seems that a majority of government subsidies, despite being justified in the political realm on grounds of equity, are actually regressive. Before moving to a discussion on why this might be the case, it is worth adding one caveat to this evidence.

Recall from our discussion above that a more in-depth understanding of the equity (and efficiency) effects of a subsidy has to take into account not only the distribution of the subsidy but also the effects of the means used to raise the funding for the subsidy. The 2004 World Bank public expenditure review for Mexico provides a nice example of this exercise. Figure 4-2 shows the incidence of *both* taxes and combined social spending.

From this figure we can see that while the benefits are somewhat progressive, taxes are sharply progressive (it is not visible on this graph, but the lowest income decile actually gets a tax credit). Thus, when we put the two together, we get a clearer idea of the net redistributive effect. Unfortunately, this kind of evidence is rare (adding up all of the subsidies is hard enough, to say nothing of tax incidence, particularly in countries with many sources of tax revenue), so we are not able to estimate the net distributional impacts of the subsidies discussed above. Yet, even if the means used to raise the funds for the subsidy are progressive, a regressive distribution of the subsidy itself undermines the goal of enhancing equity (and very few of the subsidies discussed above were justified on efficiency grounds).

If Most Subsidies Are Regressive, Why Do They Last?

Earlier we presented the arguments from economic theory as to when subsidies might be justified. However, when we seek to understand the policy outcomes that we see in practice, we are better served by arguments familiar to those who work in political science and political economy. In this section we revisit the main reasons why regressive subsidies persist, focusing on the three that seem to matter the most in practice.

Entrenched, Clear Winners with a Diffuse Set of Losers

The theory of collective action holds that when a cohesive, organized, and vocal minority faces a dispersed and unorganized majority in the political sphere, it is possible for the preferences of the minority to triumph. Thus one argument for the persistence of regressive subsidies is that these subsidies, which may even have been progressive (or efficiency enhancing) at the start, have created an organized and vocal group that has a strong interest in maintaining them. The persistence of this over time, and its detrimental development effects for the economy as a whole, are well laid out in Mancur Olson's *The Rise and Decline of Nations* (1982).

Raquel Fernandez and Dani Rodrik provide an extension to this logic that is particularly relevant to the case of subsidies.[13] In seeking to explain the failure of some obviously useful reforms to come to fruition, Fernandez and Rodrik focused on the fact that it is often difficult to identify those who will gain from the reform before the reform takes place. Given individual voter uncertainty as to whether he or she will be a gainer or a loser, a majority of voters may choose to block a reform that would in fact enjoy broad political support. This ties in with the fundamental coalitional story on subsidies in a number of ways, including the fact that when a subsidy is being proposed for reform it is often not clear who the beneficiaries of any remaining subsidy will be post reform and how the savings on the subsidy will be distributed once the subsidy is reformed (or abolished).

---

13. Fernandez and Rodrik (1991).

One example of these issues can be found in the case of electricity subsidies in the Indian state of Andhra Pradesh. As Navroz Dubash put it in discussing the national picture, "a decision to provide cheap electricity for agriculture (specifically for groundwater pumping) to stimulate India's Green Revolution quickly morphed into a highly successful populist political strategy by the late 1970s. By the mid-1980s farmers in a variety of states received either free electricity or electricity charged at a flat rate."[14] Getting rid of this subsidy in Andhra Pradesh would arguably enhance efficiency and equity. It would enhance efficiency since, because of the subsidies, the government has to roster the electricity (that is, give farmers electricity at preannounced and restricted hours). But because of energy shortages, the quality, amount, and voltage of electricity are unreliable. This leads to unpredictability of supply that can cripple yields and cause periodic blowouts of pump motors and transformers. Furthermore, since farmers in Andhra Pradesh are charged a flat rate on electricity, the marginal cost of pumping more water is zero. This leads to overuse of groundwater. This is critical in Andhra Pradesh, especially in the drought-prone areas. This flat rate also indicates the equity improvement—this is a regressive subsidy. Indeed, the lack of redeeming qualities of this subsidy (except for an increasingly entrenched group of farmers) eventually entered into the political debate in the state. Hope for change rose with the election of a reform-minded chief minister in 1995. Indeed, this chief minister was even reelected after slightly raising agricultural electricity tariffs. However, in mid-2004 he lost the election to an opponent who promised free power to farmers and whose victory was due in part to support from farmers.[15] The perceived role of electricity subsidies in contributing to the government's loss had immediate spillovers across the country—this defeat was followed by increased electrical concessions in a number of other states.

Rethinking Regressivity

Another argument for why regressive subsidies persist is that we researchers are not using a politically relevant measure of what constitutes a regressive subsidy. The figures above use a definition of *absolute regressivity,* which compares the share of expenditure received by an income decile relative to its population share. If, in fact, voters vote their pocketbook, a more useful measure would not focus on what they get relative to other groups, but rather how important the subsidy is to them individually. This leads us to the measure of *relative regressivity,* which measures the fraction of a group's total income that comes from the subsidy. The following figures, using data on a propane subsidy in the Domini-

14. Dubash (2005, p. 3).
15. As Dubash noted, the opponent also carried urban areas, so farmers only played one part in this electoral reversal.

Figure 4-3. *Propane Subsidies, Absolute Incidence*
Percentage of subsidy received

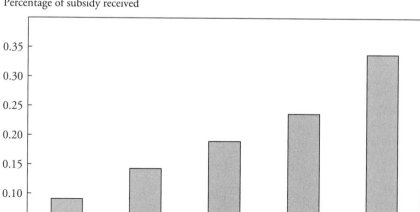

Source: World Bank (2006a).

can Republic, will help to illustrate this point. Figure 4-3 shows the distribution of the subsidy using our previous definition of absolute regressivity.

This figure shows that this subsidy is quite regressive—the share captured by the top quintile of the income distribution is more than three times that of the poorest and almost double that of the middle quintile. Figure 4-4 uses the relative measure of incidence. Here we can see that, as a fraction of income, this subsidy is much more important to the poor and middle-income groups than it is to the top group.[16] Thus, when groups decide their political support based on what this policy means to them (and not on their relative receipts), this argument can help explain why the middle class (and the poor) consistently supports subsidies that disproportionately benefit the rich.

Some Leakage Is Good, by Keeping a Bigger Chunk of Voters and Key Interest Groups on Board

Indeed, a corollary of the argument that we need to look at relative rather than absolute incidence is that some amount of leakage is good politics, as it will help sustain support for a subsidy that may be quite important for the poor.

16. Note that these graphs use 2004 data. In 2004 the government instituted reforms that capped the monthly subsidy that households could get from this subsidy. Simulations for 2006 of this reform (World Bank 2006a) showed that while the subsidy would likely become more progressive, the basic patterns shown here would not change.

Figure 4-4. *Propane Subsidies, Relative Incidence*
Subsidies as percentage of income

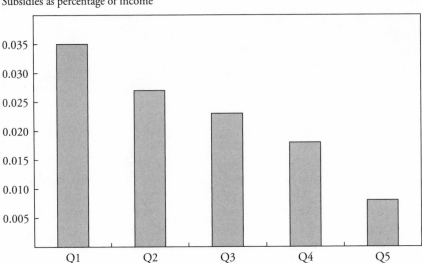

Source: World Bank (2006a).

The case of food subsidies in Sri Lanka provides a useful example of the importance of these kinds of coalitions, as well as the broader political dimensions, in reality. Sri Lanka had an almost universal food subsidy from the point of its independence.[17] In no small measure because of this universality, this subsidy enjoyed widespread support from successive governments and voters. Indeed, the subsidy was maintained by governments of significantly different ideology in the name of political stability and equity. On the voter side, there was a broad base of support, including unions. Additional political support was also provided by the fact that the subsidy targeted producers as well as consumers. The subsidy focused on rice (a staple), but it also, at one point or another, covered wheat, flour, sugar, and powdered milk. This subsidy had significant balance of payment implications since, during most of the period during which the subsidy was universal, more than 50 percent of Sri Lanka's food was imported.

During the period 1978–79, there was a large devaluation, and a new government was elected. Since this was a liberalizing government, the initial push for the reform of subsidies was part of its overall policy on subsidies and allowed policymakers to push their horizon beyond a short-run view. The main reform was the implementation of a means test. The means test was a household

---

17. Edirisinghe and Sahn (1993) demonstrate how important this subsidy was for the poor.

monthly income threshold (with some marginal allowance for household size) and reduced the number of beneficiaries to half the population. The government also shifted the benefits from rations to food stamps. In the shift to food stamps, the number of beneficiaries did not fall but actually started rising. In response the government fixed the number of beneficiaries and fixed the *nominal* amount allocated to the food stamp program in the budget. The government also protected itself from the anger of a potentially powerful interest group—wage earners—through government and parastatal wage increases. This powerful interest group had been at the heart of earlier protests.

On one level this rationalization worked: the government spending on total food (and kerosene) subsidies fell from 15 percent of government expenditure (5 percent of GNP) in the mid-1970s to 5 percent of government expenditure (2 percent of GNP) by 1982. On another level, the fact that this benefit was fixed in nominal terms meant that it was eroded considerably by the significant rates of inflation that Sri Lanka experienced. How was this erosion politically tenable when previous efforts to reduce the benefit had met with stiff opposition? Part of the explanation seems to lie in the fact that the middle class (and the rich) no longer benefited as much as it had. Recall that one of the earlier reforms had provided other benefits (wage increases) to government and parastatal workers, thereby lessening their opposition. Also, the move to means testing had some impact on reducing the provision of benefits to higher-income groups. This reduction in leakage had the effect of reducing political support as the middle and upper classes no longer had such a significant stake in the level of the subsidy.

Conclusion

Clear rationales for subsidies as an essential fiscal policy instrument to address redistribution concerns exist in economic theory—in addition to their role in correcting market failures of information or externalities. Despite the fact that this equity argument is often used in the political realm, it is evident that many of the subsidies in the developing world are, in fact, regressive, and many in the developed world have an unclear incidence. We think that three main explanations drive this phenomenon. First, entrenched, focused interest groups (which often come from the middle and upper classes) can create more political pressure than the more diffuse population that would benefit from a reform. Second, we argue that while many of these subsidies are indeed regressive in an absolute sense, when viewed from the point of view of the pocketbooks of poor and middle-class voters, they are actually relatively more important sources of income. Hence, given this relative importance, these groups will continue to provide political support for these subsidies. Finally, we utilize another facet of this second argument to argue that some amount of leakage to the middle class is likely to be necessary to sustain support for a subsidy that actually does target the poor disproportionately. When a subsidy is perfectly targeted to the poor, and when the poor do not represent a majority, political support weakens. Taken together these arguments show that while many subsidies may fail the logic of economic theory, reform in practice is likely to run afoul of the reality of political logic. And this logic gives a significant role to the middle class in ensuring that the poor get their fair share of the subsidies.

References

Aksoy, M., and J. Beghin. 2004. *Global Agricultural Trade and Developing Countries.* Washington: World Bank.

Al-Samarrai, S., and H. Zaman. 2007. "Abolishing School Fees in Malawi: The Impact on Education Access and Equity." *Education Economics* 15, no.3: 359–75.

Dubash, Navroz K. 2005. "The New Regulatory Politics of Electricity in India: Independent, Embedded or Transcendent?" Paper presented at a workshop on "The Politics of Necessity." Oxford, United Kingdom, September 9–10.

Edirisinghe, N., and D. Sahn. 1993. "The Politics of Food Policy in Sri Lanka: From Basic Human Needs to Increased Market Orientation." In *The Political Economy of Food and Nutrition Policies,* edited by Per Pinstrup-Andersen, chapter 3. Johns Hopkins University Press.

Fernandez, Raquel, and Dani Rodrik. 1991. "Resistance to Reform: Status Quo Bias in the Presence of Individual-Specific Uncertainty." *American Economic Review* 81, no. 5: 1146–155.

International Monetary Fund (IMF). 2006. *Arab Republic of Egypt.* Country Report 06/253. Washington (July).

Komives, Kristin, and others. 2005. *Water, Electricity, and the Poor: Who Benefits from Utility Subsidies?* Washington: World Bank.

Olson, Mancur. 1982. *The Rise and Decline of Nations.* Yale University Press.

Psacharopoulos, George. 1994. "Returns to Investment in Education: A Global Update." *World Development* 22, no. 9: 1325–343.

World Bank. 2004. *Mexico: Public Expenditure Review,* two volumes. Washington.

———. 2006a. *Dominican Republic Poverty Assessment: Achieving More Pro-Poor Growth.* Washington.

———. 2006b. *World Development Report 2006: Equity and Development.* Washington.

World Trade Organization (WTO). 2006. *World Trade Report 2006: Exploring the links between subsidies, trade, and the WTO.* Geneva: Switzerland.

5

Policies for Lower Global Wealth Inequality

JAMES DAVIES

This chapter is concerned with household wealth, where *wealth* is used in a strict sense to refer to net worth or the value of assets minus liabilities. Wealth in this sense is one of the central determinants of material welfare, along with income and consumption. Its separate importance has long been recognized by economists and others, but historically data on wealth were less complete than for other indicators. That situation is changing, and there is increasing evidence of the significance of wealth for household well-being.[1]

Recently, along with Susanna Sandström, Anthony Shorrocks, and Edward Wolff, I provided a first estimate of the world distribution of household wealth.[2] This distribution is highly unequal. Not only is wealth distributed very unequally within countries, but differences between countries are extreme. These differences appear to be greater, proportionally, than those in income. This is a concern since vulnerability, insecurity, and poverty are highest in poor countries. Other things equal, the greater their assets the better protected are households against such threats.

1. See Davies (2008), and in particular the overview provided in its first chapter.
2. Davies, Sandström, Shorrocks, and Wolff (hereafter, Davies and colleagues) (2006). As with the UNU-WIDER (World Institute for Development Economics Research of the United Nations University) research papers cited in this chapter, a shortened version of this paper appears in Davies (2008).

This chapter asks whether majority support is possible in low- and middle-income countries for policies that will build household wealth for the poor. The answer will be yes if such policies can be beneficial not only for the poor but for middle-income groups as well. That there is such potential is clear when one realizes that the median household in poor countries, and even in most middle-income countries, is not truly "middle class." Both the poor and middle groups *aspire* to be middle class. Being middle class means having a comfortable level of consumption but also having significant net worth and a degree of security. Owning a home, perhaps a car, and other consumer durables; being insured; not having excessive debt; and having savings to pay for health care when needed and for one's children's education—these are the indicators of being middle class. They are the things that poor and middle groups are aiming for. Policies that will help both groups achieve these goals ought to get majority support.

This study begins by using the results from the study by Davies and colleagues to estimate the size of the assets of the poor, middle class, and rich around the world.[3] I then inquire into the typical middle-class portfolio to get an idea of what assets people may aim to acquire in the quest to become middle class. This provides the background for the main task of the chapter, which is to identify effective, and popular, policies that can help people build their wealth to a middle-class level. First, the chapter looks at the developed (mainly Organization for Economic Cooperation and Development or OECD) countries to see what policies have been successful in these economies. Then it turns to the developing countries, noting policies and institutions that are already in place, asking whether past and present OECD experience is helpful, and thinking about suitable innovations that would be specific to the developing countries.

In the review of policies and institutions, I concentrate on four main areas: owner-occupied housing, land, savings institutions, and tax-sheltered personal accounts and pensions. The focus is on personal assets rather than on business assets. There are some important aspects of wealth building that are not dealt with in the chapter, either because they are specialized topics with a large literature or because they are not relevant in the current context. Assisting entrepreneurs, for example, through microfinance or conventional credit institutions, is very important and has attracted much attention in recent years. Also outside the scope of this chapter is the regulation or development of stock markets, which are of limited importance for those still aspiring to join the middle class. Finally, monetary stability is clearly crucial, but beyond the scope of this chapter. Policies and institutions that guarantee low inflation could well be the most

---

3. Davies, Sandström, Shorrocks, and Wolff (2006).

important single ingredient that allows people to build middle-class wealth, but these are not studied here.

Wealth Holding and the Middle Class

There has been much discussion over time about the definition, and theory, of the *middle class*. However, in much recent usage, the term tends to mean simply the group that is neither poor nor rich. Branko Milanovic and Shlomo Yitzhaki provide an influential example of this approach.[4] They divided the world's countries, and then the world's people, into three groups: poor, middle, and rich. *Mean income* in Brazil was used as the dividing line between poor and rich, in part on the grounds that this corresponds fairly closely to poverty lines in the rich countries—Germany and the United States are cited. The mean income of Italy is taken as the lower bound on being rich, on the grounds that Italy is the poorest of the G8 countries, aside from Russia, which in global terms are clearly all rich.

Milanovic and Yitzhaki's lower and upper bounds for the middle class were $3,470 and $8,000 per person in 1993, corresponding to $13,880 and $32,000, respectively, for a household of four people. (These amounts are in US dollars that are applied on a PPP basis to different countries. The same approach will be followed in this chapter unless indicated otherwise.) Using these bounds, 76 percent of the world's countries were poor in 1993 and only 8 percent were middle class. Looking at people instead of countries, 78 percent were poor and 11 percent were middle class. Within developing countries, the fraction that would be classified as poor would be even greater.

I will follow the lead of Milanovic and Yitzhaki and supplement their income and consumption test of the middle class status with a parallel wealth test. That is done for two reasons. First, one needs to find out if it is true for wealth, as it is for income and consumption, that the great majority of the population in most developing countries should be classified as poor. This is necessary for the idea that the majority in these countries share a common desire to build their wealth to middle-class levels. The second purpose is to see what levels of wealth and portfolio composition are typical for the middle class. This information is needed to assess the amount and kind of wealth building that the poor need to gain middle-class status in terms of assets.

The wealth data I use are from the study of the world distribution of wealth by Davies and colleagues.[5] (See box 5-1 for key features of that study.) The data from the study by Davies and colleagues are for the year 2000. The middle-class income bounds from Milanovic and Yitzhaki need to be adjusted to 2000, and

4. Milanovic and Yitzhaki (2002).
5. Davies, Sandström, Shorrocks, and Wolff (2006).

Box 5-1. *The World Distribution of Household Wealth*

With the sponsorship of the World Institute for Development Economics Research (WIDER) of the United Nations University in Helsinki, Davies, Sandström, Shorrocks, and Wolff (Davies and colleagues) have provided a first estimate of the world distribution of household wealth.[1] Global wealth is distributed less equally than world income. Using PPP exchange rates, Davies and colleagues estimated that the wealth share of the top 1 percent of households globally is 32 percent and that the wealth share of the top 10 percent is 71 percent. The corresponding Gini coefficient is 0.802, which is getting close to the maximum value of 1.0 and is significantly above the values estimated for the world distribution of income. (Milanovic estimated a world income Gini of 0.642 for 1998, for example.[2]) Globally, median wealth per adult is estimated at $8,400, and to be in the top 1 percent, a person's wealth must be at least $523,300.

Similar to estimating the world distribution of income, there are two tasks in estimating the distribution of wealth. One is to get each country's mean correct. The other is to estimate the shape of the distribution in each country. Wealth data are less complete than income data, but they are available for about 55 percent of the world's population, who hold more than 80 percent of the world's wealth according to the results of Davies and colleagues. All the large developed countries have wealth data, as do the three largest developing countries: China, India, and Indonesia. Imputations of means and distributional shapes were made for those countries that do not have data on wealth. Means were imputed separately for financial assets, nonfinancial assets, and liabilities on the basis of regression analysis of their determinants in thirty countries with household balance sheets. Wealth shares at each percentile were imputed to the missing countries on the basis of a study of the relationship between the shape of the wealth distribution and that of the income distribution in twenty countries with wealth distribution data. These methods are admittedly exploratory, but a range of checks on the results indicate that the overall results are quite robust to the imputation methods used. Results at the country level are also consistent with partial evidence on wealth distribution in many of the missing countries, for example, on land holding or wealth distribution in subnational regions or cities.

Estimated levels of wealth inequality are not systematically higher or lower in developing as opposed to developed countries. On the one hand, some developed countries, like the United States and Switzerland, have almost as much wealth inequality as Davies and colleagues estimated for the world as a whole. On the other hand, countries like Japan, Canada, Australia, Germany, and France have more moderate levels of wealth inequality. Among the developing countries, Davies and colleague found that some of the highest levels of wealth inequality are in Latin America. China still had low wealth inequality in 2000 according to its survey data, but it started from a very low level at the beginning of transition, and concentration has been increasing fairly quickly.

Also noteworthy is that the ratio of wealth to income is estimated to be lower in most developing countries than in the rich countries. The ratio of household wealth to GDP in the G8 countries is estimated to average 4.32, for example, which compares with an average value of 2.53 for China, India, South Africa, and Brazil.

1. Davies, Sandström, Shorrocks, and Wolff (2006).
2. Milanovic (2005).

one needs to assess what wealth bounds should go along with them.[6] An attractive way to do this is to start with the motivation of Milanovic and Yitzhaki in setting their lower bound on the basis of the poverty lines used in rich countries. The United States has the world's best microdata on wealth. They are collected by the Federal Reserve Board's Survey of Consumer Finances (SCF), which has been conducted every three years and in particular in 2001. A good strategy for present purposes, then, is to look at the U.S. poverty line for 2000, derive corresponding wealth with the help of the SCF data, and use the latter to divide the world's population between the wealth-poor and the wealth–middle class. An upper-income bound for the middle class in 2000 will be established simply by multiplying the lower bound by the ratio of the Milanovic and Yitzhaki 1993 upper-to-lower bounds. Also, the SCF can be used to observe the portfolio composition of the Milanovic and Yitzhaki–type middle class in the United States.[7] Although the same portfolio composition cannot be assumed to typify the middle class in developing countries, it will inform our discussion. Later in the section I will look at portfolio composition of the middle class in China and India.

Middle-Class Wealth Bounds in 2000

In 1993 the official U.S. poverty line for a family of four was $14,763, or $3,691 per person—similar to the per capita income of Brazil as Milanovic and Yitzhaki report. In 2000 this poverty line had risen to $17,600. The fraction of households below the poverty line according to the U.S. Census Bureau's Current Population Survey (CPS) was 8.7 percent in 2000 (and 9.2 percent in 2001). Using the Milanovic and Yitzhaki ratio (2.305), the corresponding upper-income bound for the middle class is $40,853, just below median income, which stood at $41,990 in 2000. Thus the Milanovic and Yitzhaki–type middle class contained approximately the bottom half of income recipients in the United States in 2000 minus the lowest decile.

To establish wealth bounds that correspond to the income bounds of the Milanovic and Yitzhaki–type middle class, we will ask what wealth-to-income

---

6. The World Bank's *Global Economic Prospects 2007* report has tables that show the Milanovic and Yitzhaki bounds for 2000. However, an announcement on the GEP website indicates that the year was mislabeled and should have appeared as 2005. See World Bank (2007a, chapter 3).

7. The Milanovic and Yitzhaki–type middle class, as we shall see, does not correspond to what Americans would call their middle class. It corresponds much better to the U.S. working class. (See, for example, the sociologist Gilbert [2002]. Sociologists commonly designate about the top 5 percent of the U.S. population as upper class, the next 15 percent as upper-middle class, and about the next third as lower-middle class. After this comes the working class.) The hope is that the wealth characteristics of the Milanovic and Yitzhaki–type middle class in the United States will have more in common with those of people at the same level of real income in other countries than would the wealth characteristics of the more prosperous group that Americans deem their middle class.

ratio was representative for households in the 10th to 50th income percentiles in the 2001 SCF.[8] The Federal Reserve Board publishes detailed information on wealth characteristics by income, grouping households into the bottom 20 percent, the 20th to 39.9th percentiles, and the 40th to 59.9th percentiles. The second of these groups centers on our Milanovic and Yitzhaki–type middle class by income. The ratio of median wealth to median income for these percentiles is 1.533, which we round off to 1.5. Using that ratio, the Milanovic and Yitzhaki–type household middle-class income bounds ($17,600, $40,583) for 2000 yield corresponding wealth bounds of $26,400 and $60,875.

I want to use middle-class wealth bounds in conjunction with the 2000 world wealth distribution from the study by Davies and colleagues. Their data are on a per adult basis. In their data there were on average 1.92 adults per household in the United States, so the middle-class wealth bounds are $13,750 and $31,706 on a per adult basis. Table 5-1 shows the division of the population between poor, middle class, and rich using these bounds, at world, regional, and country levels. The countries shown are a sampling of the larger population of developing and transition countries.

At the world level, table 5-1 shows 61.3 percent of the world's population as poor, 16.7 percent as middle class, and 22 percent as rich. The poor here are a smaller fraction of the population than in Milanovic and Yitzhaki's results, based, of course, on income rather than on wealth. Although the wealth bounds in this discussion have been developed in the spirit of Milanovic and Yitzhaki, there was nothing to guarantee that the poor would form the same fraction here. Since the fraction of wealth-poor is less than that of the income-poor in Milanovic and Yitzhaki, the world middle class, which was 11 percent in Milanovic and Yitzhaki, is 17 percent here. Given that the upper and lower bounds here differ by the same amount proportionally as those of Milanovic and Yitzhaki, this indicates that the upper tail of the Davies and colleagues' wealth distribution is thicker than that of the Milanovic and Yitzhaki world income distribution in the relevant region. It is interesting to see the size of the poor and middle-class groups in different regions and countries in table 5-1. In the high-income regions, the percentage who are poor is always less than 50 percent, and in the low-income regions, it is always more than 50 percent. The percentage that are poor varies from 61 percent in Latin America and the Caribbean to 83 percent in Africa. This suggests that there should be majority support for policies that would help the poor jump into the middle class in

8. An alternative approach would be to choose wealth bounds on the basis of the mean or median wealth for households at the Milanovic and Yitzhaki–type income bounds. That approach was rejected here, however, because the wealth-to-income ratio at the 9th or 10th income percentile in the United States is simply too low. People at this income level in the United States do not display, from any viewpoint, the wealth characteristics of what could reasonably be termed middle class.

Table 5-1. *Size of Wealth Groups in the Adult Population, by Region and Selected Countries*

Region	Mean wealth[a]	Percentage poor	Percentage poor or middle class	Percentage middle class	Percentage rich
World	43,628	61.3	78.0	16.7	22.0
North America	193,147	31.1	46.6	15.5	53.4
Asia: high income[b]	138,750	13.8	27.3	13.5	72.7
Oceania[c]	99,634	36.7	44.2	7.5	55.8
Europe	81,890	40.8	58.7	17.9	41.3
Latin America and the Caribbean	34,956	60.5	78.0	17.5	22.0
Asia: other	18,266	72.3	87.8	15.5	12.2
China	16,749	63.9	86.5	22.6	13.5
Africa	11,730	82.9	92.3	9.4	7.7
India	11,655	77.9	91.9	14.0	8.1
Selected countries					
Argentina	60,917	42.5	60.9	18.5	39.1
Turkey	40,202	50.1	71.3	21.3	28.7
Mexico	38,324	56.2	75.9	19.7	24.1
Brazil	35,188	62.0	78.4	16.5	21.6
Russia	24,011	60.8	81.7	20.9	18.3
Indonesia	13,401	80.7	93.5	12.7	6.5
Pakistan	13,214	79.0	90.9	11.9	9.1
Vietnam	10,066	82.6	94.5	11.9	5.5
Nigeria	2,194	96.5	98.4	1.9	1.6

Source: Data derived from Davies and colleagues (2006), tables 11a, 11b.
a. Purchasing power parity (PPP) adjusted US dollars.
b. "Asia: high income" includes Hong Kong, Japan, Macao, Singapore, South Korea, and Taiwan.
c. "Oceania" includes Australia, New Zealand, and the south Pacific island nations, excluding the Philippines.

these regions, even if these policies did not also help the middle class.[9] When the poor and the middle class are combined, they form a large majority in all the low-income regions. Since policies that build the wealth of the poor may also be beneficial for the middle class, this strengthens the presumption that such policies could win majority support.

Voting takes place within countries, not at the regional level, so it is important to look at the fraction of the poor and middle class at the country level as

9. Whether there would, in fact, be majority support for candidates espousing such policies in elections depends, of course, on the voting rate of the poor in relation to the rest of the population and the degree to which they vote according to their economic interests rather than their identity in ethnic, regional, religious, or other terms.

Table 5-2. *Characteristics of Poor and Middle-Class Wealth Groups in the United States, 2001*[a]

Characteristic	Poor		Middle class	
	Median	Mean	Median	Mean
Income (dollars)	19,700	24,000	34,900	39,500
Wealth (dollars)	1,100	< 50	40,900	44,300
	Percentage with asset or debt	Percentage of total assets	Percentage with asset or debt	Percentage of total assets
Transaction accounts	73.7	6.5	94.4	4.3
Stocks	5.0	0.8	9.6	0.7
Retirement accounts	18.9	4.4	46.0	6.3
Cash value life insurance	6.9	1.4	26.1	2.6
Total financial assets	78.0	15.7	96.9	16.5
Vehicles	64.8	33.9	86.7	11.7
Primary residence	14.4	46.6	69.6	51.9
Business equity	1.2	1.3	4.0	0.9
Total nonfinancial assets	68.2	84.3	100	83.5
Mortgage on home	11.2	42.5	49.5	31.2
Credit card	45.5	11.2	54.9	1.8
Total debt	68.7	99.6	80.8	40.0

Source: Federal Reserve Board, Survey of Consumer Finances (2001), tables 1, 5, 8, 11, based on internal data. See (www.federalreserve.gov/pubs/oss/oss2/scfindex.html).

a. The "poor" are households in wealth percentiles 0–24.9. The "middle class" are in percentiles 25–49.9.

well. Table 5-1 shows results for eleven of the most populous developing or transition countries. It is in only one of these countries, Argentina, that the poor are less than half the population, although Turkey is on the borderline, with 50.1 percent poor. China and India (which in the table represent regions as well as countries) have 63.9 percent and 77.9 percent poor, respectively. All of the countries have comfortable majorities of the nonrich (that is, poor and middle class together). These majorities range from 60.9 percent in Argentina to 91 to 95 percent in Pakistan, India, Indonesia, and Vietnam, and to a high of 98.4 percent in Nigeria. In principle it would seem that there should be strong electoral support for policies that would help poor households build their wealth to middle-class levels in developing countries, especially if the same policies also benefit those already in the middle class.

Portfolios of the Middle Class

In looking at portfolios of the middle class, we start with the U.S. 2001 SCF data. This provides a good reference point, even though the results can hardly be translated directly to the developing world. Table 5-2 shows characteristics of the first and second wealth quartiles in the 2001 SCF. If we are interested in portfolio composition, these groups provide the best approximation in publicly available compilations of our poor and middle-class groups.

We see from the table that even for the bottom quartile the incidence of transactions accounts, at 73.7 percent, is quite high. In the second quartile this figure rises to 94.4 percent, making a checking account or equivalent clearly typical for our middle class in the United States. The incidence of vehicle ownership is also high for both groups, at 64.8 percent for the bottom quartile and 86.7 percent for the second quartile. For other assets there is a bigger difference between the groups. For example, while 69.6 percent of the second quartile households own a house, only 14.4 percent of the poor group do so. Other useful markers for being middle class appear to be a retirement account, life insurance, or a mortgage, since these are all items for which there is a large difference between first and second quartile incidences.

Turning to portfolio composition, we see that houses and vehicles together are the dominant assets for the middle class in the SCF data. They account for almost two-thirds of total assets. If consumer durables, which are not covered by the SCF, were also included, the importance of nonfinancial assets would be even greater. Financial assets are only 16.5 percent of the average portfolio of the second quartile. Retirement accounts make up more than a third of the latter total and, on average, are almost ten times as important as the direct holding of stocks. This reflects the popularity of Individual Retirement Accounts (IRAs), Keogh plans, and 401(k) plans, all of which are included in the SCF data. On the liabilities side, note that while mortgage debt is large for the second quartile, at 31.2 percent of total assets, average credit card debt is quite small for this group (just 1.8 percent of total assets) despite the fact that more than half of the middle class (according to wealth) have a card.

Fortunately, we do not have to rely on U.S. evidence to get an idea of the portfolio composition of the middle class. We can also look at the kind of results shown in tables 5-3 and 5-4, which come from sample surveys of household wealth that have been conducted in India and China.[10] For both countries,

10. China and India have considerable experience in conducting these surveys. The first Indian survey, which looked only at rural areas, was conducted in 1961–62. Further surveys have taken place at intervals of roughly a decade and have included urban areas in addition to rural areas since 1981–82. Sample sizes are very large: the 2002–03 sample had 36,435 rural and 91,192 urban households, for example. Response rates are reported to be very high (in excess of 90 percent), as is true in China as well. Data quality is good, although debts evidently are underreported by about a factor of 3 according to Subramanian and Jayaraj (2006). The first Chinese household wealth survey was conducted in 1988 and has been followed by surveys in 1995 and 2002. Sample sizes are comparable with those used in OECD countries. The 1995 survey had 14,933 households, for example. To the best of my knowledge, the only other developing country with a full survey of wealth holding is Indonesia, where the RAND Corporation administered a survey in 1997. See Frankenberg, Smith, and Thomas (2003).

Table 5-3. *Asset Composition, Poor and Middle-Class Wealth Groups, India, 2002–03*[a]
Percentage of total assets

	Poor		Middle class	
Variable	Rural	Urban	Rural	Urban
Land	43.8	25.6	62.8	35.5
Buildings	40.2	32.9	23.5	41.8
Livestock	4.0	0.6	1.8	0.3
Agricultural machinery	0.7	0.1	2.1	0.1
Nonfarm business equipment	0.5	1.4	0.3	1.0
All transport equipment	0.9	4.1	1.4	2.8
Durable household goods	9.0	24.4	4.9	8.8
Financial assets	2.0	11.0	3.1	9.8

Source: Subramanian and Jayaraj (2006), table 5a.

a. The "poor" include households with total assets from 60,000 to 100,000 rupees. The "middle class" have total assets from 450,000 to 800,000 rupees. These asset groups center on the poor and middle-class wealth percentiles shown in table 5-1.

the tables provide separate results for rural and urban areas. Table 5-3 shows the composition of assets for asset classes that are representative for the poor and the middle class in India in 2002–03. First, it is clear that real estate is the dominant form of wealth for the poor and middle class. Land and buildings make up 84 percent of total assets for the rural poor, and 86 percent for the rural middle class. The corresponding numbers are 58 percent and 77 percent for the urban poor and middle class. These results echo the dominance of nonfinancial assets we saw in the United States. Financial assets are relatively unimportant in rural areas of India and only compose 10 percent of the assets of the middle class in urban areas, which is actually less than the figure for the poor, of 11 percent. The major differences between poor and middle class are that land is relatively more important for the middle class and consumer durables are more important for the poor, in rural and urban areas, and that buildings are less important for the middle class than for the poor in rural areas but *more* important for the middle class than for the poor in urban areas. The latter observation is suggestive of the importance of housing as a marker of middle class status in urban India.[11]

Recent media and scholarly attention has focused on the "new middle class" in India, a group that is mainly urban.[12] However, with the majority of the Indian population still living in rural areas, we cannot neglect the rural middle

11. The importance of homeownership as a middle-class goal in India is emphasized, for example, in Nijman (2006) and Doug Saunders, "Up a Slippery Slope," *Globe and Mail,* July 21, 2007, pp. F6 and F8.

12. See, for example, Scrase (2006); Fernandes (2006); Diana Farrell and Eric Beinhocker, "Next Big Spenders: India's Middle Class," *Business Week,* May 19, 2007.

Table 5-4. *Asset Composition, Rural and Urban China, 2002*

Variable	Rural China		Urban China	
	Percentage share of net worth	Concentration ratio	Percentage share of net worth	Concentration ratio
Land	30.7	0.26	n.a.	n.a.
Housing (net)	43.0	0.46	64.4	0.50
Fixed production assets	9.1	0.39	1.8	0.48
Durable consumer goods	6.1	0.38	7.2	0.32
Financial assets	12.3	0.49	25.9	0.44
Other assets	n.a.	n.a.	1.3	0.38
Nonhousing liabilities	−1.3	−0.25	−0.7	0.98

Source: Li and Zhao (2007), tables 3, 6.
n.a. Not available.

class. In summing up typical portfolios for the middle class in India, we need to take rural and urban areas into account. In rural areas, middle-class households typically own substantial amounts of land and have the buildings and equipment that go with being prosperous farmers. In urban areas, land is less important. The difference is largely taken up by buildings (mostly housing), which, as for consumer durables, are almost *twice* as important for the urban middle class as for the rural middle class. Thus being middle class in asset terms means quite different things in rural and urban areas.

Table 5-4 shows the composition of net worth in China in 2002. In this case the only available composition numbers are for all wealth classes taken together. However, Shi Li and Renwei Zhao also provide concentration indexes for each wealth component, which allow us to see which assets are more important for higher wealth groups.[13] Real estate is again the dominant asset type, but financial assets are considerably more important than in India. In rural areas in 2002, it is estimated that land holdings made up 31 percent of household wealth and that land and housing together accounted for 74 percent of wealth. In urban areas, there is no private ownership of land, but housing (net of mortgages) made up 64 percent of net worth. Financial assets were 12 percent of wealth in rural areas and 26 percent in urban areas.

The concentration ratios allow us to judge which assets are likely more important for the middle class than for the poor in China. Aside from fixed production assets in urban areas, which are a very small part of wealth, the two assets with the highest concentration ratios in rural and urban areas are financial

13. Li and Zhao (2007). The weighted sum of the concentration indexes for the different assets equals the overall Gini coefficient in which the weights are the portfolio shares of the assets. See Pyatt, Chen, and Fei (1980) for further explanation.

assets and housing. This makes sense as these are the asset types in which upwardly mobile Chinese families have been investing heavily in the last two decades.[14] In striking contrast to India, land plays an equalizing role in rural areas, as shown by its low concentration ratio.[15] It also should be noted that there is rapidly increasing ownership of vehicles in China, and owning a car can safely be said to be a typical middle-class aim, if not accomplishment.

The evidence from India and China suggests that to have a typical middle-class asset package, households need to own a house or apartment and have significant consumer durables and financial assets. Although many might, ideally, like to own a vehicle, vehicle ownership is not essential. The form of financial assets may vary and may not include shares or mutual funds, although the wide participation seen in the Chinese stock market in recent years, for example, reminds us that many middle-class people hold shares.

As a final observation, it is worth noting that homeownership is not only a goal of many poor people in developing countries, it is something that many of them have already achieved. Homeownership rates in many developing countries are higher than those in developed countries.[16] The typical aim of the poor may be to own better-quality housing, rather than to own a house for the first time.

Policies in Developed Countries

Governments in developed or OECD countries have used a range of policies to assist households in building their wealth and achieving financial security, although until recent decades the income security goal was pursued more through public pensions and income maintenance schemes than through the encouragement of private assets. Wealth-building policies range from those designed to facilitate homeownership through sheltered retirement savings, financial regulation, and the provision of savings opportunities in public institutions such as government savings banks or the post office to methods of providing secure land title and inflation control. Support and encouragement for markets in consumer durables and private transportation also support middle-class wealth. Not all these policies are used equally in all OECD countries, but most show up in some form.

14. See Gustaffson, Li, and Wei (2006); Li and Zhao (2007).

15. Although households have ownership of land in rural areas, they cannot buy or sell it. This prevents land ownership from becoming more concentrated in China. Urban land is owned by the state.

16. According to the 2007 world development indicators (World Bank 2007b, table 3.11), while the homeownership rate was 66 percent in the United States, it was 88 percent in China, 87 percent in India, 72 percent in Kenya, and 74 percent in Brazil.

Owner-Occupied Housing

Policies toward owner-occupied housing differ considerably within the OECD and have changed over time. Homeownership has been strongly encouraged in the English-speaking countries, in Scandinavia, and in some other countries. However, there are cases where large parts of the population were effectively discouraged from homeownership. While that picture is changing, the effects of the past are still evident.[17] Disincentives to homeownership have taken various forms. Cheap social housing crowded out the private housing market to an important extent in many countries. Other supply-side effects include zoning or planning regulations that reduce the availability of land for private development. Italy provides an example of demand-side effects that operate largely through the great difficulty of obtaining mortgage finance. The lack of mortgages is the result of legal procedures that make foreclosure lengthy and expensive for lenders.[18] The joint result of such factors is that homeownership rates are low in certain countries. While recently estimated homeownership rates in the United States, Norway, and Spain are 66 percent, 67 percent, and 78 percent, respectively, the rates in Japan, France, and Germany are just 61 percent, 55 percent, and 43 percent, respectively.[19]

Although it would be interesting to investigate the political economy of housing policies in the OECD, that is beyond the scope of this chapter. We can, however, discuss what policies have been effective in encouraging sustainable private homeownership. Such policies can operate on the supply or demand sides, but the most effective approach is likely a combination of the two. We will focus on Canada as an example, since it has been successful in promoting homeownership without falling into the trap of overpromotion, as seen in the United States and some other countries in recent years. In looking at these policies, we will bear in mind that while they appeal to the middle class, they may or may not also benefit the poor. Sorting out the two categories is important in the present context.

On the supply side, policies and institutions that have stimulated the supply of housing for middle-class owner occupation in Canada include

—Zoning—large urban and suburban areas set aside for low-density housing

—Relatively weak protection of green areas and heritage buildings

—Private financial institutions that provide ready finance for construction

—Favorable federal, provincial, and municipal policies toward real estate development

—Public provision of infrastructure

17. See Balchin (1996).
18. See Maclennan, Muellbauer, and Stephens (2000).
19. World Bank (2007b, table 3.11). Switzerland has the lowest reported homeownership rate among wealthy countries at 31 percent.

On the demand side there are also a range of relevant policies, including

—Insurance on approved low down payment mortgages through the Canada Mortgage and Housing Corporation (CMHC; established in 1946)[20]

—Funding for mortgages through their purchase by the Canada Housing Trust (CHT), a subsidiary of the CMHC, which has obtained finance through issuing Canada Mortgage Bonds since 2001[21]

—Various income tax breaks for home buyers

These policies and institutions have all supported middle-class housing aspirations but differed in their implications for the poor. The activities of the CMHC, like those of the Federal Housing Authority (FHA) and Fannie Mae in the United States in earlier years, succeeded in making mortgage finance broadly available and were a big success from the viewpoint of lower-income people as well as the middle class. However, many feel that zoning that emphasizes low-density housing favors the middle class at the expense of the poor. This can interact with policy failures in the form of rent control or poorly designed public housing projects or both, helping to produce bad social and housing conditions in inner cities.

In general, the Canadian experience in housing (and the U.S. experience in earlier years) illustrates the wisdom of relying on the market but at the same time ensuring that public policies and institutions that will help the market do its job (efficient land titling and mortgage insurance, for example) are in place.

The U.S. experience illustrates successful and unsuccessful approaches to housing finance. The major housing finance institutions established under Franklin Roosevelt's New Deal of the 1930s, the FHA and Fannie Mae, were very successful in making much wider homeownership possible and sustainable. However, in the late 1960s, changes began that eventually undermined the system and led to the subprime mortgage collapse of 2007–08. In 1968 Fannie Mae was privatized, and a second similar corporation, Freddie Mac, was created to give it competition. Over time these entities felt political and commercial pressure to make mortgages available to increasingly less well-qualified lenders. This is a trend that accelerated rapidly in the late 1990s and early 2000s. For a time this resulted in homeownership being extended to a wider group, including significant numbers of low-income people and minority groups. However, imprudent practices, such as payment schedules that started low and suddenly increased after a few years, doomed to failure many of the subprime mortgages created. The result was a growing number of defaults and foreclosures in 2006

20. Of some relevance in the context of this chapter, the CMHC promotes its consulting services to other countries. See the website of CMHC International, Housing Policy and Program Development and Evaluation (www.cmhc-schl.gc.ca/en/hoficlincl/cmhcin/incose/buse/buse_003.cfm).

21. On the success of the CHT, see Boyd Erman, "Good Timing; Feds Avoid Fannie-Style Mortgage Freefall," *Globe and Mail,* July 12, 2008, p. B1.

and 2007 that eventually made it clear that subprime mortgages in the United States were not sustainable.

Two important features that caused the self-destruction of subprime mortgages in the United States were very low, or zero, down payments and rising mortgage payment schedules. A valuable lesson from the U.S. experience is that other countries should regulate mortgage finance to avoid these features. Borrowers need to make significant, but not prohibitive, down payments, and payment schedules should not be steeply increasing over time. But there are at least two other features that should also be avoided. One is financial deregulation allowing mortgages to be packaged and repackaged and sold to investors in such a way that they could not properly evaluate the riskiness of the assets they were acquiring. The whole world has learned a bitter lesson from the meltdown in the value of the "asset-backed commercial paper" and other investment vehicles so created.

The second feature to avoid is no-recourse mortgages, which are the general rule in the United States but not in many other developed countries, such as Canada. Under recourse mortgages, lenders not only can repossess a house when the mortgagee is in default but can also pursue repayment by going after the borrower's other assets. Under no-recourse mortgages, the mortgagor's effective liability is limited to the value of the house. This means that borrowers may begin to face a strong financial incentive to default when housing prices fall and they find that they have negative equity in their homes. This effect is, of course, stronger, the smaller the down payment is, which has been one of the crucial problems in the subprime mortgage market.[22] The incentive to default results in more foreclosures and resulting house sales, making crashes in housing prices more likely to occur and likely to be larger when they do occur. The lesson for other countries is clear: avoid no-recourse mortgages if you want stability in housing markets, housing finance, and homeownership.

Land Ownership and Titling

As pointed out dramatically by Hernando De Soto, one way the developed countries differ from many developing countries is in their secure systems of land ownership and land titling.[23] As explained by James MacGee, there are two essential elements in such systems.[24] One is a registry that tracks land ownership and transactions. The other is a cadastre, which is a public database that records who has what legal rights to each piece of land and which often has additional information such as the value of the land and structures built on it. Reporting

---

22. Martin Feldstein, "A Home Price Firewall," *Washington Post,* June 19, 2008, p. A19.
23. De Soto (2000).
24. MacGee (2006). See also Deininger (2003).

all land transactions and interests in land is compulsory, and the rules are enforced. But in addition, these services are provided with sufficiently low fees, and with enough convenience to the public, that there is little temptation to avoidance or evasion.

De Soto argued that even when people have good access to financial institutions in developing countries, the amount they can borrow may be severely restricted by a lack of collateral if they do not have formal title to their property. However, research has shown that merely giving people title does not necessarily make it easier for them to borrow and that in fact many people who lack formal title do borrow successfully.[25] The key is that good credit market institutions are needed before property can be readily used as collateral to secure loans. As shown by the case of Italy, if it is difficult or expensive for lenders to foreclose, mortgage finance will be hard to obtain. Thus, while a good system of land administration is no doubt helpful in supporting borrowing opportunities, it is not a magic bullet.

Finally, there has been so much recent emphasis on the importance of titling in helping people borrow that a more basic and substantial benefit of efficient land administration is sometimes overlooked. Suppose there was no possibility of borrowing. People would still want to own and purchase land and construct buildings. However, if secure title cannot be obtained, these investments become vulnerable to counterclaims of ownership. A good system of land administration fosters investment in real estate by eliminating this risk and is therefore a necessary element in any battery of policies intended to encourage household wealth building.

Savings Institutions

We are used to thinking that households in developed countries have ready access to finance. In large measure they do, but this is not universal in all respects, and it is easy to forget that some forms of access, for example credit cards, have only come to the fore relatively recently. Since most developed countries have been rich and have had a large middle class for a long time, it would seem that the full panoply of financial institutions and opportunities now seen are not a *necessary* requirement for people to build middle-class wealth.

One thing that is common across the developing countries, however, is that people had opportunities to save in secure form, through either private institutions including banks, building societies, cooperatives, and so on, or public services such as post office savings banks or savings bonds. So while borrowing has been difficult in many times and places, opportunities to save were generally not lacking. This likely was key, particularly for an increasingly urbanized popula-

---

25. See, for example, Woodruff (2001).

tion, in allowing consumption smoothing, household formation, saving for education, and geographic and occupational mobility.[26]

The particular institutions that became important savings vehicles differed across countries. Banks have, of course, generally been important, but this has differed across countries and over time. In the United States, while there were many banks and they were not difficult to find, historically they often were not regarded as very safe. In many other countries, the banking industry became concentrated and uncompetitive over time. To earn higher returns, and sometimes for ideological reasons, many households deposited their savings in trust companies, credit unions, or cooperative banks, or public institutions. In the latter category, in a number of countries, postal savings banks were very popular and successful. While postal savings banks have declined in importance in recent years, this form of saving is still significant in a number of developed countries and is very important in a least one of them, Japan. Postal savings banks offer convenience and trustworthiness, but also in some cases tax advantages.

Another significant feature in a number of countries is the savings bond. During the Second World War, governments launched large campaigns to sell bonds to raise war finance. After the war they found it convenient to continue selling savings bonds, and these proved very popular in Canada, the United States, the United Kingdom, and several other countries. These bonds provide complete security (aside from inflation risk), reasonable interest rates, and great convenience.

A final point to note is that most developed countries provide some form of deposit insurance, which protects depositors against the failure of private savings institutions. In Canada, for example, the first $100,000 of deposits in commercial banks is insured federally, and the same amount of deposits in credit unions is insured provincially.[27] Similar deposit insurance has been provided in the United States, also with a limit of $100,000. The U.S. limit was raised in October 2008 to $250,000 as part of the worldwide effort to stabilize financial conditions. It was announced that the higher limit would stay in place until December 31, 2009.

Tax-Sheltered Personal Accounts and Pensions

Tax-sheltered retirement saving through contributory public pensions, or employer-based pensions, has been common in developed countries and the

---

26. Honohan (2006) examined patterns of financial access in 150 countries and concluded that "despite [a] policy focus on the value of credit instruments, it is deposit products that tend to be the first to be used as prosperity increases."

27. The $100,000 in insurance is provided for each institution that one banks with. This has encouraged some middle-class people, particularly older people who have significant liquid assets, to use several institutions rather than just one. This is somewhat inconvenient for savers, but it is a help to smaller financial institutions, which is perhaps a benefit given the high level of concentration in the banking system.

formal sector of developing countries for many years. The need for such schemes is hardly a matter of controversy. In some English-speaking countries, such as Canada and the United States, these systems have been complemented for a number of years by tax-sheltered personal retirement accounts. Although the latter are sometimes confused with "pension accounts," personal retirement accounts are distinctly different. Employers as well as employees normally contribute to pension accounts, and participation is generally mandatory. In contrast, a personal retirement account is a private and voluntary, but tax-advantaged, savings instrument. Such accounts allow people who do not have employer-based pensions access to a comparable form of retirement saving but also allow those with employer-based pensions to supplement them if those pensions are not deemed sufficient.

Although personal accounts are far from universally available in developed countries, they are spreading. As in the case of public or private pensions, the need and desirability for this form of tax-sheltered saving is not particularly controversial. There is, however, a substantial cost to government, in the form of reduced revenue, since contributions are generally tax deductible and interest accrues tax free within the plans. These revenue consequences perhaps explain why personal accounts are not available in all countries. While the desirability of tax sheltering for pensions and personal accounts is not really controversial, there has been a lot of controversy about form and function in recent years. The following trends have been taking place in pensions: unfunded public pension schemes are being replaced, at least partially, by funded schemes in many countries; defined benefit (DB) pension plans at the employer level are being replaced by defined contribution (DC) schemes; individual workers are being given more freedom and responsibility to direct the investment of their pension funds; and workers are in some cases being given the opportunity to make early withdrawals to fund such nonretirement needs as home buying, education, and medical expenses. The latter two trends are also seen in personal accounts: savers are seeing a greater choice of how their savings are directed, and early withdrawals are becoming more common.

Whether public pensions should be funded, and whether DC plans should be supplanting DB plans, are issues we will not address here. It is important, however, to address the two aspects that are common to pensions and personal accounts: self-direction of savings and early withdrawal.

In the United States today, the most important form of tax-sheltered personal account, or TSPA, for employees is the Individual Retirement Account (IRA).[28] There are several different types of IRAs. In the Traditional IRA, contributions are deductible, interest or other investment income in the plan

---

28. Keogh plans are an analogous instrument for the self-employed; however, they come with higher contribution limits.

accrues tax free, and withdrawals are taxed. Investments are placed in instruments equivalent to certificates of deposit or, increasingly, in stock or mutual funds. A variant is the Self-Directed IRA, under which the saver has great freedom to choose and alter the composition of assets in the plan over time. Normally, preretirement withdrawals are subject to a 10 percent penalty, but this may be waived in the case of withdrawals for large uninsured medical bills; education expenses; or to buy, build, or rebuild a first house.

Allowing early withdrawals from IRAs without penalty for medical, education, or home-buying expenses makes the instrument strikingly more suitable for middle-class savers and those aspiring to be middle class. The reasons for nonpenalized withdrawals are all to satisfy what we have identified as middle-class objectives.

Although what has been happening with IRAs in the United States is interesting, much more dramatic has been the growth of 401(k) pension plans. These were introduced through the addition of a new section, 401(k), to the Income Tax Act in 1978. Originally it was thought that these plans would only be of interest to executives, but they have spread much more widely. A 401(k) is an employer-based DC pension plan. The most common form is the "participant-directed plan," which allows the worker a choice about how the funds are invested. Employers have considerable freedom in designing the provisions of these plans, however, and may limit the choices available to workers. As in the case of IRAs, early withdrawals are normally subject to a 10 percent penalty, but penalty-free withdrawals can be made in the case of "hardship" situations. Hardship includes buying a primary residence or paying education expenses or uninsured medical bills. Workers may also take a loan from their 401(k) plan, but only for a period of five years or less.

The 401(k)-type plans are spreading among developed countries. In October 2001, Japan enacted an analogous plan with the title "Japan-version 401(k)." These types of plans are also a centerpiece of pension policy in the United Kingdom and the Australian Superannuation System, although in these countries participation in some form by all workers is expected (unlike in the United States where an employer is not required to offer a pension plan).

Does it make sense to turn a pension system into a generalized savings vehicle, with generous provisions for early withdrawals and loans? Is this something that increases the value of these plans in building middle-class wealth, or the opposite?

On the one hand, it may seem that the opportunity for early withdrawals for education, housing, or medical expenses must be a good thing since it allows people to make investments that they believe have higher returns at the margin than retirement saving has. And the ends are all middle-class aims, so it would seem the policy is a fit for us. On the other hand, secure retirement income is also a standard middle-class aim, and if people are allowed to withdraw before they arrive at retirement will their pensions be smaller and their retirement incomes less secure?

The issue is a difficult one for an economist. We are constitutionally inclined to believe that people will make the best choices given their circumstances and that paternalism is a mistake. However, there has now been considerable research by behavioral economists that has established a large psychological element in decisions about saving. Saving requires self-restraint, and that is a difficult thing for many people to apply. This is no doubt why we do not allow early withdrawals from pension schemes for consumption purposes. But is it okay to allow those withdrawals if they are for investment purposes? Yes, there will be less in the pension account, but there will be more wealth in the form of housing or human capital. This is a reasonable argument, and it would seem that allowing some early withdrawals for these purposes is appropriate. However, it may also be appropriate to require repayment in the case of housing or education. Repayment could also be required in the case of medical expenses, contingent on a return to good health.

In addition to being able to access their pension savings and TSPAs for medical expenses, Americans are now able to utilize tax-sheltered Health Savings Accounts. With many Americans very concerned about the financial and other consequences of future health problems, this innovation is naturally of serious interest to many in the United States. It is less attractive to citizens of other developed countries who have access to either free public health care (as in Canada) or public health insurance. Health Savings Accounts may, however, be attractive in developing countries, which generally lack public health programs that would meet middle-class standards. The advantages and disadvantages of these accounts are discussed in the context of developing countries in the next section.

Finally, while TSPAs are clearly popular with the middle class in developed countries, one may question their value to the poor. This value is reduced by at least three things: the low saving rate of the poor; a small advantage of deducting contributions against taxes due to a low, or zero, marginal tax rate at contribution time; and a heavy, effective tax burden on withdrawals in retirement due to a higher marginal tax rate than what existed earlier in the retiree's lifetime and to clawbacks of other benefits. These disadvantages may lead the poor to make little use of TSPAs.[29] A response was the creation of Individual Development Accounts (IDAs) a decade ago in the United States, and the introduction of Personal Accounts in the United Kingdom, slated to come into effect in 2012. IDAs provide matching contributions that could be as much as 1 to 1

29. In the United States, Roth IRAs may be more suitable for the poor. They differ from other IRAs in having nondeductible contributions but also no tax on withdrawals. The introduction of Roth-type plans has been advocated in Canada specifically to help lower-income savers.

or 2 to 1. Matching is meant to provide an incentive that will overcome the disadvantages of TSPAs for the poor, but the spread of IDAs has been disappointingly slow. Part of the reason is that there is a patchwork of IDA programs sponsored by financial institutions or community organizations that have obtained support from government (typically at the state level) or private donors. The British system would seem to have a better chance of success, as participation in a Personal Account or pension will be compulsory for eligible workers. Targeting at lower-income workers is achieved by the requirement for employers to make partially matching contributions in the earnings range of £5,000 to £33,500.

Policies for Developing Countries

In this section we have three tasks. One is to summarize briefly the kind of policies and institutions that we see in developing countries, in the same areas as discussed above for OECD countries. Another is to ask what successful policies from the developed countries could be transplanted usefully to the developing world. The third is to discuss the possible value of institutions as builders of middle-class wealth that may be special to the developing world.

Owner-Occupied Housing

There has been a revolution in the approach to housing policy in the developing world in the last three decades. As of the 1970s, housing markets in poor countries were stifled by excessive regulation in the formal sector and lack of finance and secure ownership in the informal sector. Housing finance systems, as known in the developed world, did not exist. This picture began to change in the 1980s and has now been largely overturned in many developing countries, including the most populous. Large changes have been made, for example, in Chile, China, India, Malaysia, Mexico, Singapore, Jordan, and South Korea.[30] The emphasis is on letting markets work, with appropriate support from government policy and public institutions. Mortgage credit, while still far less extensive than in the developed world, is growing. And in the informal sector, there has been a recognition that people need more security of tenure. There is also a thriving movement to provide microfinance for shelter, which is helping many poor households build or improve their homes with small loans.

What are the possibilities for housing policies that can help the poor work toward middle-class status? What policies will be embraced by the middle class and the poor? Are the new policies that are now in place, or are spreading in the developing world, of this type? What other policies could be followed?

---

30. See, for example, Buckley and Kalarickal (2005).

The new housing policies in developing countries appear to fall into separate pro-poor and pro-middle-class categories. More supportive and tolerant policies toward informal sector housing, and microfinance for shelter, help the poor but not the middle class on the one hand. Improved mortgage markets, on the other hand, help mainly the rich and middle class. It might appear that there is little scope for policies that will win the support of poor *and* middle-class voters. However, if the poor are a majority and exercise their voting rights in their own interests, this apparent lack of common cause with other groups may not interfere with them getting appropriate policies. And to the extent that the more upwardly mobile among the poor can see the advantages that they may reap in the future from better mortgage finance, they may make common cause with those higher in the distribution to support improvements in that area as well.

Land Ownership and Titling

There is no doubt that developing countries need good systems of land administration and that the experience and success of developed countries in this area provide guidance to what is required. A land registry and a cadastre are needed, but of course, almost all developing countries already have these. What is crucial is to deliver their services cheaply, conveniently, and efficiently. This requires investments to open additional branches, inform the public, and prosecute in cases in which, for example, land transactions are not registered. Political will is needed to ensure that the requirements to register transactions and provide other information and documents are not flouted. Although some may find this an unwelcome intrusion by government, such improvements ought, in principle, to win broad electoral support. The land registry and cadastre provide greater security of property ownership and can make real estate transactions possible that would otherwise not occur because of insufficient trust between buyers and sellers.

An issue that generally does not arise in developed countries, but which is important in many developing countries, is the actual or perceived legitimacy of current land ownership. This raises the difficult issue of land reform, as well as questions about the implications of squatting. In many developing countries, one still sees the pattern of large landed estates. Research indicates that countries, like Bolivia, Ethiopia, Japan, Korea, and Taiwan, that implemented rigorous land reforms appear to have benefited in terms of reduced inequality and more rapid growth.[31] However, there are also many examples of failed land reforms. The nature of agriculture in a country has an effect on the prospects for successful reform, and land reform is normally a very sensitive political issue. This is an example of a situation in which merely having the support of a majority of the public does not necessarily make a policy politically implementable.

31. See, for example, Deininger (2002).

Careful approaches, involving much negotiation and study, however, have been successful in certain cases and provide an indication of how land reform can work in other cases.[32]

Squatting is interesting in this context since its acceptance creates some tension between the interests of the poor and the middle class. The poor generally benefit from policies or expenditures that recognize the rights of squatters and raise living standards in informal communities. The property-owning middle class, however, may in some cases regard these initiatives as a threat, since it may be feared that they will weaken the security of their property rights. The situation parallels the one we saw in the case of housing policy. Since the poor are in the majority, policies that tolerate squatting and support the informal sector should, in principle, win electoral support. However, the more upwardly mobile among the poor may regard policies that weaken property rights too much as undesirable, which may restrict somewhat the degree of generosity toward squatting that will emerge from the democratic process.

Savings Institutions

Having a good system of savings institutions and savings products is in everyone's interest. Further, having access to such a system is an important element in allowing people to climb into, or stay in, the middle class. It should not be hard to construct policies in this area that will unite the poor and the middle class. The promotion of competition among private financial institutions as well as the encouragement of cooperative banks and microfinance institutions, postal savings banks, and national savings bonds are all examples of what should be popular policies. And, in fact, we see examples of at least some of these policies in place in most developing countries. One has only to look at India, with its rich array of financial institutions, active microfinance, and highly successful postal savings bank to see an impressive example.[33] Also striking is the recent expansion of deposit-taking by microfinance institutions, of which Bank Rakyat Indonesia, with its 25 million depositors, is a leading example.[34]

There are, however, several political threats that may interfere with the achievement of a good system of savings institutions. First, many countries have a fairly concentrated banking system. Bankers and bank shareholders, who may include many people in the middle class, have an interest in restricting competition. Thus postal savings banks, cooperative banks, or savings bonds may be absent or only tolerated if they offer relatively low interest rates and provide a restricted range of products. Second, if middle-class and rich taxpayers feel overburdened they may simply oppose the provision of nonessential public services,

32. See Deininger (2002); Deininger and Binswanger (2002).
33. For details on the wide range of saving products offered by the post office savings bank in India, see (www.iloveindia.com/finance/post-office/saving-accounts.html).
34. See Armendáriz de Aghion and Morduch (2005).

which may act to limit the scope and size of public savings institutions. Finally, usury laws and the difficulty of enforcing loan provisions or collecting collateral in the event of default limit the amount of finance that private institutions can provide and the interest rates they can offer. Raising or eliminating limits on loan interest rates, or making loan provisions more enforceable, may be unpopular moves, however, especially if there is insufficient competition among private financial institutions.

One factor that greatly increases the potential for savings institutions in developing countries is the sharp decline in rates of inflation that has been seen in recent years. The average rate of inflation in Brazil from 1990 to 2000 was 199.5 percent, but was only 9.1 percent from 2000 to 2005, for example. While the inflation rate from 1900 to 2000 was lower in most developing countries than in Brazil, almost all saw a decline during the 2000–05 period, and a large majority had inflation rates in that latter period of less than 10 percent. Rates in China and India, for example, were 1.3 percent and 4.0 percent, respectively. Particularly given that many developing countries still have controls on nominal interest rates, getting inflation down to low levels is potentially very useful in encouraging saving. Public savings products in India, for example, are currently yielding interest of 8 percent, which allows a reasonable real rate of return, if recent inflation rates continue or decline.

While, broadly speaking, recent inflation experience in developing countries is favorable, and savers can be more confident in earning a positive real rate of return than in the past, there is still significant inflation and currency risk in many countries. The rich deal with this in part by sending their savings abroad, but this is an alternative that is unavailable to the poor. That difference may help to explain the continued high inequality of wealth and the difficulty that the poor have in building up their wealth. It therefore may be reasonable to ask whether it would be possible to give the poor the ability to save in foreign currency accounts. The amount held in these accounts could, of course, be regulated. Although there would be a negative effect on a country's capital account, it would not be large. The outflow of funds would likely be small in comparison with the offshore holdings of the rich. Such a system could perhaps be facilitated by our international financial institutions in cooperation with a consortium of G8 or OECD countries, which might be able to provide a guarantee for these deposits under suitable conditions.

Tax-Sheltered Personal Accounts and Pensions

Like developed countries, most developing countries in effect have long allowed tax-sheltered saving for retirement through pension funds. Typical among these funds has been a national provident fund, with mandatory contributions for workers in establishments of some predetermined minimum size (for example, in India, 20 employees at present). Because of the large size of the informal sector and the large number of small establishments, it is generally a minority of workers who are covered by these pensions.

There are two main ways in which this typical pattern has changed in some countries. One is that funded plans with some element of participant choice in how funds are directed have emerged. The other is that individual tax-sheltered nonpension savings vehicles have been developed.[35]

Latin America provides a striking example of the liberalization of pension schemes and their growing use for purposes other than retirement income. Chile blazed the way, adopting an individual-based pension scheme in 1981 with a large element of choice in how personal pension funds are invested.[36] This development was contemporaneous with the rise of 401(k) plans in the United States, but whereas the takeover of pensions in the United States by this new form of saving reflected choice on the part of employers, in Chile the change was imposed. The Chilean initiative was instrumental in the rise of the "multipillar" approach to pensions, which has spread to eleven other Latin American countries. Similar reforms have been instituted in eight eastern European countries.

In Singapore, one sees another variant on the theme, which is now a high-income country but was a developing country not so long ago and whose example is influential in the developing world. Workers younger than fifty contribute 14.5 percent of their earnings to accounts in the Central Provident Fund. Employers add 20 percent of workers' earnings to these contributions. Contributions are allocated to an Ordinary account, used for housing, insurance, investment, and education; a Special account, used for retirement-related financial products; and a Medisave account, used to cover medical expenses. In 2008 and 2009, the interest rate on these accounts is slated to rise by 1 percentage point, to 3.5 percent for Ordinary accounts and 5.0 percent for the other two account types. Initial contributions are allocated according to fixed ratios for those in an age band. For example, currently for workers aged 35 to 45, the shares are 60.9 percent for an Ordinary account, 17.4 percent for a Special account, and 21.7 percent for the Medisave account.

The Medisave aspect of Singapore's system has aroused interest elsewhere, with the promotion of tax-sheltered medical savings accounts perhaps being seen as an affordable alternative to a universal system of medical insurance like that seen in most developed countries other than the United States. From an economic viewpoint, this is a somewhat odd development. The private market for medical insurance does not work well because of adverse selection and moral

---

35. In India, the Public Provident Fund is advertising TSPAs with a minimum deposit of 500 rupees per financial year and a maximum deposit of Rs 70,000. These can be established at designated post offices or public sector banks. National Savings Certificates also seem to provide substantial tax relief on personal savings.

36. See Gill, Packard, and Yermo (2005).

hazard problems. Without public intervention, individuals try to cope in various ways, one of which is through personal saving. This is inherently imperfect, however, since it does not reduce the cost of risk, as would true insurance. There is also a serious problem of lack of protection against catastrophic medical expenses. Further, the burden sharing across individuals and families that occurs with true insurance is missing. Appropriate policy responses would seem to be regulation and perhaps subsidies for private insurance, or substitution of a public insurance system. These measures would get at the root of the problem. Nevertheless, in the context of developing countries, where providing good public health care or health insurance may be prohibitively costly, the health savings account approach is attractive from the viewpoint of helping people to build the assets that will help them weather difficult health episodes.

Conclusion

This chapter has suggested that policies and institutions that allow people an opportunity to build and maintain middle-class wealth are effective in fighting poverty and can gain strong majority support in developing countries. We have looked at the current and historical experience of the now-developed countries to see what policies worked in their case and have asked which of these policies, and what others, can be productively employed in the developing world. One has seen that some of the successful initiatives in developed countries, such as tax-sheltered savings, for example, have begun to spread in the developing world. And important innovations, such as microfinance and pension reforms, have been pioneered in the developing countries themselves. Yet, because of deficiencies in land administration, underdeveloped financial institutions, and a lack of mortgage insurance, loans for home buying or building are difficult to obtain in many developing countries, holding people back from acquiring the quintessential middle-class asset, a well-built private house or apartment. There is a lot of room for further improvements in giving ordinary people the tools they need to build their personal wealth.

Further development of savings opportunities and mortgage finance is one of the most promising initiatives for wealth building that will benefit a significant number of the poor and at the same time find majority electoral support. Fostering competition among financial institutions and ensuring that microfinance organizations are not impeded are very important, as is ensuring that tax-sheltered savings vehicles are available for the full range of saving purposes. To make housing finance effective, it is important to have effective land administration and the possibility of mortgage foreclosures that are not too expensive to enforce or too long delayed. A system of mortgage insurance is needed to make possible reasonably low down payments without threatening the stability of the lending institutions. Also popular and useful in wealth building would be measures directed more squarely at the poor. More secure tenure and better services for those in informal housing fall in this category. Land reform, although always a difficult process, may also be very helpful if pursued carefully.

Although the developed countries have generally helped people become middle class through asset accumulation, it should be noted that they have also employed an alternative strategy to help the poor raise their living standards to a middle-class level. The alternative strategy is to subsidize key goods and services, such as education, housing, or student loans, and to provide forms of insurance and related products, such as unemployment insurance, medical insurance, and annuities (in the form of state pensions), that are either missing or under-provided in private markets. Free public education has been provided in most developed countries for a long time, and with only a few exceptions, either free or low-cost public health care or health insurance has also been provided. Such policies allow people to achieve a middle-class standard of life without so much of the asset accumulation we have discussed in this chapter.

In much of the developing world today, public education and health care are not of a high standard. This means that to be truly middle class one has to have the income and wealth to finance private education and private health care, which is a tall order. Improvements to public education and health care can reduce this burden by making more reliance on public systems acceptable as part of middle-class life. Such improvements may be seen as complementary with the policies aimed at fostering private wealth that have been discussed in this chapter.

References

Armendáriz de Aghion, Beatriz, and Jonathan Morduch. 2005. *The Economics of Micro-finance.* MIT Press.

Balchin, Paul, ed. 1996. *Housing Policy in Europe.* London: Routledge.

Buckley, Robert M., and Jerry Kalarickal. 2005. "Housing Policy in Developing Countries: Conjectures and Refutations." *World Bank Research Observer* 20, no. 2: 233–57.

Davies, James B., ed. 2008. *Personal Wealth from a Global Perspective.* Oxford University Press for UNU-WIDER (World Institute for Development Economics Research of the United Nations University).

Davies, James B., Susanna Sandström, Anthony Shorrocks, and Edward N. Wolff. 2006. "The World Distribution of Household Wealth." Helsinki: UNU-WIDER (December 5).

Deininger, Klaus. 2002. "Negotiating Land Reform as One Way of Land Access: Experiences from Colombia, Brazil and South Africa." In *Access to Land, Rural Poverty and Public Action,* edited by Alain De Janvry and others, pp. 315–48. Oxford University Press for UNU-WIDER.

———. 2003. *Land Policies for Growth and Poverty Reduction.* Oxford University Press and the World Bank.

Deininger, Klaus, and Hans Binswanger. 2002. "The Evolution of the World Bank's Land Policy." In *Access to Land, Rural Poverty and Public Action,* edited by Alain De Janvry and others, pp. 406–40. Oxford University Press for UNU-WIDER.

De Soto, Hernando. 2000. *The Mystery of Capital: Why Capitalism Triumphs in the West and Fails Everywhere Else.* New York: Basic Books.

Federal Reserve Board. Various years. Survey of Consumer Finances. Washington (www.federalreserve.gov/pubs/oss/oss2/scfindex.html).

Fernandes, Leela. 2006. *India's New Middle Class: Democratic Politics in an Era of Economic Reform.* University of Minnesota Press.

Frankenberg, Elizabeth, James P. Smith, and Duncan Thomas. 2003. "Economic Shocks, Wealth and Welfare." *Journal of Human Resources* 38, no. 2: 280–323.

Gilbert, Dennis. 2002. *The American Class Structure.* New York: Wadsworth.

Gill, Indermit S., Truman Packard, and Juan Yermo. 2005. *Keeping the Promise of Social Security in Latin America.* Stanford University Press and the World Bank.

Gustafsson, Bjorn, Shi Li, and Zhao Wei. 2006. "The Distribution of Wealth in Urban China and in Chin as a Whole 1995." *Review of Income and Wealth* 52, no. 2: 173–88.

Honohan, Patrick. 2006. "Household Financial Assets in the Process of Development." Working Paper 3965. Washington: World Bank.

Li, Shi, and Renwei Zhao. 2007. "Changes in the Distribution of Wealth in China, 1995–2002." Research Paper 2007/03. Helsinki, Finland: UNU-WIDER.

MacGee, James C. 2006. "Land Titles, Credit Markets and Wealth Distributions." Research Paper 2006/150. Helsinki, Finland: UNU-WIDER.

Maclennan, Duncan, John Muellbauer, and Mark Stephens. 2000. "Asymmetries in Housing and Financial Market Institutions and EMU." In *Readings in Macroeconomics,* edited by Tim Jenkinson, chapter 5. Oxford University Press.

Milanovic, Branko. 2005. *Worlds Apart: Measuring International and Global Inequality.* Princeton University Press.

Milanovic, Branko, and Shlomo Yitzhaki. 2002. "Decomposing World Income Distribution: Does the World Have a Middle Class?" *Review of Income and Wealth* 48, no. 2: 155–78.

Nijman, Jan. 2006. "Mumbai's Mysterious Middle Class." *International Journal of Urban and Regional Research* 30, no. 4: 758–75.

Pyatt, G., C. N. Chen, and J. Fei. 1980. "The Distribution of Income by Factor Components." *Quarterly Journal of Economics* 95: 451–73.

Scrase, Tim. 2006. "The 'New' Middle Class in India: A Re-Assessment." Paper presented at the 16th biennial conference of the Asian Studies Association of Australia. University of Wollongong, June 26–29.

Subramanian, S., and D. Jayaraj. 2006. "The Distribution of Household Wealth in India." Research Paper 2006/116. Helsinki, Finland: UNU-WIDER.

World Bank. 2007a. *Global Economic Prospects 2007: Managing the Next Wave of Globalization.* Washington.

———. 2007b. *World Development Indicators 2007.* Washington.

Woodruff, Christopher. 2001. "Review of de Soto's *The Mystery of Capital.*" *Journal of Economic Literature* 39, no. 4: 1215–223.

6

Can Happiness Research Help Fiscal Policy?

CAROL GRAHAM

Economists have increasingly been questioning the extent to which traditional measures of utility and welfare that are based on income and consumption fully capture important elements of individual welfare. At the same
time, behavioral economists have been using experiments and other tools to
explore how individuals depart from standard notions of rationality and welfare
maximization. An outgrowth of these developments has been the new interest in
happiness surveys as a tool for measuring welfare and well-being.

This chapter explores the extent to which happiness surveys can shed light on
the seeming disconnect between the record of policy reforms (at least as gauged
by economic assessments) on the one hand and the very low levels of public
support for them on the other, with a focus on Latin America. More specifically, speaking to the topic of fiscal incidence, happiness surveys allow researchers
to gain some insights into the relative importance that respondents attach to
various public policies and to the allocation of public expenditures as well as to
isolate the views of middle-class respondents in particular. The chapter first
reviews the basic determinants of happiness and how Latin America compares
with other regions. It then highlights research that has found high levels of
unhappiness and frustration among the middle class relative to the poor and the
rich, as well as some research that highlights the role of inequality and insecurity,
among other factors. Finally, the chapter reviews the promises and pitfalls of
applying the findings of happiness surveys to policy.

The Economics of Happiness: A Novel Approach to Measuring Welfare

Happiness economics combines techniques typically used by psychologists with standard econometric tools more common to economists.[1] The most important departure of happiness economics from conventional economic analysis is that it relies on surveys in which individuals report their happiness levels as a measure of welfare rather than relying on the standard approach of *revealed preferences,* which is based on measuring what people purchase or consume.

Economists have traditionally shied away from survey data, which, like much other data, are rift with problems of bias and measurement error. Yet increased usage of such data in recent years has resulted in improved econometric techniques for accounting for the errors. In addition, the results of large sample studies demonstrate remarkable consistency in the determinants of well-being or happiness across hundreds of thousands of individuals across countries and over time. There are, no doubt, cross-cultural differences in the definition of happiness. It is important for the robustness of the studies that no attempt is made to define the term *happiness.* Each respondent does so on his or her own.

The lack of an externally imposed definition of happiness allows for the use of such surveys as a research tool across diverse populations and cultures. Yet it presents challenges when applied to policy. The importance that is assigned to happiness as a policy objective will vary depending on how it is defined, and that in turn will vary across cultures and countries. Addressing those challenges will be critical to the successful application of happiness surveys to policy questions. This chapter will discuss the specific problems associated with doing so. Notwithstanding these challenges, this approach has the potential to significantly enhance the field's understanding of human well-being.

Early economists and philosophers, ranging from Aristotle to Bentham, Mill, and Smith, incorporated the pursuit of happiness in their work. Yet, as economics grew more rigorous and quantitative, more parsimonious definitions of welfare took hold. Utility was considered to depend only on income, mediated by individual choices or preferences within a rational individual's monetary budget constraint.

The economics of happiness does not purport to replace income-based measures of welfare but instead to complement them with broader measures of well-being. These measures are based on the results of large-scale surveys, across countries and over time, of hundreds of thousands of individuals who were asked to assess their own welfare. The surveys provide information about the importance of a range of factors that affect well-being, which include

---

1. This section of the paper draws on Carol Graham's "The Economics of Happiness" (2008).

income but also others, such as health, marital and employment status, and civic trust.

The approach of happiness surveys, which relies on expressed preferences rather than on revealed choices, is particularly well suited to answering questions in areas in which a revealed preferences approach provides limited information. Indeed, it often uncovers discrepancies between expressed and revealed preferences. Revealed preferences cannot fully gauge the welfare effects of particular policies or institutional arrangements that individuals are powerless to change. Examples of these include the effects on welfare of inequality, environmental degradation, and macroeconomic policies, such as inflation and unemployment. Amartya Sen's capabilities-based approach to poverty, for example, highlights the lack of capacity of the poor to make choices or to take certain actions.[2] Another area in which a choice approach is limited and happiness surveys can shed light is the welfare effects of addictive behaviors such as smoking and drug abuse or of public health problems such as obesity, in which differences in social norms and in future expectations and related variance in discount rates may be at play.[3]

Happiness surveys are based on questions in which the individual is asked, "Generally speaking, how happy are you with your life?" or "How satisfied are you with your life?" with possible answers on a 4–7 point ordinal scale. Psychologists have a preference for life satisfaction questions. Yet answers to questions on happiness and life satisfaction correlate quite closely. The correlation coefficient between the two ranges between 0.56 and 0.50.[4]

This approach presents several methodological challenges.[5] To minimize order bias, happiness questions must be placed at the beginning of surveys. As with all economic measurements, the answer of any specific individual may be biased by idiosyncratic, unobserved events. Bias in answers to happiness surveys can also result from unobserved personality traits and correlated measurement errors (which can be corrected using individual fixed effects if and when panel data are available).

Despite the potential pitfalls, cross sections of large samples across countries and over time find remarkably consistent patterns in the determinants of happiness. Many errors are uncorrelated with the observed variables and do not

2. Sen (1999).

3. For an application of this line of thinking to the obesity problem, see Felton and Graham (2005); Graham and Ladkawalla (2006).

4. Blanchflower and Oswald (2004), based on British data from 1975 to 1992 that included both questions; Graham and Pettinato (2002), based on Latin American data from 2000 to 2001, in which alternative phrasing was used in different years.

5. For a fuller description of these methodological challenges, see Bertrand and Mullainathan (2001); Frey and Stutzer (2002).

systematically bias the results. Psychologists, meanwhile, find validation in the way that people answer these surveys that are based on physiological measures of happiness, such as the frontal movements in the brain and in the number of "genuine"—Duchenne—smiles.[6]

Microeconometric happiness equations have the standard form $W_{it} = \alpha + \beta X_{it} + \epsilon_{it}$, where W is the reported well-being of individual i at time t, and X is a vector of known variables including sociodemographic and socioeconomic characteristics. Unobserved characteristics and measurement errors are captured in the error term. Because the answers to happiness surveys are ordinal rather than cardinal, they are best analyzed using ordered logit or probit estimations. These regressions typically yield lower R squares than economists are used to, reflecting the extent to which emotions and other components of true well-being, some of which may be ephemeral, are driving the results as opposed to the variables that we are able to measure, such as income, education, and marital and employment status.

The availability of panel data in some instances, as well as advances in econometric techniques, are increasingly allowing for sounder analysis.[7] The coefficients produced from ordered probit or logistic regressions are remarkably similar to those from OLS regressions based on the same equations. Although it is impossible to measure the precise effects of independent variables on true well-being, happiness researchers have used the OLS coefficients as a basis for assigning relative weights to them. They can estimate how much income a typical individual in the United States or Britain would need to produce the same change in stated happiness that comes from the loss in well-being resulting from, for example, divorce ($100,000) or job loss ($60,000).[8]

The Easterlin Paradox

In his original study, Richard Easterlin revealed a paradox that sparked interest in the topic but is as yet unresolved.[9] While most happiness studies find that *within* countries wealthier people are, on average, happier than poor ones, studies across countries and over time find very little, if any, relationship between increases in per capita income and average happiness levels. On average, wealthier countries (as a group) are happier than poor ones (as a group); happiness seems to rise with income up to a point, but not beyond it. Yet even among the less happy, poorer countries, there is not a clear relationship between average income and average happiness levels, which suggests that many other factors— including cultural traits—are at play (see figure 6-1).

6. Diener and Seligman (2004).
7. Van Praag and Ferrer-i-Carbonell (2004).
8. Blanchflower and Oswald (2004).
9. Easterlin (1974).

Figure 6-1. *Happiness and Income Per Capita, 1990s*[a]

Percentage above neutral on life satisfaction

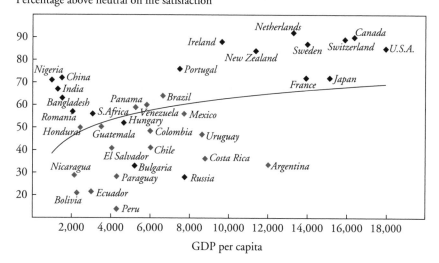

Source: Graham and Pettinato (2002).

a. $R^2 = 0.14$.

b. GDP per capita based on 1998 purchasing power parity dollars.

Within countries, income matters to happiness.[10] Deprivation and abject poverty in particular are very bad for happiness. Yet, after basic needs are met, other factors such as rising aspirations, relative income differences, and the security of gains become increasingly important, in addition to income. A common interpretation of the Easterlin paradox is that humans are on a "hedonic treadmill": aspirations increase along with income and, after basic needs are met, relative rather than absolute levels of income matter to well-being. Another interpretation of the paradox is the psychologists' *set point* theory of happiness, in which every individual is presumed to have a happiness level that he or she goes back to over time, even after major events such as winning the lottery or getting divorced.[11] The implication of this theory for policy is that nothing much can be done to increase happiness.

Individuals are remarkably adaptable and in the end can get used to most things, and in particular to income gains. The behavioral economics literature, for example, shows that individuals value losses more than gains.[12] Easterlin argues that individuals adapt more in the pecuniary arena than in the nonpecuniary arena, while life-changing events, such as bereavement, have lasting effects on happiness.

10. Oswald (1997); Diener and others (1993); among others.

11. Easterlin (1974).

12. See Kahneman, Diener, and Schwarz (1999), among others.

There is no consensus about which interpretation is most accurate. Yet numerous studies showing that happiness levels can change significantly in response to a variety of factors suggest that research can yield insights into human well-being, providing in turn important, if complementary, information for policymakers. More recent studies by psychologists, meanwhile, suggest that there are some events that individuals never adapt back from.[13] Even under the rubric of set point theory, meanwhile, accepting that levels *eventually* adapt upward to a longer-term equilibrium, mitigating or preventing the unhappiness and disruption that individuals experience for months, or even years, certainly seems a worthwhile objective for policy.

Selected Applications of Happiness Economics

Happiness research has been applied to a range of issues that are relevant to the topic of this volume. These include the relationship between income and happiness, the relationship between inequality and poverty, and the effects of macropolicies on individual welfare. Some studies have attempted to separate the effects of income from those of other endogenous factors, such as satisfaction in the workplace. Studies of unexpected lottery gains have found that these isolated gains have positive effects on happiness, although it is not clear that they are of a lasting nature.[14] A recent study based on the German Socio-Economic Panel (GSEOP) found that individuals adapt to the positive effects of income gains very quickly but, in contrast, status changes have more lasting effects on well-being.[15] Other studies have explored the reverse direction of causality and found that people with higher happiness levels tend to perform better in the labor market and to earn more income in the future.[16]

A related question, and one which is still debated in economics, is how income inequality affects individual welfare. It is interesting that the results differ between developed and developing economies. Most studies of the United States and Europe have found that inequality has modest or insignificant effects on happiness. The mixed results may reflect the fact that inequality can be a signal of future opportunity and mobility as much as it can be a sign of injustice.[17] In contrast, recent research by Graham and Andrew Felton on Latin America found that inequality has a negative effect on the well-being of the poor and a positive one for the rich. In a region where inequality is much higher and where public institutions and labor markets are notoriously inefficient, inequality signals

13. Diener, Lucas, and Scollen (2006).
14. Gardner and Oswald (2001).
15. DiTella, Haisken-DeNew, and MacCulloch (2004).
16. Diener and others (1993); Graham, Eggers, and Sukhtankar (2004).
17. Alesina, Di Tella, and MacCulloch (2004).

persistent disadvantage or advantage rather than opportunity and mobility.[18] This is a particularly important question in the context of the middle class in Latin America, where inequality in general is worsened by fiscal policy and it seems to be the middle class that is most squeezed.[19]

Happiness research can deepen the understanding of the relationship between the poor and the middle class. The set point theory suggests that a destitute peasant can be very happy. While this contradicts a standard finding in the literature—namely, that poor people are less happy than wealthier people within countries—it is suggestive of the role that low expectations play in explaining persistent poverty in some cases. Work on social mobility by Nancy Birdsall and Graham, meanwhile, suggests that high and persistent levels of inequality— which they distinguish from the kind of inequality that rewards productivity and innovation—can exacerbate the low expectations and poverty trap.[20]

The well-being of those who have escaped poverty is often undermined by insecurity and the risk of falling back into poverty. Income data do not reveal this vulnerability, yet happiness data show that it has strong negative effects on their welfare. Indeed, the reported well-being of middle-income groups is often lower than that of the poor. The former's exit from poverty is typically accompanied by higher expectations that are, in turn, more likely to be frustrated in the face of insecurity or limited upward mobility.[21]

Happiness surveys can be used to examine the effects of different macropolicy arrangements on well-being. Most studies find that inflation and unemployment have negative effects on happiness. The effects of unemployment are stronger than those of inflation, and they hold, above and beyond those of forgone income.[22] The standard misery index, which assigns equal weight to inflation and unemployment, may be underestimating the effects of the latter on well-being.[23] Political arrangements also matter. Well-being literature shows that trust and freedom have positive effects on happiness.[24] Research based on variance in voting rights across cantons in Switzerland found that there are positive effects from *participating* in direct democracy.[25] Research by Graham and Sandip Sukhtankar in Latin America found a strong positive correlation between happiness and preference for democracy.[26]

Given the wide range of potential applications for happiness surveys, they can and should provide important insights into the perceived welfare effects of

18. Graham and Felton (2006).
19. Estache (2008).
20. Birdsall and Graham (1999).
21. Graham and Pettinato (2002).
22. Di Tella, MacCulloch, and Oswald (2001).
23. Frey and Stutzer (2002).
24. Helliwell (2005); Layard (2005).
25. Frey and Stutzer (2002).
26. Graham and Sukhtankar (2004).

policy reforms, as well as serve as a tool for measuring their impact. At the same time, for a number of reasons discussed below, caution is necessary when applying the research findings to policy directly. Before that discussion, however, it is necessary to see how the determinants of happiness in Latin America compare with those in other places where happiness has been studied and how the middle class, in particular, fares.

The Determinants of Happiness: Latin America in Comparative Perspective

The 2002 study of happiness in Latin America by Graham and Stefano Pettinato was the first study of happiness in such a large sample of developing countries and certainly the first for the region. The general direction of those findings has been confirmed in a number of studies since then.[27] In the 2002 study, we compared the determinants of happiness in Latin America with those of the United States. For the United States, we used the pooled data for the period 1973–98 from the General Social Survey (GSS). We also compared the determinants of happiness in Latin America with those in another large sample of respondents in a very different context, Russia. For Russia, we relied on the most recent available survey (2000) from the Russia Longitudinal Monitoring Survey (RLMS). For Latin America, we relied on the 2001 Latinobarómetro public opinion survey. We used data from 2001 as it is the one year for which we have variables for self-reported health status and minority status, which makes it comparable with the U.S. and Russia surveys. (See annex tables A-1, A-2, A-3.) Studies based on a pooled sample for several years of Latinobarómetro rather than on cross sections for particular years show essentially the same results.

We found a remarkable degree of similarity: there are similar age, income, education, marriage, employment, and health effects.[28] In all contexts, unemployed people are less happy than others. Self-employed people are happier in the United States and in Russia on average, while in Latin America, they were less happy. In the United States, self-employment is a choice; in Latin America, the self-employed are often in the informal sector by default. Another difference is that women are happier than men in the United States, while in Russia men are happier than women (because of disparities in status?), and in Latin America, there is no gender difference. Blacks are less happy than other races in the United States, and similarly, those that identify as minorities in Latin America are less happy. In contrast, minorities are happier than ethnic Russians.

27. Graham and Pettinato (2002). See, for example, Graham and Sukhtankar (2004); Graham and Felton (2006).

28. The coefficient on marriage for Latin America is positive but short of statistical significance for the 2001 sample. For other years for which we have data, the coefficient on marriage is positive and significant.

We also find that in Latin America and Russia happier people are more likely to support market policies, to be satisfied with how democracy was working, and to prefer democracy to any other system of government. Happier people, on average, have higher prospects for their own and their children's future mobility, are more likely to believe that the distribution of income in their country was fair, place themselves higher on a notional economic ladder, and have lower fear of unemployment.[29]

Bottom Line: What Makes People Happy?

In summary, happiness studies show remarkable consistency in the effects of certain variables on happiness, as our studies in Latin America, Russia, and the United States suggest. Income, for example, clearly matters to happiness, and the wealthy are, on average, happier than poorer people. But the effect is not a linear one. Health, meanwhile, matters as much as, if not more than, income to people's happiness. Education has more mixed effects, most likely because education and income are so closely correlated in most contexts. While the sign on education is usually positive, it is not significant when income is included in the equation. The income variable likely overpowers the effects of education. An additional explanation, though, may be that returns to education are not always as predicted, particularly in rapidly changing developing economies, as discussed above. Therefore there is probably a significant subsample of the more educated population that is frustrated with the returns on education.

Unemployment, meanwhile, has deleterious effects on happiness everywhere it is studied. There are, however, some differences surrounding employment status across countries and regions. While self-employment is positively correlated to happiness in Russia and the United States, it is negatively correlated in Latin America, most likely as the self-employed in Latin America are not so by choice. And retirees are significantly less happy in Russia than they are in other contexts, reflecting the oft-cited plight of Russian pensioners during the transition, no doubt.

Meanwhile, related to unemployment and health, is social insurance. People who have access to health insurance and to social or economic mechanisms to protect themselves from unemployment and other kinds of insecurity are, typically, happier than others. To some extent these findings reflect higher levels of socioeconomic status, but they hold even when controlling for respondents' income levels. Fear of unemployment, meanwhile, is closely correlated with

29. The Economic Ladder Question (ELQ) asked respondents to place themselves on a 9-step ladder representing their society, where the poor are on step 1 and the rich are on step 9. Support for market policies was measured by an index based on several scaled questions about the private sector, foreign investment, free trade, and privatization. For details, see Graham and Pettinato (2002).

unhappiness in all contexts. Most individuals seem to be loss averse, and insecurity seems to have the potential to erode the positive effects of income gains in most contexts. And, for the reasons discussed above, those in the middle are most likely to experience these effects, rather than the very poor who are less likely to have made income gains to begin with. Finally, there is some evidence that Africa may be somewhat of an outlier, on the basis of some preliminary work on cross-sectional data from the Afrobarometer public opinion survey.[30] Although the survey does not have direct happiness questions, there are a number of questions that are good proxies for optimism about the future, including questions about respondents' children, which typically are closely correlated with happiness. In every other context where we have studied optimism and prospects of upward mobility, respondents who think that their children will live better than they will are wealthier and more educated, on average. They are the most likely to predict accurately that they will be able to provide their children with the means necessary to take up opportunities.

In Africa, in contrast, Graham and Matthew Hoover found that respondents who are the most optimistic about their *children's* future are the poorest and least educated in the sample. (The poorest are not more optimistic about their own future, which is more typical of other contexts.) However, data over an extended period of time, which would be necessary to better explain such a result, are not yet available. On the one hand, one could posit that this result is driven by selection bias: in a context as difficult as Africa, people have to be optimistic to survive. On the other, the finding may reflect a very human capacity to adapt one's own expectations downward in the face of adversity but to retain hope and optimism for one's children. Finally, given the rather bleak macroeconomic prospects in Africa, it may also be a realistic assessment on the part of the wealthy that their children are likely to have limited opportunities to better their status.

The Frustrated Middle: Findings from Panel Data

The above studies are based on cross sections from the Latinobarómetro, the GSS, the RLMS, and the Afrobarometer. For one country in Latin America, Peru, we have data on both reported and objective well-being for the same respondents over a ten-year period. This allows us to get a picture of the effects over time of income on happiness, as well as to begin to separate out what is driven by contextual factors as opposed to what is driven by specific personality traits. We also have similar data for Russia.

In Peru, Graham and Pettinato reinterviewed a subsample (500) of respondents in a large, nationally representative panel for the period 1991–2000 and

---

30. For details, see Graham and Hoover (2007).

Figure 6-2. *Long-Term Perceived Mobility Compared with 1991–2000 Income Mobility, Peru, 2000*[a]

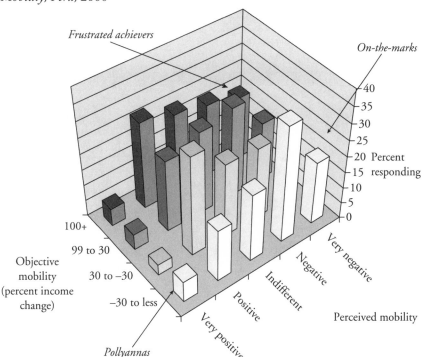

Source: Graham and Pettinato (2002).
a. Similar findings when using observations are limited to only those with above-median wealth.

asked a number of questions about their perceptions of their past progress and for their future prospects. We repeated this perceptions survey three years in a row. The most significant and surprising finding was that almost half of the most upwardly mobile respondents perceived that their economic situation was negative or very negative compared with ten years prior. (See figure 6-2.)

We conducted a similar analysis that was based on comparable data for Russia and found an even higher percentage of frustrated respondents—or "frustrated achievers" as we now call them (figure 6-3).

These frustrated achievers (FAs) were at or just about at average income (and therefore not the poorest in the sample)—roughly middle class. They were slightly older on average than upwardly mobile nonfrustrated respondents, but without any significant gender or education differences.[31] The FAs scored lower

31. For a complete picture of the statistically significant differences between frustrated and nonfrustrated upwardly mobile respondents, see Graham and Pettinato (2002, chapter 4).

Figure 6-3. *Perceived Past Mobility Compared with 1995–99 Income Mobility, Russia, 1999*

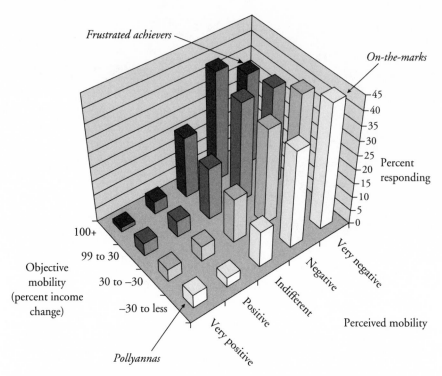

Source: Graham and Pettinato (2002).

on a whole host of perception questions, such as their perceived prospects of upward mobility and their position on a notional economic ladder. They also had a greater fear of being unemployed in the future. In addition, the Russian FAs were more likely to want to restrict the incomes of the rich and were less satisfied with the market process and with democracy (we did not have the same questions in the original survey for Peru).[32]

In Peru, the likelihood of having upward mobility and being frustrated (that is, being a frustrated achiever) is negatively related to initial income levels.[33] In

32. In an initial, and at this point cursory, analysis of the 2003 Peru survey data, Graham and Margaret MacLeod (2004) found that the frustrated achievers are less likely to favor democracy, but there is no link with market policies. Yet, the results are also not fully comparable because a much lower number of respondents had upward mobility during this latter period, and thus there was a far lower percentage of frustrated achievers.

33. This finding is based on a logit regression on the probability of being a frustrated achiever. For results, see Graham (2005).

other words, the frustrated achievers started from lower income levels, on average, even though they were not the poorest in the sample at the time of our survey. This is not surprising, since even large percentage increases in their incomes will seem insufficient to reach the levels of wealthier groups, particularly if the perception is that their mobility is limited. The Peruvian FAs were also more likely to be urban and therefore more informed about the lifestyles of others, including those of the very wealthy.

Relative income differences could certainly be a plausible explanation for these frustrations. Peru and Russia both have high degrees of inequality. The FAs were more likely to score lower on the notional economic ladder in both surveys, as well as to compare their situation negatively with that of others in their community and, in Peru specifically, in their country (this latter question was not in the Russian survey).

Insecurity and a lack of adequate social insurance could be another explanation. As noted above, the FAs had a higher fear of unemployment than non-frustrated achievers had. Even though the FAs were doing well by objective income measures, they perceive that there is no guarantee of stability or maintaining their earnings level. This was not surprising, given that both surveys were conducted in very volatile economic contexts, and the objective mobility data revealed a remarkable degree of vulnerability.[34] The FAs in Russia also reported less satisfaction with the process of market reform and lower support for democracy in relation to questions about returning to pre-perestroika times (we did not have these same type of questions for Peru).

Most of the FAs were at mean levels of education. In Latin America, with trade and capital market liberalization in the 1990s, people with higher levels of education gained high marginal returns compared with the rest of society, while people with secondary education experienced decreasing marginal returns when compared with those with primary education.[35] Before this period of increased trade and expanded capital markets, people with secondary education were able to lead relatively stable middle-class lives. Yet, by the end of the 1990s, the income gaps between the middle and the poor had narrowed, and the public sector jobs that many of this cohort held were far fewer and less desirable.[36] The unemployed, for example, are disproportionately represented among those with completed or almost-completed secondary education.[37]

---

34. A higher percentage of respondents went from "rags to riches"—or from the bottom to the top quintile in a ten-year period in Peru (5 percent) than in a similar period in the United States (1 percent), for example. Yet a surprising 11 percent of respondents in the middle of the distribution (quintile 4 in Peru) fell back all the way to the bottom quintile during the same period, which is analogous to falling from the middle class into extreme poverty.

35. See Behrman, Birdsall, and Székely (2001).

36. We discuss this in detail and introduce a measure of "middle-income stress" (MIS) in Birdsall, Graham, and Pettinato (2001).

37. Graham and Felton (2006).

Last, it is quite plausible that some of the frustrations that we have found are driven by individual character traits. There is probably some percentage of every sample that will always be unhappy or negative, regardless of objective conditions. We do not have the data over time that are necessary to test this proposition. Some intersect of contextual variables and character traits is likely driving the frustrations of our achievers.

Inequality and Opportunity

Clearly the findings for the frustrated achievers highlight the role of insecurity and inequality in undermining well-being—and possibly support for policy reforms—in the region. The effect of inequality on individual welfare remains a debated question in economics. In a separate study, Graham and Felton looked at the effects of inequality on happiness in Latin America and found that this is one important area where the region appears to differ markedly from the Organization for Economic Cooperation and Development (OECD) countries.[38] In Europe and the United States, inequality does not seem to have significant effects on happiness, one way or the other. In those contexts, and particularly in the United States, inequality seems to signal mobility and opportunity as much as it suggests injustice. In stark contrast, we found that it has significant effects on well-being in Latin America, making those in the highest quintiles 5 percent happier and those in the poorest quintile 3 percent less happy than the average. Indeed, the effects of relative income differences in the region—measured as each respondent's distance from the mean wealth level for his or her country—held regardless of average country-level incomes, which had no effect. (See table 6-1.)

In a simple illustration, we show how a respondent in the poorest quintile in Honduras, whose distance from the country mean is half that of a respondent in the poorest quintile in Chile, is happier than the respondent in Chile because of smaller relative differences. Yet the poor Honduran is twice as poor in objective terms.

We conducted the same analysis using different reference norms and compared respondents in large-, medium-, and small-sized cities. Our results were similar, except that in small cities, average income levels still had a significant positive effect, in addition to relative income levels, suggesting that at lower levels of income, concerns for relative income are still mediated by absolute levels, a finding that is consistent with the broader literature (and the Easterlin paradox). Our findings on inequality in Latin America run in the opposite direction of the interpretation in which inequality signals opportunity and mobility, which is more typical for the United States and for Europe.

---

38. Graham and Felton (2006). For a study of U.S. inequality at the neighborhood level, see Luttmer (2005).

Table 6-1a. *Average versus Relative Wealth*[a]

| | Average wealth calculated by cluster | | | | | |
	Country	Country	Country and city size	Country and city size	Country and city size	Country and city size
Individual wealth	0.106557 (5.52**)		0.111905 (11.78**)		0.094951 (12.60**)	
Average wealth	−0.044854 (0.70)	0.0617034 (0.81)	0.053104 (−1.5)	0.0588004 (1.65*)	−0.063055 (−1.48)	0.0318961 (0.73)
Relative wealth		0.106557 (5.52**)		0.111905 (11.78**)		0.094951 (12.60**)
Country dummies[b]	no	no	no	no	yes	yes
Citysize dummies	yes	yes	yes	yes	yes	yes

Source: Author's calculations based on data from Latinobarómetro (1997–2004).
**Significant at the 5 percent level.
a. Ordered logit estimation of a 1–4 scale of happiness. Demographic variables in all regressions: age, years of education, marital status, gender, health status, employment status and type, selfemp (self-employed), retired, and student. Numbers in parentheses are the t statistic.
b. When calculating average wealth at the country level, country dummies cannot be included in the regression due to multicollinearity. When we split the data sample by city size, the coefficient for average wealth is positive and significant for small cities.

Table 6-1b. *Average versus Relative Wealth*[a]

| | Average wealth calculated by cluster | | | | | |
	Country	Country	Country and city size	Country and city size	Country and city size	Country and city size
Individual wealth	0.104796 (5.43**)		0.111883 (12.2**)		0.094975 (12.60**)	
Average wealth	−0.044854 (−0.60)	0.060438 (0.78)	0.051717 (−1.37)	0.060166 (1.45)	−0.069826 (−2.69**)	0.025149 (0.94)
Relative wealth		0.104796 (5.43**)		0.111883 (12.2**)		0.094975 (12.60**)
Country dummies[b]	no	no	no	no	yes	yes
Citysize dummies	no	no	no	no	no	no

Source: Author's calculations based on data from Latinobarómetro (1997–2004).
**Significant at the 5 percent level.
a. Ordered logit estimation on a 1–4 scale of happiness. Demographic variables in all regressions: age, years of education, marital status, gender, health status, employment status and type, selfemp (self-employed), retired, and student. Numbers in parentheses are the t statistic.
b. When calculating average wealth at the country level, country dummies cannot be included in the regression because of multicollinearity. When we split the data sample by city size, the coefficient for average wealth is positive and significant for small cities.

Unemployment

One of the most important variables affecting well-being or happiness is employment status. An obvious question is how the region compares. Previous happiness research has found that unemployment is one of the most traumatic events that can happen to people. One of the reasons is the loss of income; however, there is also a cultural stigma to unemployment that affects happiness. The typical unemployed person in our study is a male who has attended some high school (has ten years of education on average). The percentage of the unemployed population increases with city size. This may be an artifact of the data, however, because people in rural areas are more likely to be outside the formal labor force altogether, and unemployment is a less relevant concept for them.

The strength of these effects—for example, the "costs" of unemployment—tend to vary across countries and regions. We build from the work of others. Rafael Di Tella, Robert MacCulloch, and Andrew Oswald found that respondents in the United States and Europe are made more unhappy by higher unemployment rates than they are by inflation.[39] In other words, the typical respondent—including employed respondents—would accept higher levels of inflation if it would eliminate the insecurity associated with higher unemployment rates.

Several studies have shown that increased unemployment in general lessens the impact on unemployed individuals. Andrew Clark and Oswald found that the unemployed in Britain are less unhappy in districts with higher unemployment rates.[40] The loss of happiness due to the decreased probability of finding a job seems to be lower than the gains to happiness that come from being less stigmatized and surrounded by more unemployed individuals. Similarly, Alois Stutzer and Rafael Lalive found that unemployed respondents are less happy in cantons that have voted to reduce unemployment benefits in Switzerland (controlling for benefit levels) when the stigma from unemployment is higher. Andrew Eggers, Clifford Gaddy, and Graham found that employed and unemployed respondents in Russia are happier in regions with higher unemployment rates.[41]

We, too, find positive effects of general unemployment on happiness in Latin America, using an unemployment rate calculated from our own data and the latest statistics available from the United Nations Economic Commission for Latin America and the Caribbean. These are country-wide unemployment rates and have statistically significant positive effects on happiness. As in the

39. DiTella, MacCulloch, and Oswald (2001).
40. Clark and Oswald (1994).
41. Stutzer and Lalive (2004); Eggers, Gaddy, and Graham (2006).

Table 6-2a. *Cost of Unemployment*[a]
Ordered logit regression of a 1–5 scale of happiness for 2004 dataset[b]

	Coefficient	z score
Unemployed	−0.342	−6.05**

OLS estimation of a 1–5 scale of happiness for 2004 dataset[b]

	Coefficient	z score
Unemployed	−0.174	−6.57**

Ordered logit regression of a 1–5 scale of happiness for pooled 1997–2004 dataset[c]

	Coefficient	z score
Unemployed	−1.375	−5.07**
Unemployed*Gini coefficient	0.020	3.93**

Ordered logit regression of a 1–5 scale of happiness[b]

Costs of unemployment by education level[d]	Coefficient	z score
Unemployed (incomplete primary)	−0.485	−3.83**
Unemployed (completed primary)	−0.205	−1.63
Unemployed (incomplete secondary)	−0.511	−4.46**
Unemployed (completed secondary)	−0.562	−5.17**
Unemployed (incomplete tertiary)	0.027	0.13
Unemployed (completed tertiary)	−0.246	−1.39

Source: Author's calculations based on data from Latinobarómetro (1997–2004) and OECD (matching years).

**Significant at the 5 percent level.

a. Results of regressions with "happiness" (on a 1–5 scale) as the dependent variable.

b. Controls include standard demographic variables and country dummies.

c. Controls include standard demographic variables, country dummies, and year dummies.

d. Base case is illiterate.

above cited studies, higher overall unemployment may reduce the stigma effect on individuals. The results must be tempered, though, by the limited information that open unemployment rates can provide in a region with high levels of informal employment (exceeding 50 percent in a few countries).

Inequality in countries also has an effect on happiness among the unemployed. Using our pooled dataset from the period 1997–2004, we ran a standard happiness regression, including a control variable for being unemployed and then added interaction terms for being unemployed in a high or low Gini country. We found that the costs to happiness of being unemployed are lower in higher Gini countries (table 6-2a). In other words, unemployed respondents in countries with higher inequality are actually happier than the unemployed in countries with low inequality. Countries with high inequality are also poorer, on balance, than other countries, so the unemployed may have less far (and less fear) to fall.

Table 6-2b. *Fear of Unemployment*[a]
Ordered logit regression of a 1–5 scale of fear of unemployment[b]

	Coefficient	z score
Small town	−0.256	−4.34**
Big city	0.081	1.87

Ordered logit regression of a 1–5 scale of fear of unemployment[c]

	Coefficient	z score
Gini coefficient	0.017	4.45**

Source: Author's calculations based on data from Latinobarómetro (1997–2004) and OECD (matching years).

**Significant at the 5 percent level.

a. Results of regressions with "fear of unemployment" (on a 1–5 scale) as the dependent variable.

b. Controls include standard demographic variables, except dummy variables for jobs that are not in the workforce, and country dummies.

c. Controls include standard demographic variables, except dummy variables for jobs that are not in the workforce.

Another possible explanation is the high level of informal employment in the poorer and more unequal countries in the region, resulting in less stigma for the unemployed. However, this finding may be due to some other unobservable country-level variable that we have not accounted for. And while the costs of being unemployed are *lower* in higher Gini countries, fear of unemployment (among the employed) is *higher,* in keeping with our intuition about greater levels of informality and associated insecurity. Thus, in higher inequality countries, the lower stigma for the unemployed is accompanied by greater insecurity for the employed.

With the opening of trade and capital markets, job instability has particularly affected those with a high school education. If we look at the impact on happiness of unemployment among different educational groups, it turns out that, in addition to having the highest rate of unemployment, those with a high school education are made most unhappy by unemployment, again providing some evidence for a middle-class squeeze of sorts. In fact, unemployment has a statistically insignificant effect on happiness on the ends of the education spectrum. College-educated people are less likely to fear unemployment than those with less education. And unemployment is a less relevant concept for the illiterate, who are most likely to be outside the formal labor market to begin with, and those with higher education are more likely to be able to find another job than those with secondary school education (table 6-2a).

We also looked at the costs to unemployment by city size. As in the case of our Gini coefficients, we found that the costs of unemployment are lower in big cities than they are in small towns, suggesting that there is a lower stigma effect in big cities. Yet again, as in the case of inequality (as measured by the Gini), fear of unemployment is higher in the big cities, presumably because labor markets are more integrated into the international economy and volatility is more of a factor, while relying on farming as a safety net is not an option the way it is in smaller towns (table 6-2b).

Our findings are suggestive of how the costs of being unemployed can vary across and within countries and according to different measures of inequality. Inequality seems to be correlated with a lower stigma for the unemployed, but with a higher fear of unemployment for the employed.

Policy Implications

In his 2005 book, Richard Layard made a bold statement about the potential of happiness research to improve people's lives directly through changes in public policy.[42] He highlighted the extent to which people's happiness was affected by status—resulting in a rat race approach to work and to income gains, which in the end reduces well-being. He also noted the strong positive role of security in the workplace and at the home and of the quality of social relationships and trust. He identified direct implications for fiscal and labor market policy— in the form of taxation on excessive income gains and through reevaluation of the merits of performance-based pay.

While many economists would not agree with Layard's specific recommendations, there is nascent consensus that happiness surveys can serve as an important complementary tool for public policy. Scholars such as Ed Diener and Martin Seligman and Daniel Kahneman and others advocated the creation of national well-being accounts to complement national income accounts.[43]

In terms of fiscal incidence, happiness surveys are an important tool for helping policymakers understand what sorts of expenditures contribute most to reported well-being and the relative weights that respondents attach to those (and how these expenditures and weights may vary across countries and socioeconomic cohorts). Income matters to happiness, but that relationship seems to be mediated by how much income respondents have relative to others in their respective reference group. Health matters across the board, but again, that relationship may be mediated by people's expectations of the level and quality of health care. And social safety nets and social insurance also seem to matter a great deal to people's happiness. Rapid but volatile growth that produces a lot of insecurity seems to have less of an impact on happiness than do lower levels of steadier growth. Those insights from happiness surveys are important for policymakers.

---

42. Layard (2005).
43. Diener and Seligman (2004); Kahneman and others (2004).

That said, there are many reasons why policymakers cannot directly apply the findings of happiness surveys to policy choices. One is the potential biases in survey data and the difficulties associated with analyzing these kinds of data in the absence of controls for unobservable personality traits. Happier people may, for example, be healthier on average and at the same time less demanding of health care. That does not mean that they are less deserving of it.

In addition, happiness surveys at times yield anomalous results that provide novel insights into human psychology—such as adaptation and coping during economic crises—but do not translate into viable policy recommendations. One example is the finding (discussed above) that unemployed respondents are happier (or less unhappy) in contexts with higher unemployment rates. The positive effect that reduced stigma of being unemployed has on the well-being of the unemployed seems to outweigh the negative effects of a lower probability of future employment.[44] One interpretation of these results for policy—for example, raising unemployment rates—would obviously be a mistake. At the same time, the research suggests a new focus on the effects of stigma on the welfare of the unemployed.

The findings may also be a result of a combined effect of loss aversion and fear of reform, as the regions with higher unemployment rates were also those which had, in general, made less progress toward implementing economic reforms. There are intertemporal choices involved in supporting reforms, which entail making short-term sacrifices for an unknown, although hopefully better, future. Building better safety nets in the long term, for example, might entail raising the fiscal burden in the short term. It is not surprising that making such reforms or changes may decrease reported happiness in the short term, particularly for individuals who are risk averse. But avoiding necessary structural economic changes is unlikely to enhance welfare in the longer term. This is a clear instance in which happiness surveys can help policymakers understand the public's psychology in the context of policy changes, but they are not a useful guide to policy choices.

The promises and pitfalls of applying happiness research to policy also apply more generally to questions of fiscal incidence and the distribution of income and of public expenditures. There is great promise in understanding a variety of phenomena about which revealed preferences cannot tell us much. As noted above, two sets of questions along these lines come to the fore. The first of these is the welfare effects of macro and institutional arrangements that individuals are powerless to change, such as macroeconomic volatility, inequality, or weak governance structures. The poor who live in a region where access to political as well as economic opportunities is unequally shared are obviously least able to express their preferences (as they are the least able to either circumvent the sys-

---

44. Clark and Oswald (1994); Stutzer and Lalive (2004); Eggers, Gaddy, and Graham (2006).

tem or vote with their feet and emigrate or put their assets abroad). Yet they may well suffer negative welfare effects from inequality.

The other set of questions deals with behaviors that are not the result of preferences but of norms, addiction, or self-control problems. Any number of public health–related issues, such as obesity, cigarette smoking, and other phenomena, can and have been addressed by happiness surveys and could be usefully analyzed in a region that is suffering from many of them. Equally important, though, are those behaviors that are driven by low expectations. If the poor and even the middle-income segments of the population have low expectations for their own and their children's future—and if that is exacerbated by high and persistent levels of inequality as in Latin America—their behavior and attitudes on any number of fronts, ranging from investing in their children's education to saving to public health, could be compromised. If those behaviors are merely analyzed as a result of revealed preferences, then the policy implications will be very different than if these behaviors are analyzed in the context of the costs associated with those behaviors to one's welfare.[45]

A second area of much promise for applying well-being surveys to policy is in the exploration and understanding of the importance of nonincome variables, such as health, education, employment status, gender rights, environment, and any number of other variables related to welfare and quality of life. Standard approaches, which rely on income-based measures of well-being, tend to underweight the importance of these variables. Happiness surveys not only highlight their importance but also allow us to attach relative weights to them.

While there are certainly many promises for applying the results of happiness surveys to policy, there are also many caveats. Three in particular stand out in the context of Latin America and other regions attempting to implement policy reforms or deciding on the allocation of public expenditures. The first is the extent to which individuals adapt to many situations, both upward and downward. Javier Herrera and coauthors, for example, using panel data for Peru and Madagascar, found that people's expectations adapt upward during periods of high growth and downward during recessions and that this adaptation is reflected in their assessments of their life satisfaction.[46] People are less likely to be satisfied with the status quo when expectations are adapting upward. Graham and Pettinato had similar findings for Peru; more recent work on China by Whyte and Hun confirmed the direction of these findings.[47] A number of studies have suggested that people's expectations rise with rapid GDP growth or income gains and then drop with recessions and income losses. That will obviously

---

45. Felton and Graham (2005); Graham and Ladkawalla (2006); Gruber and Mullainathan (2002).

46. Herrera, Razafindrakoto, and Roubaud (2006).

47. Graham and Pettinato (2002); Whyte and Hun (2006).

affect trends in well-being indicators as reforms are implemented and economies change throughout the region.

A related issue, which was alluded to above, is the so-called happy peasant problem. In this instance, very poor and uninformed respondents, who happen to have a high set point (cheery nature), might report that they are very happy, even though they live in destitute poverty. The implications of this information for policy are very unclear. Should policy raise the peasant's awareness of how bad his or her situation is in order to raise expectations, although risk making him or her miserable in the process? Should policy leave the peasant ignorant? How policy factors into differences between set point and character is another difficult normative question. Should policy listen to the naturally unhappy respondents who have a tendency to complain more than others? How much of the expressed unhappiness is due to expectations and how much to character, for example?

Another issue is one of cardinal versus ordinal measures. Happiness surveys are ordinal in nature and do not attach cardinal weights to the responses. Thus no distinction is made between the answers "very happy" and "happy" or "happy" and "unhappy." Yet if these measures are really used to guide policy, does it become necessary to attach such weights? Does unhappiness matter more than happiness, for example? How does one choose between a policy that raises a happy person to the status of very happy compared with one that raises an unhappy person to just being happy? Many of these choices require normative judgments.

Perhaps a more fundamental question is whether happiness should be a policy objective. Are happy people successful or complacent, for example? There is some evidence that happier people perform better in the labor market and are healthier, on average.[48] In other words, being happy seems to have positive causal effects on behavior. And certainly very unhappy or depressed people have all sorts of related negative externalities. But the evidence also suggests that there is a top limit to this. Psychologists find that those that answer happiness questions near the top end of a 10-point scale are indeed more successful, but the effects are stronger around the 7–9 range rather than at the very top of the scale.[49] And there are certainly examples of very successful and creative people who are miserable for most of their lives. On average, though, it seems that happiness is correlated with better outcomes than is unhappiness or misery and that eliminating the latter seems a worthwhile objective for policy.

The definition of happiness is fundamental to resolving these questions. Attempting such a definition is clearly beyond the scope of this chapter—and of the author's expertise. Philosophers have provided a range of definitions over centuries. A more recent attempt to define happiness, by Anthony and

48. Graham, Eggers, and Sukhtankar (2004).
49. See Diener, Lucas, and Scollon (2006); Diener and others (1999).

Charles Kenny, seems particularly well suited to policy.[50] Kenny and Kenny define happiness as having three separate components: contentment, welfare, and dignity. Happiness defined simply as contentment seems an inappropriate objective for public policy. Yet when it is defined as a combination of these three factors, it seems more relevant, particularly for a region where the major policy challenge is not extreme poverty but relative poverty, vulnerability, and inequality of income and opportunity.

Happiness and Policy Reform

Imposing a definition of happiness does not answer the question of how much weight policymakers should put on happiness as an objective in relation to other objectives such as growth, policy reforms, and fiscal stability. There are intertemporal considerations as well. Reforms can and do make people unhappy in the short term, but in the long run, reforms are likely to guarantee people more prosperity and possibly greater happiness. There is a significant body of evidence, from the behavioral economics and the happiness literatures, that reports that individuals are loss averse and that they value losses disproportionately to gains. And the happiness literature shows that individuals adapt very quickly to income gains but much less quickly to losses. Meanwhile, there is more adaptation to changes in income than to changes in status.

There is also significant evidence of hyperbolic discounting: individuals trade off much larger future benefits for much shorter-term ones. It is not a coincidence that most developed economies have forced savings schemes. Our own work, meanwhile, which is in the initial stages, suggests that high levels of inequality or low levels of social mobility and related low expectations can result in higher discount rates (and therefore more hyperbolic discounting) for those in the lower-income ranks. This discounting can apply to other areas besides income and savings, such as public health, and may help explain why phenomena such as obesity are concentrated among lower-income cohorts, at least in the developed economies.[51]

Certainly, understanding these behaviors is important information for policymakers. But can short-term happiness questions and measures be used as a gauge for policy? The information may be more useful for explaining lack of public support for optimal policies than it is as a guide to policy choice (although it may help resolve debates about the appropriate pace and scope of change). Structural policy reforms, for example, can result in major changes in income and status and related unhappiness for particular cohorts, at least in the short

50. Kenny and Kenny (2006).
51. Graham and Felton (2006); Felton and Graham (2005); Graham, Chattopadhyay, and Picon (forthcoming).

term, while producing gains in the aggregate in the long term. Raising the fiscal burden, meanwhile, may impose financial costs—and reduce happiness—in the short term but result in better public services over the long term.

This may help explain the disconnect between the record of certain policy reforms, such as privatization, in making long-term improvements in access to services and the public's assessments or opinions of those reforms. If the reforms entail visible short-term losses or dislocation for particular groups, thereby generating widespread public anxiety and risk aversion, public assessments are likely to be influenced by those very visible dynamics rather than by longer-term aggregate gains from reform. Inequality, meanwhile, remains a challenge that defies established policy prescriptions and likely undermines support for reform.

Happiness surveys could, at least in theory, lend support to populist politicians. If the results of a national happiness survey show that the majority of citizens prefer inflation to unemployment (as happiness surveys suggest in most contexts, including Latin America), those results could fuel irresponsible fiscal policies in countries that are very vulnerable to hyperinflation (which indeed makes people very unhappy). The kinds of structural reforms that are necessary for long-term growth, meanwhile, are unlikely to be supported by a population that has a high tendency for hyperbolic discounting. How many voters will report that they are happier than before while in the throes of a controversial privatization or tax reform, the benefits of which are not immediately clear, for example? How can happiness surveys be useful?

Surely there are risks. Yet previous work by Graham and Sukhtankar also shows that economic crisis makes people very unhappy, and that happier people are more supportive of democracy and market reforms.[52] Although the direction of causality is not clear (happier people may be more supportive of whatever policy context they live in), it does suggest that happiness is not inherently linked to support for irresponsible or antireform politics. And the same literature that finds that crises reduce happiness in Latin America also finds that crises are linked to decreased support for how markets and democracy are working but *increased* support for markets and democracies as systems.

Perhaps the most useful role for happiness surveys is in helping us understand and better navigate the political outcomes that can result, especially in contexts such as Latin American economic policy, where there is reform fatigue; risk and loss aversion due to past experience with macroeconomic volatility and other crises; and a large proportion of the population that is, at least in theory, vulnerable to hyperbolic discounting. Is it really irrational if one is poor and unemployed in Ecuador, for example, to support an antisystem politician in the hope of change and a possible short-term improvement? And understanding what makes people most unhappy with the policy context, through well-being surveys,

---

52. Graham and Sukhtankar (2004).

might also help reformists avert the kind of policy mistakes that lead to populist or hyperbolic politics. In addition, well-being surveys provide a metric to measure perceptions of welfare—across countries and over time—and their relation to a range of policy reforms such as privatization and new forms of social insurance.

There are a number of areas where happiness surveys could yield valuable insights into areas that may be key to the success of policy reforms; however, more work remains to be done. One area of concern is social safety nets and other forms of social insurance. Our work on frustrated achievers and fear of unemployment suggests that insecurity and volatility are major causes of unhappiness in Latin America.[53] But are respondents with access to better social welfare systems and other safety nets happier? Are they more supportive of policy reforms in such contexts? This is an open question for research and could help provide insights into the kinds of social arrangements that best mediate this insecurity.

Another area is inequality. We have some sense that inequality and perceived differences in rank, status, and access to opportunities have negative effects on happiness (at least for the poor) in the region. Do other kinds of inequality, such as racial and gender inequality, have similar effects? Which kinds of inequality are most important? How do the dynamics of inequality relate to those of public support for policy reforms?

Finally, happiness surveys could help in tracking the effects of different policy arrangements on well-being, such as inflation versus unemployment and local- versus central-level governments and democracy, and thereby help determine priorities in the reform agenda. Bruno Frey and Stutzer, cited earlier, showed that participating in direct democracy has positive effects on happiness, above and beyond the benefits of living in a direct democracy. John Helliwell and Robert Putnam found that citizens who live in contexts in which social capital is greater are also happier.[54] Public health policy—such as access to health insurance, particularly in a context where many people lack it—may also matter to happiness. Analysis of such variables using happiness surveys allows for one way to weight their relative importance in the design of policy reforms.

Conclusions

Happiness studies can provide critical insights into the determinants of human well-being, in areas ranging from income, poverty and inequality, public health, and fiscal policy.[55] The studies are also a way to gain insights into many other questions, such as the effects of particular policy reforms on perceived well-being and on public opinion more generally. They provide researchers with a

53. Graham and Felton (2006); Graham and Pettinato (2002); Graham, Chattopadhyay, and Picon (2008).

54. Helliwell and Putnam (2005).

55. Dolan, Peasgood, and White (2006).

tool to assess the relative weights that particular populations—and socio-economic cohorts—attach to various public expenditures, such as health, education, and social insurance, which can—indirectly—help inform the design of fiscal policy. They also highlight high levels of frustration—about insecurity and inequality—among the middle class in many developing economies. On one level, this frustration is likely the result of the middle class having low-quality public services and weak social insurance. On another, it may be the result of natural heightened expectations as these cohorts exit poverty, a result policymakers cannot control, but which they can take into account.

For all of the reasons cited above, including the "happy peasant" problem, adaptations and set points, hyperbolic discounting, and the absence of clarity on a definition of happiness, caution is necessary before directly applying the results of happiness surveys to policy and, in this instance, using them as a basis for the design of fiscal policy. Because people are loss averse, for example, more expenditure on social insurance and safety nets may result in higher reported happiness. Such expenditures may be necessary, and happiness surveys surely support the intuition that they are welfare enhancing. Yet because of inter-temporal problems, the same surveys cannot guide how much people *trade off* these kinds of expenditures for those with longer-term returns, for example, in children's education or in retirement savings.

Happiness economics opens a field of research questions that still need to be addressed, more generally and as applied to policy reforms. These include the implications of well-being findings for national indicators and economic growth patterns; the effects of happiness on behavior such as work effort, consumption, and investment; and the effects of happiness on political behavior. In the case of the latter, surveys of unhappiness or frustration may be useful to gauge the potential for social unrest or political backlash against reforms in various contexts.

To answer many of these questions, researchers need more and better-quality data on well-being, particularly panel data, which allow for the correction of unobserved personality traits and correlated measurement errors, as well as for a better determination of the direction of causality. These are major challenges in most happiness studies. It is hoped that the combination of better data and increased sophistication in econometric techniques will allow economists to better address these questions in the future and to increase the potential of such surveys to contribute to the better design of policy reforms and to help inform fiscal choices in developing countries.

References

Alesina, A., Rafael Di Tella, and Robert MacCulloch. 2004. "Inequality and Happiness: Are Europeans and Americans Different?" *Journal of Public Economics* 88, nos. 9–10: 2009–042.

Behrman, Jere, Nancy Birdsall, and Miguel Székely. 2001. "Economic Policy and Wage Differentials in Latin America." Working Paper 01-048. University of Pennsylvania, Penn Institute for Economic Research.

Bertrand, Marianne, and Sendhil Mullainathan. 2001. "Do People Mean What They Say? Implications for Subjective Survey Data." *American Economic Review* 91, no. 2: 67–72.

Birdsall, Nancy and Carol Graham. 1999. "New Markets, New Opportunities? Economic and Social Mobility in a Changing World." Brookings and Carnegie Endowment for International Peace.

Birdsall, Nancy, Carol Graham, and Stefano Pettinato. 2001. "Stuck in the Tunnel: Has Globalization Muddled the Middle Class?" Working Paper 13. Brookings, Center on Social and Economic Dynamics (August).

Blanchflower, D., and A. Oswald. 2004. "Well-Being over Time in Britain and the USA." *Journal of Public Economics* 88, nos. 7–8: 1359–387.

Clark, Andrew E., and Andrew J. Oswald. 1994. "Unhappiness and Unemployment." *Economic Journal* 104, no. 424: 648–59.

Diener, Ed, R. E. Lucas, and C. N. Scollon. 2006. "Beyond the Hedonic Treadmill: Revisions to the Adaptation Theory of Well-Being." *American Psychologist* 61, no. 2: 305–14.

Diener, Ed, and Martin E. P. Seligman. 2004. "Beyond Money: Toward an Economy of Well-Being." *Psychological Science in the Public Interest* 5, no. 1: 1–31.

Diener, Ed, E. M. Suh, R. E. Lucas, and H. Smith. 1999. "Subjective Well-Being: Three Decades of Progress." *Psychological Bulletin* 125, no. 22: 276–302.

Diener, Ed, and others. 1993. "The Relationship between Income and Subjective Well-Being: Relative or Absolute?" *Social Indicators Research* 28, no. 3: 195–223.

Di Tella, Rafael, John P. Haisken-DeNew, and Robert MacCulloch. 2004. "Happiness Adaptation to Income and to Status in an Individual Panel." (http://ssrn.com/abstract= 760368).

Di Tella, Rafael, Robert J. MacCulloch, and Andrew J. Oswald. 2001. "Preferences over Inflation and Unemployment: Evidence from Surveys of Happiness." *American Economic Review* 91, no. 1: 335–41.

Dolan, Paul, Tessa Peasgood, and Mathew White. 2006. "Review of Research on the Influences of Well-Being and Application to Policy-Making." Report for the Department for Environment, Food and Rural Affairs (DEFRA), United Kingdom.

Easterlin, Richard. 1974. "Explaining Happiness." *Proceedings of the National Academy of Sciences* 100, no. 19: 11176–1183.

Eggers, Andrew, Clifford Gaddy, and Carol Graham. 2006. "Well-Being and Unemployment in Russia in the 1990's: Can Society's Suffering Be Individuals' Solace?" *Journal of Socioeconomics* 35, no. 2 (April): 209–42.

Estache, Antonio. 2008. "The Middle Class and the Sustainability of Fiscal Policies: An Overview," presentation at a World Bank seminar, Washington, June.

Felton, Andrew, and Carol Graham. 2005. "Variance in Obesity across Countries and Cohorts: Some Initial Evidence from Happiness Surveys." Working Paper Series 45. Brookings, Center on Social and Economic Dynamics (January).

Frey, Bruno S., and Alois Stutzer. 2002. "What Can Economists Learn from Happiness Research?" *Journal of Economic Literature* 40, no. 2: 401–35.

Gardner, J., and Andrew Oswald. 2001. "Does Money Buy Happiness? Some Evidence from Windfalls." Mimeo. Coventry, United Kingdom: University of Warwick.

Graham, Carol. 2008. "The Economics of Happiness." In *The New Palgrave Dictionary of Economics,* 2nd ed., edited by Steven Durlauf and Laurence E. Blume. Basingstoke, Hampshire, United Kingdom: Palgrave Macmillan.

———. 2005. "Insights on Development from the Economics of Happiness." *World Bank Research Observer* 20, no. 2: 201–31.

Graham, Carol, Soumya Chattopadhyay, and Mario Picon. Forthcoming. "The Easterlin and Other Paradoxes: Why Both Sides of the Debate May Be Correct." In *International Differences in Well-Being*, edited by Ed Diener, John Helliwell, and Daniel Kahneman. Oxford University Press.

Graham, Carol, Andrew Eggers, and Sandip Sukhtankar. 2004. "Does Happiness Pay? An Initial Exploration based on Panel Data from Russia." *Journal of Economic Behavior and Organization* 55, no. 3: 319–42.

Graham, Carol, and Andrew Felton. 2006. "Does Inequality Matter to Individual Welfare: An Exploration Based on Happiness Surveys in Latin America." *Journal of Economic Inequality* 4, no. 1 (April): 107–22.

Graham, Carol, and Matthew Hoover. 2007. "Optimism and Poverty in Africa: Adaptation or a Means to Survival?" Afrobarometer Working Paper 76. Pretoria, South Africa: Institute for Democracy in South Africa (IDASA).

Graham, Carol, and Darius Ladkawalla. 2006. "Cheap Food, Societal Norms, and the Economics of Obesity." wsj.com (*Wall Street Journal* online) (August 25).

Graham, Carol, and Margaret MacLeod. 2004. "Curmudgeons or Frustrated Achievers? Economic Adjustment, Mobility, and Unhappiness in Peru, 2000–2003." Working Paper. Brookings.

Graham, Carol, and Stefano Pettinato. 2002. *Happiness and Hardship: Opportunity and Insecurity in New Market Economies.* Brookings.

Graham, Carol, and Sandip Sukhtankar. 2004. "Does Economic Crisis Reduce Support For Markets and Democracy in Latin America? Some Evidence from Surveys of Public Opinion and Well-Being." *Journal of Latin American Studies* 36, no. 2: 349–77.

Gruber, J., and S. Mullainathan. 2002. "Do Cigarette Taxes Make Smokers Happier?" Working Paper 8872. Cambridge, Mass.: National Bureau of Economic Research.

Helliwell, John. 2005. "Well-Being and Social Capital: Does Suicide Pose a Puzzle?" Working Paper 11807. Cambridge, Mass.: National Bureau of Economic Research.

Helliwell, John, and Robert D. Putnam. 2005. "The Social Context of Well-Being." In *The Science of Well-Being,* edited by Felicia Huppert, Nick Baylis, and Barry Keverne, chapter 17. Oxford University Press.

Herrera, Javier, Mireille Razafindrakoto, François Roubaud. 2006. "The Determinants of Subjective Poverty: A Comparative Analysis in Madagascar and Peru." Working Paper DT/2006-01. Paris: Développement, Institutions & Analyses de Long terme (DIAL).

Kahneman, D., E. Diener, and N. Schwarz. 1999. *Well-being: The Foundations of Hedonic Psychology.* New York: Russell Sage.

Kahneman, D., and others. 2004. "Toward National Well-Being Accounts." *AEA Papers and Proceedings:* 429–34.

Kenny, Anthony, and Charles Kenny. 2006. *Life, Liberty, and the Pursuit of Utility: Happiness in Philosophical and Economic Thought.* Exeter, United Kingdom (Charlottesville, Va.): Imprint Academic.

Layard, Richard. 2005. *Happiness: Lessons from a New Science.* New York: Penguin Press.

Luttmer, Erzo. 2005. "Neighbors as Negatives: Relative Earnings and Well Being." *Quarterly Journal of Economics* 120, no. 3: 963–1002.

Oswald, Andrew. 1997. "Happiness and Economic Performance." *Economic Journal* 107 (445): 1815–831.

Sen, Amartya K. 1999. *Development as Freedom.* New York: Knopf.

Stutzer, Alois, and Rafael Lalive. 2004. "The Role of Social Work Norms in Job Searching and Subjective Well-Being." *Journal of the European Economic Association* 2, no. 4: 696–719.

Van Praag, B., and A. Ferrer-i-Carbonell. 2004. *Happiness Quantified: A Satisfaction Calculus Approach.* Oxford University Press.

Whyte, Martin, and Byong-Hun. 2006. "Memo on China." Mimeo. Harvard University.

Table 6A-1. *What Drives Happiness in Latin America, 2001*

Independent variable	Ordered logit[a]		OLS[b]	
	Coef.	z	Coef.	z
Age	−0.025	−4.21	−0.010	−4.04
Age squared	0.000	4.72	0.000	4.58
Male	−0.002	−0.07	0.000	0.03
Married	0.056	1.63	0.022	1.56
Log wealth index	0.395	10.56	0.166	10.70
Years of education	−0.003	−0.64	−0.001	−0.29
Minority	−0.083	−2.49	−0.041	−2.95
Student	0.066	1.01	0.032	1.17
Retired	−0.005	−0.06	−0.002	−0.06
Homemaker	−0.053	−1.04	−0.025	−1.19
Unemployed	−0.485	−7.54	−0.206	−7.66
Self-employed	−0.098	−2.33	−0.041	−2.31
Health (self-reported)	0.468	24.58	0.194	25.11
Pseudo R^2	0.062		0.136	
No. obs.	15,209		15,209	

Source: Author's calculations based on data from Latinobarómetro (2001).
a. Ordered logit estimation: country dummies included but not shown.
b. Ordinary least squares estimation: country dummies included but not shown.

Table 6A-2. *Happiness in Russia, 2000*

Independent variable	Ordered logit[a]		OLS[b]	
	Coef.	z	Coef.	z
Age	−0.085	−11.27	−0.047	−10.94
Age squared	0.001	9.97	0.000	9.67
Male	0.040	0.90	0.031	1.20
Married	0.192	4.19	0.094	3.58
Log equivalent income	0.399	17.18	0.231	17.85
Education level	0.018	1.37	0.007	0.91
Minority	0.254	4.16	0.142	4.08
Student	0.481	3.03	0.304	3.29
Retired	−0.244	−3.25	−0.124	−2.89
Housewife	0.363	2.21	0.238	2.53
Unemployed	−0.437	−4.03	−0.225	−3.64
Self-employed	0.270	1.82	0.159	1.85
Health index	0.387	4.09	0.207	3.80
Constant			1.44	8.59
Pseudo R^2	0.032		0.084	
No. obs.	7,666		7,666	

Source: Graham, Eggers, Sukhtankar (2004).
a. Ordered logit estimation: country dummies included but not shown.
b. Ordinary least squares estimation: country dummies included but not shown.

Table 6A-3. *Happiness in the United States, 1972–98*

Independent variable	Ordered logit[a]		OLS[b]	
	Coef.	z	Coef.	z
Age	−0.025	−5.20	−0.007	−5.13
Age squared	0.038	7.53	0.011	7.39
Male	−0.199	−6.80	−0.058	−6.66
Married	0.775	25.32	0.232	25.89
Log income	0.163	9.48	0.049	9.55
Education	0.007	1.49	0.003	1.81
Black	−0.400	−10.02	−0.120	−10.27
Other race	0.049	0.59	0.011	0.45
Student	0.291	3.63	0.085	3.59
Retired	0.219	3.93	0.064	3.90
Housekeeper	0.065	1.66	0.019	1.61
Unemployed	−0.684	−8.72	−0.205	−8.93
Self-employed	0.098	2.29	0.030	2.38
Health	0.623	35.91	0.181	36.58
Pseudo R^2	0.075		0.075	
No. obs.	24,128		24,128	

Source: Author's calculations based on data from the General Social Survey (1973–98).

a. Ordered logit estimation: year dummies included but not shown.

b. Ordinary least squares estimation: year dummies included but not shown.

7

The Politics of Effective and Sustainable Redistribution

EVELYNE HUBER, JENNIFER PRIBBLE, AND JOHN D. STEPHENS

O ne of the primary activities of states around the world is to provide public policies aimed at protecting citizens from falling into poverty and providing assistance to those individuals who have already fallen victim to risk. The
nature and scope of redistributive policies vary across countries and regions, as
do the political sustainability of and popular support for the programs. Research
on social protection in advanced industrialized democracies has found that the
(Nordic) social democratic and, to a lesser extent, (continental) Christian democratic welfare states are very effective at reducing poverty and income inequality.
By contrast, the Anglo-American liberal welfare state regimes reduce poverty
and inequality to a much smaller extent.[1] The political sustainability of social
protection policies in the Organization for Economic Cooperation and Development (OECD) countries follows a similar pattern, with the more universal
(Nordic) welfare states exhibiting high levels of public support for state responsibility for people's welfare among the working and middle classes. In the more
residual (liberal) welfare states, however, support for extensive government
intervention in the form of transfers and services is lower.[2]

In this chapter, we explore the variation in the effectiveness of redistributive policies and in the level of popular support enjoyed by such programs.
Specifically, we consider two questions: What kinds of social policies are most

1. Bradley and others (2003); Moller and others (2003).
2. Mehrtens (2004).

effective at reducing poverty and improving human capital among society's most vulnerable sectors? And second, how are these social policy configurations constructed politically, and how do they then shape political support for their own maintenance across social classes? To answer these questions, we summarize the lessons learned from the well-researched experiences of advanced industrialized democracies. We then discuss the degree to which these lessons are applicable to Latin America and what modifications, if any, should be made to make these experiences more relevant to the region's experience. To some extent, these lessons and modifications apply to other middle-income countries as well. However, differences in economic and social structure (size of the informal sector), political history (strength of the democratic record), and policy legacies (degree of involvement of the private sector in the provision of transfers and services) argue against sweeping generalizations.

The Effectiveness of Social Expenditure

All welfare states in advanced industrial democracies redistribute income, though they do so to greatly varying degrees. Table 7-1 presents our own calculations, based on Luxembourg Income Studies (LIS) data, of income redistribution among the working-aged population to counter the criticism that welfare states only redistribute income across generations. The first three columns document reduction in inequality due to taxes and transfers, the next three columns do the same for poverty reduction. The Nordic countries, with social democratic welfare states, effect the most reduction in inequality and poverty and end up with the lowest levels of poverty and inequality. The Anglo-American countries, with liberal welfare states, are at the opposite end, and the continental European countries, with Christian democratic welfare states, are in the middle. The Anglo-American countries rely more heavily on targeting than the other two types of welfare states do, but they spend much less and thus reduce poverty and inequality less.[3] The targeting in and of itself is the reason why spending is low, because targeted programs benefit a comparatively small proportion of the population and thus have restricted political support.

What is important to understand here is the paradox of redistribution, and this paradox is best illustrated with the example of pensions, the largest public transfer program.[4] The paradox is that the countries with the most unequal public transfers (Norway and Sweden) achieve the greatest amount of redistribution and the most equal posttax and transfer income distribution among the elderly. The solution to the paradox is the fact that all other sources of income are vastly more unequal than public transfers and that highly generous public

3. Huber and Stephens (2001).
4. Korpi and Palme (1998).

Table 7-1. *Inequality and Poverty, by Welfare State Regimes*

	Inequality among working-aged population			Poverty among working-aged population		
	1	*2*	*3*	*4*	*5*	*6*
Welfare state	*Pretax and transfer Gini*	*Posttax and transfer Gini*	*Reduction in Gini due to taxes and transfers*	*Pretax and transfer*	*Posttax and transfer*	*Reduction in poverty due to taxes and transfers*
Social democratic welfare states						
Sweden, 1995	38	20	47	22	4	82
Norway, 1995	32	22	31	16	4	72
Denmark, 1992	34	21	38	19	4	77
Finland, 1995	36	20	44	18	4	80
Mean	35.0	20.8	40.0	18.8	4.0	77.8
Christian democratic welfare states						
Belgium, 1992	35	21	40	15	4	75
Netherlands, 1994	36	25	31	18	7	62
Germany, 1989[a]	32	25	22	8	5	38
France, 1994	39	28	28	24	8	67
Switzerland, 1992	33	30	9	13	11	16
Mean	35.0	25.8	26.0	15.6	7.0	51.6
Liberal welfare states						
Australia, 1994	40	29	28	19	9	51
Canada, 1994	38	28	26	19	11	42
Ireland, 1995	44	33	25			
United Kingdom, 1995	46	35	24	25	12	52
United States, 1994	43	35	19	19	16	13
Mean	42.2	32.0	24.4	20.5	12.0	39.5
Grand mean	37.6	26.6	29.4	18.1	7.6	55.9

Source: Authors' calculations, based on data from the Luxembourg Income Study.

a. The figures for Germany are for 1989 because the figures in 1994 show large changes due to unification that are unrepresentative of the rest of the German data.

Table 7-2. *Income Inequality among the Aged Population*[a]

Country	Public transfers	Earnings	Private pensions	Capital income	Gross income	Net income (after tax)	Public pensions as percentage of total income
	1	2	3	4	5	6	7
Australia	−.07	.74	.61	.63	.34	.28	59
Canada	−.02	.61	.53	.58	.33	.30	58
Finland	.19	.66	.36	.53	.29	. .	69
Germany	.12	.73	.61	.41	.29	.28	70
Netherlands	.04	.67	.66	.82	.33	.27	69
Norway	.11	.77	.60	.54	.30	.24	82
Sweden	.15	.78	.49	.44	.24	.14	86
United Kingdom	−.01	.73	.53	.61	.31	.26	67
United States	.08	.63	.52	.60	.38	.34	60

Source: Kangas and Palme (1993); Esping-Andersen (1990, p. 85); Palme, personal communication.
a. All cell entries are Gini coefficients except column 7.

transfers crowd out private pensions and capital income. To put it in different words: In countries with comprehensive earnings–related social transfer systems, social spending is much larger than in countries with residual welfare states that rely heavily on means testing, and the size factor overwhelms the distributive profile in determining redistribution.

Table 7-2 demonstrates this paradox. The figures were calculated by Olli Kangas and Joakim Palme using LIS data.[5] For columns 1 to 4, income units are ranked according to the size of gross income, and then the income in question is distributed along this continuum. The index varies from −1 to 1, with −1 indicating that the poorest income group receives all of the income of this type, 0 indicating that all income groups receive the same amount, and 1 indicating that the richest income group receives all of this type of income. Australia, Canada, and the United Kingdom have pension systems with benefits most clearly targeted to lower-income groups, yet they end up with the most unequal income distributions behind the United States. The public pensions systems in Sweden and Norway have the most unequal profile, but they account for more than 80 percent of total income of the elderly and thus produce the most egalitarian final income distributions.

Although the social democratic and Christian democratic welfare states are generous in transfers, they differ markedly in two respects that make social democratic welfare states significantly more redistributive. First, social assistance is much better developed in social democratic welfare states; that is, people with a

5. Kangas and Palme (1993).

tenuous attachment to the labor market have citizenship rights to higher basic transfers compared with their counterparts in the Christian democratic welfare states. Second, the former provide more free or subsidized social services than the latter do, particularly in the areas of health and child care.

The relationship between social policy generosity and redistribution is different in Latin America from that in advanced industrial democracies. Indeed, a growing body of research on the incidence and impact of social spending in the region underscores the fact that the bulk of social expenditure—that is, funding used to finance social security programs such as pensions—is largely ineffective at protecting the poor and heavily favors the upper two quintiles of income earners.[6] There is no size effect overwhelming the distributive profile here. First of all, Latin American countries spend much less on social transfers than advanced industrial democracies spend. Second, the distributive profile is much worse because very large sectors of the population are excluded from (contribution-based) social security altogether, and (noncontributory) social assistance accounts for a small percentage of transfer spending only.[7] The character of Latin American labor markets, namely the fact that formal sector employment is limited in scope, means that social insurance programs linked to payroll contributions will leave a large share of the population unprotected. Since workers in the informal sector have lower salaries on average, and because the nature of informal sector work is inherently more precarious, the exclusion of these individuals means that it is precisely the poorest and most vulnerable sectors of society that are left out of the system. In fact, the region's social security systems reproduce segmentation of the labor market.

Several studies of the region's social policy regimes have uncovered evidence of the ineffectiveness of contributory social insurance policies to protect the poor in Latin America.[8] In an analysis of the redistributive impact of social spending in the region, the United Nations' Economic Commission on Latin America and the Caribbean (ECLAC) found that a very small share of social security spending is received by the bottom 20 percent of income earners. As demonstrated in figure 7-1, even the best-performing country in the region, Costa Rica, distributes only 12 percent of social security spending to the bottom income quintile, while 45 percent of funds are allocated to the top 20 percent of

6. Lindert, Skoufias, and Shapiro (2006); ECLAC (2005); Uthoff (2006).

7. Huber and others (2008) estimated that, on average, Latin American states allocated 5.24 percent of GDP to social security and welfare spending in the period 1999–2000. By contrast, during the same time frame, countries in the region allocated 3.98 percent and 2.86 percent of GDP, respectively, to education and health care spending (calculations by authors). It should be noted that these averages mask wide variation across the region. For example, Guatemala allocated just less than 1 percent of GDP to social security and welfare programs in 1998, while Uruguay spent 19.2 percent of GDP on such programs in 1999.

8. Lindert, Skoufias, and Shapiro (2006); ECLAC (2005); Uthoff (2006).

Figure 7-1. *Social Security Expenditure, by Income Quintile, 1997–2003*
Percent

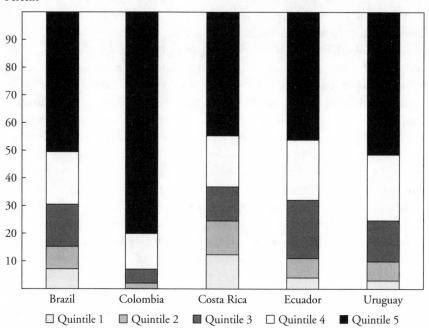

Source: ECLAC (2005, p. 144–46).

the income distribution.[9] The top quintiles in Brazil and Uruguay receive 50 percent of total social security expenditure. The skewed nature of spending is even more dramatic in the region's less-developed social policy regimes. In Colombia, for example, 80 percent of social security expenditure is delivered to individuals in the top income quintile.[10]

A recent World Bank study of public transfers in Latin America reached a similar conclusion about the impact of social insurance policies on poverty reduction.[11] This study analyzed sixteen social insurance programs in the region and found that all were regressive. The sixteen programs included pensions and other labor-related benefits, such as unemployment insurance and severance pay. Among social insurance programs, Kathy Lindert, Emmanuel Skoufias, and Joseph Shapiro found that net pension benefits, or the benefits received minus total contributions, are the most regressive form of social insurance. Specifically, the authors found that on average in Latin America, the top 20 per-

9. ECLAC (2005, p. 144).
10. ECLAC (2005, p. 146).
11. Lindert, Skoufias, and Shapiro (2006).

cent of income earners receive 61 percent of net pension subsidies, while the bottom quintile receives a mere 3 percent.[12]

In contrast to the skewed character of contributory social insurance, the authors found strong evidence to suggest that noncontributory social assistance spending, and more specifically conditional cash transfer programs (CCTs), is highly progressive and quite effective at protecting the poorest sectors of society.[13] Noncontributory social assistance policies come in a variety of forms ranging from old-age poverty pensions, school feeding programs, to targeted income supplements. The programs differ from social insurance schemes in their funding and eligibility requirements. Social assistance policies are funded out of general revenue, while social insurance is typically financed with a combination of worker contributions and state revenue. While social insurance provides access to individuals working in the formal labor market, individuals receiving social assistance are usually selected using some form of means testing (or proxy means testing).

Lindert, Skoufias, and Shapiro found that CCT programs provide the most progressive outcomes. CCT policies provide an income supplement to individuals or households that agree to uphold certain established conditions, such as enrolling children in school and ensuring attendance or visiting the local health clinic.[14] The programs, therefore, combine income support with strategies to improve the human capital endowments of the poorest sectors of society.[15]

ECLAC's 2005 study of Latin American social spending uncovers additional evidence of the effectiveness of noncontributory social assistance to reduce poverty.[16] As displayed in figure 7-2, the bulk of noncontributory social assistance spending is consumed by the bottom of the income distribution.

In other words, there is significant evidence to suggest that noncontributory social assistance is much more effective than social insurance at protecting Latin America's poor. Still, such policies make up only a minimal share of spending. Lindert, Skoufias, and Shapiro reported that for their sample of eight countries, spending on noncontributory social assistance as a share of total social spending in 2000 was about 7.7 percent.[17] This is even less impressive if one considers this category of spending as a share of GDP. The highest social assistance spender was Argentina, which allocated 1.2 percent of GDP to such programs,

12. Lindert, Skoufias, and Shapiro (2006, p. 27).
13. Lindert, Skoufias, and Shapiro (2006, p. 28).
14. Lindert, Skoufias, and Shapiro (2006).
15. A study by Villatoro (2004) of five CCT programs in Latin America found that while the actual cash transfer in some programs was insufficient to bring households above the poverty line, the schooling and health care requirements had important effects for long-term poverty prevention (p. 31).
16. ECLAC (2005).
17. Calculations by authors using data from Lindert, Skoufias, and Shapiro (2006).

Figure 7-2. *Social Assistance Expenditure, by Income Quintile, 1997–2003*
Percent

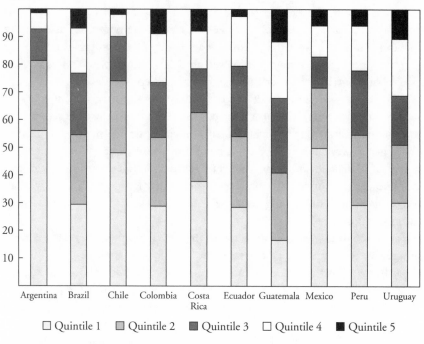

□ Quintile 1   ■ Quintile 2   ■ Quintile 3   □ Quintile 4   ■ Quintile 5

Source: ECLAC (2005, p. 158).

which is still significantly lower than state expenditure on social insurance (8.9 percent of GDP).[18]

States in the region also provide social services that offer an additional layer of protection to the poor. In particular, the provision of education and health care services, which develop the human capital endowments of citizens, helps to alleviate poverty through a short- and long-term mechanism. In the long term, state investment in education and health care equips individuals with the necessary skills and health to obtain employment and escape poverty or keep themselves from falling below the poverty line. In the shorter term, state provision of education and health care can reduce poverty by easing the financial burden that families face when sending children to school or if a member of the household falls ill.

Studies on education and health care in the region show that certain categories of spending are particularly redistributive and thus effective at protecting the poor. Specifically, Fernando Filgueira and others contend that investment in

18. Lindert, Skoufias, and Shapiro (2006, p. 86).

Figure 7-3. *Health Care Expenditure, by Income Quintile, 1997–2003*
Percent

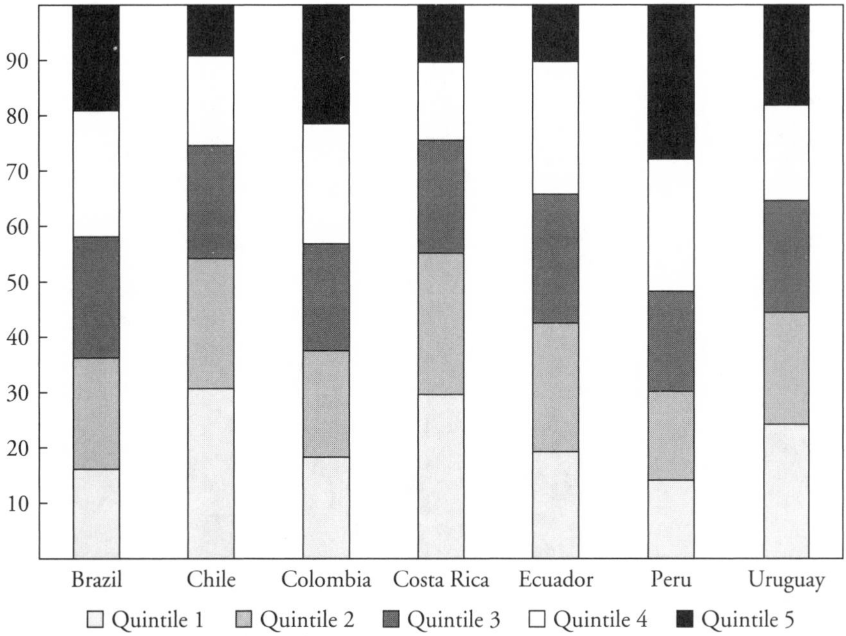

Source: ECLAC (2005, p. 143–46).

preschool and primary education as well as spending on primary health care is most important for protecting the most vulnerable sectors of the population.[19] The 2005 study by ECLAC supports this assertion, finding that health care spending in Costa Rica, a country noted for its focus on primary care and preventive public health programs, is extremely pro-poor in nature.[20] Specifically, about 29 percent of Costa Rica's health care spending is received by the bottom 20 percent of income earners.[21] As shown in figure 7-3, not all countries in the region exhibit progressive health spending patterns. ECLAC's study revealed that the poorest income quintile in Brazil received 16 percent of health care expenditure, while in Colombia and Peru that same group received 18 and 14 percent, respectively.[22] Still, this is much greater than their share of income. Thus the way in which health spending is allocated, namely, whether the state focuses its energy on primary care and public health programs or costly curative

19. Filgueira and others (2006, pp. 43–44).
20. Costa Rica has a comparatively highly unified health care system, with the public sector accounting for around 80 percent of all health spending.
21. ECLAC (2005, p. 144).
22. ECLAC (2005, pp. 143–46).

Figure 7-4. *Share of Education Spending Received by the Lowest Income Quintile*
Percent

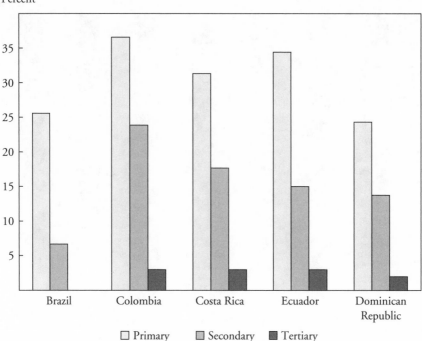

Source: ECLAC (2005, p. 143–46).

care and the manner in which individuals gain access to health care—as a right of citizenship or through a contributory insurance scheme—will influence how redistributive the programs are.

As illustrated in figure 7-4, in those cases for which disaggregated spending data are available, it is clear that the poorest sectors of the population benefit the most from expenditures on primary education.[23] While spending on secondary school is also progressive on average, state expenditure on tertiary education has almost no impact among the poor.[24]

Our research provides additional evidence about how the structure and level of state expenditure influence variation in poverty levels across Latin America.[25] In particular, we find that aggregate education expenditure is not a significant predictor of variation in poverty levels across the region. By contrast, our proxy measure of education coverage, average years of education of the population

23. ECLAC (2005, p. 132).
24. ECLAC (2005, p. 132).
25. Pribble, Huber, and Stephens (forthcoming).

aged twenty-five and older, is a significant and negative predictor of poverty. We conclude, therefore, that it is not the level of education expenditure per se but how the funds are distributed that determines poverty levels. In countries where funding is concentrated at the preschool, primary, and secondary levels, poverty levels are significantly lower.

In summary, it would seem that the basic lesson that emerges from studies of advanced industrialized democracies—that the most effective welfare states are those that invest heavily in social services and provide benefits as a right of citizenship—also holds true in Latin America. Where things differ is with regard to social policy configurations such as those seen in the Christian democratic (continental) welfare states. While in the setting of OECD countries these insurance-based systems tied to employment provide significant protection against poverty, albeit less than in the Nordic countries, the same is not true in Latin America. Indeed, the informal nature of Latin American labor markets and high levels of inequality put limits on the Christian democratic model that are less dramatic in the setting of advanced industrialized states. Even the liberal residual welfare state works differently in Latin America than in the Anglo-American OECD countries. That is because unemployment and underemployment tend to be much higher in Latin America than in the Anglo-American residual welfare states. As a result, the requirement that citizens purchase social protection from private providers is even less feasible than in advanced industrialized states.

In light of the nature of Latin American labor markets and the presence of deep structural inequalities, the most effective model of social protection for the region is what Filgueira and his colleagues call *basic universalism*.[26] They define basic universalism as a system that guarantees universal coverage of a group of essential services and transfers. They contend that the state must play a central role in guaranteeing access to and the effective usage of these services and transfers. Moreover, the same quality of benefits would be provided to all citizens. Policy proposals that would fulfill the goals of basic universalism include a flat-rate citizenship pension, a guaranteed minimum citizenship income, a public preschool education system, and state guarantees to cover health threats.[27]

Examples of social programs that move in the direction of basic universalism have emerged recently in Latin America. One such example is Chile's 2004 health care reform that guarantees coverage of fifty-six illnesses for all Chileans regardless of whether they are covered by the private or public system.[28]

26. Filgueira and others (2006).
27. Huber (2006); Isuani (2006); Medici (2006).
28. The current government of President Michelle Bachelet, Socialist Party, has announced its intent to cover eighty illnesses by 2010.

Another example is Uruguay's 1995 reform of education, which established a national system of public preschool. Finally, Brazil's *Bolsa Familia* program provides an example of a minimum income program that grants assistance to families regardless of their labor market status. These three programs all exhibit elements of basic universalism and have been quite effective at delivering social protection to the most vulnerable sectors of society. Moreover, the three policies enjoy significant popular support—an issue that we discuss in more detail in the next section of this paper.

Underlying the highly limited commitment to social spending in Latin America are weak tax systems. Several studies find that Latin American states undertax their populations. Specifically, Latin American states imposed an average tax burden of just 15 percent of GDP during the 1990–2005 period.[29] Moreover, the level of tax burden varies greatly across the region. While Brazil imposed taxes equal to 32.5 percent of GDP in 2000, the burden was a mere 12.1 percent of GDP in Mexico and 9.4 percent of GDP in Venezuela.[30] These figures differ greatly from the average tax burden in OECD countries in 2000, which was equal to 36.3 percent of GDP.[31] This variation is even more dramatic if we consider only fifteen member states of the European Union, where the tax burden, on average, was equal to 40.6 percent of GDP.[32] Direct taxes in Latin America account for only about 25 percent of total revenue, with 60 to 80 percent of those direct taxes coming from corporate payments, while only 10 to 15 percent is paid by private individuals.[33]

The distributive effects of taxes are minimal. In a comparison of pre- and posttax income distribution, Juan Carlos Gómez-Sabaini found that the Gini coefficient increases after taxes in seven of the nine countries analyzed. The other two cases (Brazil, 2000–01, and Costa Rica, 2000) exhibited no effect.[34] In other words, Latin America's tax system is proportional at best and outright regressive at worst.

It is important to keep in mind here that tax systems in advanced industrial democracies are not progressive either. Progressive income taxes are counterbalanced by high and regressive value-added taxes, so that the total tax incidence is roughly proportional.[35] The significant redistribution documented in table 7-1 is effected on the expenditure side. Our data take into account only transfers; if we were to include public services as well, the redistributive effect would be larger, particularly in the service-heavy social democratic welfare states.

29. Gómez-Sabaini (2006, p. 16).
30. Gómez-Sabaini (2006, pp. 17–18).
31. Gómez-Sabaini (2006, p. 20).
32. Gómez-Sabaini (2006, p. 20).
33. ECLAC (1998, p. 72).
34. Gómez-Sabaini (2006, p. 32).
35. Mahler and Jesuit (2005).

Constructing and Sustaining Social Policy: Political Coalitions and Popular Support

There are several ways to think about the construction and sustainability of social policy regimes or welfare states. One is to take a historical perspective and analyze the social and political alliances that have shaped and sustained different types of social policy regimes. A second one is to look at support for social policy in public opinion polls to try and map the demand side. The limitation of this second approach is, of course, that policies that enjoy wide popular support are not necessarily legislated and implemented. A strong case in point is health insurance in the United States: For the past forty years, a majority of the American public has favored health insurance for all, yet the numbers of uninsured Americans continue to grow.[36] This leads us to look at the supply side, at politicians who make social policy an important part of their platform and at parties committing a sufficient number of representatives to these platforms to get them enacted once the elections are won.

On the supply side, there is a lot of slippage between voter demand and legislative output. The factors that intervene are the nature of the parties and the party system (consolidation of parties as organization, party discipline, number of parties), party-voter linkages (programmatic or clientelistic or charismatic), constitutional concentration or dispersion of power (presidentialism, federalism, bicameralism), and strength of interest groups. Parties that are weak organizationally and have low party discipline, party systems that are composed of a large number of parties, clientelistic or charismatic party-voter linkages, and power dispersion through federalism, presidentialism, and strong bicameralism all militate against the translation of voters' social policy preferences into legislation. Interest groups find more access points in political systems with higher power dispersion (through presidentialism, federalism, bicameralism, and the existence of referenda), and their strength is an additional factor increasing the slippage between voter demand and legislative outcomes. Such factors as weak parties with low discipline, a large number of parties, and clientelistic or charismatic linkages between parties and voters tend to be prevalent in new democracies, and these make progress on expansion of social programs difficult, even if they are desired by a majority of the population.

An additional fundamental question for this mode of analysis is whether issues such as social policy proposals decide elections. Essentially, the problem of endogeneity makes it impossible for scholars of electoral behavior to answer

---

36. In a study of U.S. public opinion, Gilens (2005) found that there is a moderately strong relationship between voter preferences and public policy outcomes. When, however, the author considered only issues in which different income groups have divergent preferences, he found that policy outcomes tend to favor the preferences of the wealthiest sectors and do not reflect the interests of the poor and middle sectors (p. 778).

the question of how much of an election outcome is due to a particular issue. As James Stimson, an authority in this field, puts it: "The discouraging fact of human attitudes is that all attitudes cause all other attitudes."[37] Partisanship and ideology predispose a voter to perceive an issue in a certain way, which leads to high correlations between party, ideology, and issue attitudes and thus introduce multicollinearity into statistical models. Instrumental variable approaches are not possible because data cannot be found that satisfy the assumptions of instruments being uncorrelated with one side of the equation. The Downsian world, in which voters have an issue position and vote for the candidate or party closest to that position, is for the most part psychologically unrealistic.[38] When preferences are weak and information imperfect, projection (the voter attributes his or her preferences to his or her preferred party and candidate) or persuasion (the voter adopts the position on an issue that is held by the candidate and party that he or she prefers for other reasons) are at least equally likely.[39]

All of these caveats are not to say that voter support for social policies does not matter—they are simply to warn against the assumption that the correct design of social policy (the one that benefits the median voter) will ensure the adoption of this policy because the candidate and party that espouse that policy will win elections. Election outcomes are shaped by a large number of factors, and for social policy to be decisive, the issue has to have huge saliency. Saliency in turn is a result of at least three factors: personal experience of voters, emphasis put on an issue by candidates and parties, and coverage given to the issue by the media. In many elections, "the economy" is said to be decisive. Indeed, opinion polls find that retrospective and prospective perceptions of the economic situation of respondents' families are important for approval of incumbents. However, again, the impact of such perceptions on voting decisions depends on what other attitudes and perceptions they are competing or combining with and thus, in part, on the intensity of the personal experience and on the intensity and diversity of the political messages with which the voter is confronted. These observations underline the importance of media influence, particularly in new democracies where parties are relatively weak at forming opinion.

37. Stimson (2007, p. 1); see also Carmines and Stimson (1986).
38. It should be noted that Downs's (1957) economic proximity voting model is highly contested and challenged by alternative models. MacDonald and Rabinowitz (1989) argued that citizens are not as sophisticated as the proximity model purports, that, in fact, voters are often unclear about exact issue positions. For this reason, MacDonald and Rabinowitz argued that voting is a *directional process.* By directional, the authors mean citizens do not stake out a precise position on any given issue, but rather voters decide which side of the issue they stand on. They then select a candidate on the basis of the direction and intensity of the position of the candidate and the party. In this way, candidates are rewarded for moving away from the center (so long as they do not exit the domain of acceptability). Any politician who moves outside of this range is punished by losing votes. The directional model, then, predicts an empty center.
39. Carsey and Layman (1999).

Even if it cannot be conclusively demonstrated that social policy issues decide elections, there is still the possibility that politicians believe it to be true and act accordingly. In particular, incumbent politicians may believe that they can ensure reelection by introducing social policies supported by a majority of voters. This may be the most realistic view, but only if the policies in question benefit large sectors of the population in a tangible way. Indeed, interpretations of the 2006 presidential election in Brazil suggest that *Bolsa Familia* was decisive in generating support for Lula (we shall return to this case below).

The impact of social policy on election outcomes becomes potentially stronger in the case of cutbacks of programs that are in place. Before something is in place, voters lack the experience of the benefits, and their preferences for or against a given social policy proposal are not as firm. Once a program is in place that benefits a majority or a politically influential (well-organized or well-financed) minority of voters in tangible ways, it becomes extremely difficult and costly in terms of political support to reduce those benefits.[40] In contrast, programs that are targeted at smaller and less politically influential groups (such as single mothers) are more vulnerable to attack. The contrast between Social Security and Aid to Families with Dependent Children in the United States illustrates this point extremely well. The many failed attempts to reform the regressive social security systems in Latin America further support the point. There have been cuts to programs that benefit majorities in advanced industrial societies, but typically only once all major parties have accepted that the existing system had become unsustainable because of long-term economic and demographic trends. To put it differently—inclusive designs of social policy are more likely to sustain themselves than to get adopted in the first place.

Still, inclusive designs have been adopted in many countries, and we now turn to an examination of the political coalitions that were successful in implementing them. The political histories of the OECD democracies that have successfully reduced poverty and redistributed income illuminate the political preconditions for such policies. From table 7-1, one can see that the Nordic countries, followed by Belgium, the Netherlands, and Germany, have been most successful in this regard. Australia does not quite make it into this group, but since the unusual structure and extensive reach of its income-tested transfers make it an interesting case for less-developed countries, we will also examine the politics of social policy development in that country.

The lesson that most clearly emerges from the experiences of these countries is that universal social policies were made possible in settings where broad cross-class alliances were established. In the Nordic countries, the first stage of the development of the modern welfare state began with the cementing of the red-

40. Pierson (1996).

green (worker–small farmer) alliances in the 1930s. Consistent with power resources theory, the now dominant theory of welfare state development in OECD countries, it was the social democrats who were the main initiators of social policy expansion.[41] However, it was their agrarian party allies who were responsible for pushing the design of transfers from the contribution-based, income-related structure covering only employees, which was favored by some unions and social democrats, toward a universalistic, flat-rate, tax-financed structure. This structure was obviously favorable to the small farmers who were the primary base of the agrarian parties. As a result, all of the Nordic countries adopted flat-rate, universalistic, tax-financed basic pensions in the decade after World War II. The same coalition passed universal health insurance in this period and began a process of educational reform that resulted in universal secondary education in comprehensive schools by the 1960s and relatively open admissions to universities a decade later.

The decline of the agrarian population and later of manual manufacturing occupations meant that the farmer-worker coalition began progressively to lose its sociological majority. In the second phase of Nordic welfare state development, the social democrats consciously attempted to forge a new wage earner coalition including blue- and white-collar employees. This involved turning from flat-rate benefits to earnings-related benefits in all of the major transfer systems, either by adding an earnings-related tier in the case of pensions or by making the earnings-related transfers the primary public program in the case of other transfers. The conscious appeal to white-collar workers can be seen in the Swedish Social Democrats' revision of their original earnings-related pension proposal in the late 1950s. To gain the support of TCO, the confederation of white-collar unions, the Social Democrats reduced the number of years of contributions required for a full pension and reduced the number of years on which the benefit was calculated, from the twenty-five best earning years to the fifteen best earning years. As one can see from a comparison of table 7-1, column 1, and table 7-2, column 1, this did not mean that the resultant structure was not redistributive. Because of minima and ceilings in the structure of benefits, public pension income is much more equally distributed than is market income among working-aged adults.

The Swedish Social Democrats' decisive victory in the 1960 election, which was attributed to their pension reform, indicated the breadth of popular support for the welfare state. The other Nordic welfare states experienced similar phenomena, and by the late 1960s, the centrist parties in all of these countries abandoned any pretense of opposition to the welfare state, which was a reflection of the underlying broad support for the welfare state across classes. The final stage of Nordic welfare state development added a new support con-

41. Stephens (1979); Korpi (1983); Huber and Stephens (2001).

stituency, women. Beginning in the 1960s in Sweden and accelerating in the 1970s and 1980s in all of the Nordic countries, the social democrats, often in alliance with the liberals as well as with left socialists greatly expanded policies, such as day care, elderly care, and parental leave, that facilitate combining work responsibilities and family commitments. These policies not only freed women to work, but the public health, education, and welfare jobs created demand for women's employment since they were filled disproportionately by women. In the case of day care, these policies had an additional, and intended, side effect: they also resulted in an improvement of the human capital base, as Nordic public day care is not simply child minding but also early childhood education.

The development of the welfare state in Germany, the Netherlands, and Belgium was complicated by the existence of large Christian democratic parties with a cross-class base and a pro–welfare state ideology rooted in Catholic social thought.[42] The coalition dynamics in Belgium and the Netherlands are different from those in Germany, but the outcomes are rather similar. In the low countries, the religious parties are centrist with secular liberals occupying the right of the political spectrum. In these two countries, coalitions of Christian democratic parties and social democrats developed during the depression (as did the red-green Nordic coalitions) and spearheaded welfare state development in the postwar period. In Germany, the center right Christian Democrats competed rather than coalesced with the Social Democrats on welfare state issues and, with Christian Democrat dominance of the government, this predictably produced very low levels of poverty but less redistribution (see table 7-1). In all three countries, the multiclass base of the Christian democrats ensured that resultant policy configurations enjoyed broad support. Indeed, the current problem in Germany and Belgium is that the welfare states, particularly the pay-as-you-go (PAYG) pension systems, are not demographically viable, but they are difficult to change because they are so popular.

Australia is interesting for developing countries because two of its principal transfer programs, pension and unemployment benefits, were income tested but not targeted at the poor. Rather, they were (and are in the case of unemployment benefits) structured to exclude upper-income groups but include middle-income groups.[43] In the case of pensions, this public system was the primary source of income for retirees. More than two-thirds of the elderly are covered in the system. The replacement rates, 31 percent of a standard production worker's income for a single retiree and 45 percent for a couple, are modest, and they are flat rate so the replacement rate declines with rising income. Benefits begin to be phased out somewhat below median income and taper off steeply. On the basis of the OECD conventional poverty line of 50 percent of the median

42. Van Kersbergen (1995).
43. Castles (1985).

income, 22 percent of Australian elderly are poor, while only 5 percent are below 40 percent of the median and fully 45 percent are below 60 percent of the median. The distributive effect of the system can clearly be seen in table 7-2. It is apparent that the system enjoyed popular support: Even during the long period of conservative government from 1949 to 1972, coverage was expanded from 40 percent to two-thirds of the elderly, while replacement rates were stable.[44] However, from the point of view of organized labor, the benefits were inadequate, so unions pushed for and received an earnings-related, funded, individual account pension plan in the 1986 round of compulsory arbitration, and the plan was subsequently expanded and made statutory by the Labor government.

The lesson that most clearly emerges from the experiences of advanced industrialized democracies is that universalistic and redistributive social policies were made possible in settings in which broad cross-class alliances including workers and farmers or blue- and white-collar workers were established (that is, urban and rural working classes and sectors of the urban middle classes). In Latin America, we find no comparable cases of universalistic welfare states. Still, we can identify more and less successful social policy regimes if we look at outcomes in the 1990s in terms of poverty, inequality, education, and health as well as at efforts in terms of sustained social expenditures from the 1970s on. On all of these indicators, by calculating averages for the 1990s on the outcome indicators and decade averages since the 1970s for effort indicators, Argentina, Chile, Costa Rica, and Uruguay emerge as comparatively successful cases.[45]

If we turn to the political conditions in the period between 1945 and 1970, when major social policy schemes were shaped, three of our four countries had by far the longest records of democratic rule. Chile and Uruguay were the leaders with 26 years, followed by Costa Rica with 25 years. Argentina with 12 lagged behind Brazil, 19; Colombia, 16; Peru, 15; and Venezuela, 14. Moreover, three of the four countries had strong left-of-center parties with significant legislative influence. In the period leading up to the 1970s, legislative strength of the Left was dominant in Uruguay, followed by Costa Rica, and then Chile. In Argentina, the situation was very different, as the Peronists were essentially banned from elections after the overthrow of Perón in 1955.

The PLN in Costa Rica dominated the legislature in 1961 when the constitutional amendment for universalization of social security was passed.[46] The Colorados inspired by reformist President José Batlle y Ordóñez (1903–07 and 1911–16) dominated in Uruguay during the early decades of the twentieth century, when the social security system was first established, and in the period

44. Huber and Stephens (2001, p. 176).
45. Huber and Stephens (2007).
46. Partido Liberción Nacional or PLN. Rosenberg (1979).

1948–54, when it was expanded and reorganized.[47] In Chile, the origins of the social security system for blue-collar workers are in the period of turmoil in 1925, when military intervention terminated the stalemate between reformist President Alessandri and the conservative congress, but significant efforts to expand coverage came in the 1960s and early 1970s in the competition between the Christian Democrats and the Left and under pressure from unions.[48] Argentina illustrates an alternative to democracy, the path to a social security system with wide coverage through populist authoritarianism and semidemocracy. The social security system was established by Perón, as part of his popular mobilization and support-building strategy, beginning in 1944 as minister of labor under the military government and extending through his democratic and then authoritarian periods as president. However, subsequently the Peronist party and the unions did become the key defenders of the system.

Essentially, then, we can identify two political paths to comparatively high social expenditures, high average educational achievement, and low poverty as of the 1970s: democracy and left-of-center party strength (Uruguay, Costa Rica, and Chile) or populism on the borderline between restricted democracy and authoritarianism (Argentina). The latter path by the 1970s did not entail the same commitment to social expenditure as the former; rather, the low levels of poverty in Argentina were explained to a larger extent than in the other three countries by high GDP per capita, low inequality, low urban unemployment, and low informal sector employment, all linked to the strength of the import substitution industrialization (ISI) thrust.

Our quantitative analyses of pooled time series data for eighteen Latin American and Caribbean countries show that these observations about the relationship between democracy and parties and social policy, poverty, and inequality are generalizable. The cumulative records of democracy and the strength of the left are negatively related to inequality and poverty, and the cumulative record of democracy is positively related to spending on social security and welfare and on health and education.[49] Social security and welfare spending is positively related to inequality, but when it takes place in a democratic context (measured with an interaction term), it is negatively related to inequality.[50] This makes sense in the light of our discussion above about the distributive profile of social security spending.

Whereas the social policy regimes in Argentina, Chile, Uruguay, and Costa Rica still produced better results at the turn of the century than other social policy regimes did in Latin America, they were all under financial pressure, and

47. Filgueira (1995); Papadópoulos (1992).
48. Borzutzky (2002, pp. 48, 97–120, 139–45).
49. Huber, Mustillo, and Stephens (2008).
50. Huber and others (2006).

their effectiveness in the first three countries had declined during this period compared with their effectiveness during the 1970s. By the early 1970s, Argentina, Chile, and Uruguay had reached comparatively high coverage in their social security systems, close to 70 percent of the economically active population in Argentina, about 75 percent in Chile, and more than 90 percent in Uruguay; whereas Costa Rica lagged far behind, with just below 40 percent.[51] Costa Rica's push for expansion began in earnest only in the 1960s. Social security schemes in all four countries covered sickness and maternity (health care and often some cash subsidy as well), pensions, employment injury, and family allowances. In Costa Rica, the bulk of the spending went to sickness and maternity, close to 80 percent, which in part reflects the fact that the pension system had not matured yet.

The reason for the wide coverage in Argentina, Chile, and Uruguay was the strength of the import substitution industrialization thrust. The prevailing form of social policy was social security, dominant in advanced industrial societies and internationally promoted by the International Labor Office. As noted, social security is tied to formal sector employment, and in those three countries, unemployment and informal sector employment were comparatively low at that point in time. These conditions deteriorated in the course of the debt crisis and the implementation of structural adjustment programs, and as a result, coverage by social security programs shrank. The military regimes in the 1970s and 1980s reduced expenditures on health and education, so that the new democratic regimes had much ground to make up. Whereas they did increase social expenditures, adaptation in the form of greater emphasis on nonemployment-based social assistance and citizenship-based access to quality health and education services was slow. The severe economic crisis, starting in 2001, in Argentina and then affecting Uruguay as well, and the election of the *Frente Amplio* (FA) government in Uruguay, propelled such adaptation efforts forward in the form of emergency employment programs in both countries and citizenship income in Uruguay.

The example of the partial erosion and reform of these comparatively most successful social policy regimes in Latin America highlights the importance of the changing class structure in the region. The Latin American class structure of the early twenty-first century is completely different from that of the OECD countries, and therefore it cannot be assumed that the median voter, or the crucial sector to be included in a majority coalition, is represented by the middle

---

51. Mesa-Lago (1994, p. 22). These figures have to be taken with some caution. In general, Mesa-Lago's figures are on the high side, because he looked at legal coverage, whereas other scholars have looked at actual contributors to social security schemes. Isuani (1985, p. 95) gave coverage for Argentina in 1970 as 68 percent and Chile as 69 percent and Papadópoulos (1992, pp. 55ff) for Uruguay as somewhat more than 80 percent. Still, the figures give a reasonable picture of the relative position of these countries.

Figure 7-5. *Share of the Population That Earns below the Average Income and below Half of Average Income, 1990–99*

Percent

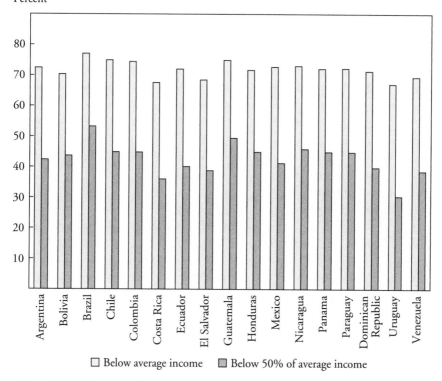

☐ Below average income   ■ Below 50% of average income

Source: ECLAC (2001, p. 71).

sectors, conceptualized as average income earners. This assumption does not hold because of the high levels of income inequality and informal employment in the region. It is well known that Latin America is one of the most unequal regions in the world, but an often overlooked consequence of this fact is that high income inequality makes it difficult, if not impossible, to identify the median voter on the sole basis of income level. As illustrated by figure 7-5, mean salaries in the region are well above the median for all countries for which data were available in the period 1990–99. In fact, in most of the countries, around 40 percent of the population does not even earn *half* of the national average.[52] In other words, if we assume that voting preferences track closely with one's income level, it is clear that Latin America's median voter does not belong to the middle-income sectors but rather to the lower-income group.

52. ECLAC (2001, p. 71).

To arrive at a judgment regarding possible political alliances, we need to go beyond mere income levels to begin with. Reading off political preferences from income levels is a rather asociological and ahistorical way of thinking. First, classes as potential political actors need to be delineated, and second, the construction of class interests needs to be analyzed. Classes are made up of "people who by virtue of what they possess are compelled to engage in the same activities if they want to make the best use of their endowments," and their boundaries are defined by social interaction and mobility.[53] Within class boundaries, social interaction and social mobility are easy and typical; across class boundaries, they are rare and difficult. Thus we need to begin with the occupational profile of individuals who fall into the different income sectors in an attempt to understand which groups form social classes and could potentially be mobilized in support of social programs.

The Latin American class categories distinguished by Alejandro Portes and Kelly Hoffman are rooted in a sociological view.[54] The authors distinguished between the informal proletariat (urban and rural), the formal proletariat (manual and lower nonmanual), the petty bourgeoisie, and the dominant classes (professionals, executives, and capitalists). A comparison of Latin America's class structure with that of the OECD reveals that, yet again, the lessons learned in OECD countries are difficult to apply in the region because the traditional class categories of blue- and white-collar workers are small in Latin America. Instead, informal (urban and rural) workers constitute the largest occupational category in the region. Portes and Hoffman estimated that, on average, 45.9 percent of the region's workers operate in the informal sector and are—in their formulation—part of the informal proletariat.[55] The flip side of this statistic is that the more traditional categories of manual labor or nonmanual white-collar workers make up a small share of the occupational structure, just 23.4 percent and 12.4 percent, respectively. A similar conclusion regarding the size of the lowest categories emerges from ECLAC's comparative analysis of Brazil, Colombia, Costa Rica, El Salvador, Mexico, Panama, and Venezuela. The study found that occupational categories in the region can be divided, on the basis of the income they generate, into three fairly homogenous groups: lower, intermediate, and higher, with the higher category covering just 9 percent of the population. The intermediate sector, meanwhile, groups 14 percent of the population, while 75 percent of working-aged individuals fall into lower-income occupational categories.[56]

53. Elster (1985, pp. 330–31).
54. Portes and Hoffman (2003).
55. Portes and Hoffman (2003, pp. 46–49).
56. ECLAC (1999, p. 61). Additionally, Sémbler (2006) found that since the mid-1990s there has been a growing polarization within Latin America's small middle class. The author contends that there has been a distancing between winners and losers, which has resulted in a segmented and weakened middle sector (p. 58).

Figure 7-6. *Brazil's Class Structure in 2000*

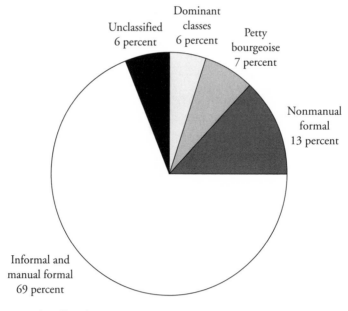

Source: Portes and Hoffman (2003, p. 52).

In other words, the median voter in most countries is found within the informal sector (urban and rural) and manual working class category. As illustrated in figures 7-6, 7-7, 7-8, and 7-9, the relative size of distinct class groups is fairly similar across Latin American countries, regardless of the level of economic development. Indeed, the informal and manual (formal) working class sectors of society make up more than 60 percent of the working-aged population, while the (sociologically defined) middle sectors—the nonmanual formal sector and the petty bourgeoisie—account for about 20 to 25 percent of the working-aged population. Therefore, the challenge for policymakers interested in building a majority coalition (or appealing to the median voter) is to enact programs that respond to the risks faced by informal sector workers and formal manual laborers. Put differently, the challenge for politicians interested in effective social policy is to craft appeals to these groups that raise the saliency of the benefits of universalistic social policies.

If Allan Meltzer and Scott Richard's theory of redistribution were correct, such a coalition should emerge easily in the Latin American setting because of the high levels of income inequality that exist in the region. Meltzer and Richard argued that the larger the ratio of mean to median income, the greater is the incentive for the median voter to demand redistribution, and thus the larger is the size of government.[57] A consideration of empirical facts in the

57. Meltzer and Richard (1981).

Figure 7-7. *Mexico's Class Structure in 2000*

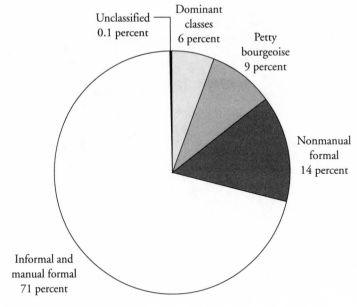

Source: Portes and Hoffman (2003, p. 52).

Figure 7-8. *El Salvador's Class Structure in 2000*

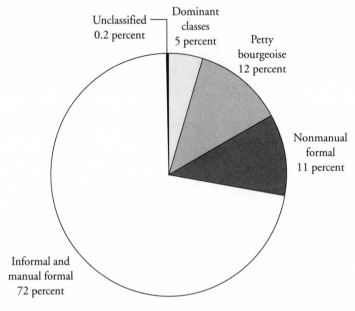

Source: Portes and Hoffman (2003, p. 52).

Figure 7-9. *Chile's Class Structure in 2000*

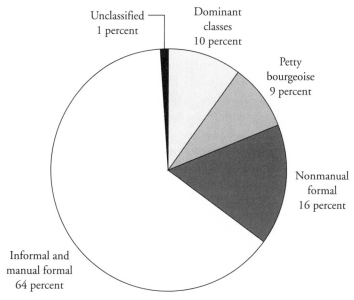

Source: Portes and Hoffman (2003, p. 52).

countries across the region reveals just how erroneous this assumption is. Even if these demands were articulated, our discussion above highlighted just how much slippage there is between voter demands (even majority voter demands), elections, and policy output. In contemporary Latin America, high levels of income inequality serve to undermine rather than strengthen attempts to even articulate demands for redistribution.

We are not the first to disagree with Meltzer and Richard's theory. Although the authors found empirical support for their hypothesis using time series data for the United States, other scholars have refuted the argument, and yet others have found that the exact opposite is true: that high inequality leads to less redistribution.[58] A final body of research has worked to stipulate the conditions under which the Meltzer and Richard theory holds.[59] Certainly, as demonstrated in table 7-1, in the OECD countries, the greatest reduction of income inequality through the tax and transfer system occurs in the social democratic welfare states, where income inequality is lowest to begin with.[60] This is the case

58. Meltzer and Richard (1983); Perotti (1996); Bassett, Burkett, and Putterman (1999); Persson (1995); Bénabou (2000).

59. Borge and Rattsø (2004).

60. Bradley and others (2003, p. 210).

because in societies where high levels of income inequality exist, the relative power of the median voter is low compared with the political power of the middle and upper sectors, and therefore, effective demands for redistribution are weak.

As noted by Jacob Hacker and Paul Pierson, modern day politics is not simply about the relationship between politicians and voters, but it also involves the connection between interest groups and policymakers.[61] Increasingly, politicians rely on funding from such organizations to run campaigns, and thus the policy demands of these groups are hard to ignore. Moreover, as policy issues become more complex, interest groups are better able to stay informed and, therefore, are more effective at pressuring politicians.

In Latin America, the role and profile of organized interests have changed rather dramatically in the past few decades. Beginning in the 1970s, the composition of interest groups began to shift, as blue-collar unions, peasant leagues, and rural workers' organizations declined, while public sector unions and business organizations increased their power share. With the wave of privatizations and free trade agreements that were negotiated during the 1980s and 1990s, the formal sector working class and its organizations declined further, while the private sector developed its political experience and clout. Judith Teichman argues that business groups during this period consolidated special links to the policy-making process, while "such links for other groups, such as labor, rural workers, small farmers, and small business, are either weak or absent, raising the specter that policy formulation will likely ignore the interests of these groups."[62] In other words, while the median voter in most Latin American states works in the informal or manual formal sector and earns an income below the national average, the median interest group appears to represent upper-income sectors. Since politicians face incentives to balance the demands of individual voters and interest groups, this means that an analysis of coalition building must look beyond the individual median voter to include organized interests.

Other aspects of Latin American politics also contribute to skew the distribution of power in favor of elite sectors over the median voter. In particular, the power of wealthy individuals has been strengthened by the region's poor regulations on campaign finance. While many countries in Latin America have introduced legislation on campaign finance since the 1990s, limits on private funding remain comparatively weak.[63] The country that places the greatest limit on individual campaign donations is Argentina, which allows donors to contribute up to 1 percent of the full amount raised by a party. In Bolivia and Ecuador, by contrast, that limit is set at 10 percent of the total.[64] Countries

61. Hacker and Pierson (2007, p. 19).
62. Teichman (2001, p. 8).
63. Speck (2004, p. 32).
64. Speck (2004, p. 33).

vary in how they set caps on donations. While Costa Rica allows donations equal to forty-five times the monthly minimum wage, Paraguay limits that amount to six times the minimum salary.[65] There is also significant diversity in the enforcement of these laws, as some states require information to be made public, while other countries do not require parties to publish details about their financing.[66]

Yet another issue that strengthens the voice of elite sectors in Latin America is the concentration of media ownership. As noted by the Carter Center, the majority of mass media outlets are weakly regulated and are commercial (that is, they operate for profit). As a result, these media conglomerates stand to profit from elections, and perhaps unsurprisingly, the cost of advertising has grown in recent years.[67] Consequently, wealthy candidates (or candidates who have access to significant sources of private funding) enjoy an advantage. Additionally, it is likely that the impact of media concentration is felt far beyond the electoral period and influences agenda setting and framing of policy issues on a day-to-day basis. The power of the media to structure the political playing field has profound effects on the role of the median voter.

The obstacles to the construction of effective social policy regimes in Latin America, then, are formidable. However, this is not to say that the adoption of basic universalism is impossible in Latin America. In fact, recent developments such as the success of Brazil's *Bolsa Familia* program and popular support for Chile's 2004 AUGE health care reform provide evidence of how policies that provide effective protection to the poor can simultaneously enjoy high levels of political sustainability.

In an analysis of the 2006 Brazilian presidential elections, Wendy Hunter and Timothy Power found that the *Bolsa Familia* program, a policy of conditional cash transfers created by the administration of Luiz Inácio Lula da Silva, was crucial for the president's reelection. Specifically, the authors found that at the state level, voting for the incumbent president correlated at 0.621 with the coverage of families in *Bolsa Familia*.[68] It appears that the policy even allowed Lula's Workers' Party (PT) to make inroads in regions that had previously been controlled by oligarchic families. Additionally, and of particular interest in light of the previous discussion about the waning power of the median voter, *Bolsa Familia* appears to have increased voter turnout. In an analysis of turnout in the second round of the 2006 election, the authors found that the share of families receiving *Bolsa* benefits was a better predictor of voting levels than whether the state had a gubernatorial runoff. Based on this analysis, Hunter and Power

65. Speck (2004, p. 33).
66. Speck (2004, p. 35).
67. Carter Center, "Political Finance in the Americas: Mapping the Media," p.1.
68. Hunter and Power (2007, p. 20).

concluded that the political support for *Bolsa Familia* is so widespread that "like social security in the United States or the National Health Service in Britain, the *Bolsa Familia* may indeed become the third rail of Brazilian politics, a political totem that self-styled reformers can touch only at their own peril."[69] In other words, the adoption of *Bolsa Familia,* a policy in the line of those promoted by basic universalism may have generated a strong support base and thus may serve as a crucial case study for understanding how policies that are effective at protecting the poor can be made politically sustainable in the Latin American context.

This still leaves us with the question of how such policies come to be implemented to begin with, given the relative weakness of organizations representing the interests of the bottom three quintiles of income earners. The answer has to be sought in party politics; that is, the prime agents for the implementation of inclusive and redistributive social policy regimes are political parties with a commitment to solidarity and equity. The evidence for the importance of such parties in partnership with labor movements in the construction of welfare states in Europe is conclusive.[70] Even for Latin America, despite the comparative weakness of parties, there is evidence that in the long run, incumbency of left-of-center parties reduces poverty and inequality.[71]

In Latin America at the beginning of the twenty-first century, left-of-center parties in Brazil, Chile, and Uruguay have been at the forefront of pushing social policy toward basic universalism. They have been the central actors in emphasizing the importance of social policy and demonstrating that high poverty and inequality are not immutable conditions but subject to modification through policy. Further progress in this task requires appealing to the informal sector and blue-collar workers with programs that improve universalistic public primary and secondary education and health care. It is very clear that members of both sectors have a great interest in an improvement of these services. Severing the link between formal sector employment and transfer payments and strengthening social assistance, essential parts of a successful strategy, require a gradual and differentiated approach, because formal blue-collar workers have a stake in the social security systems and can potentially be mobilized by more privileged sectors in defense of these systems. One feasible approach is to maintain a basic public tier with flat-rate benefits and gradually reduce the difference between those benefits and social assistance. Finally, at least in the short-to-medium run, the means-tested conditional cash transfer (CCT) programs will have an important role to play in dealing with acute poverty and human capital deficits.

69. Hunter and Power (2007, p. 24).
70. For example, Hicks (1999); Huber and Stephens (2001).
71. Pribble, Huber, and Stephens (forthcoming); Huber and others (2008).

As we noted, it may be difficult for parties to win elections on the basis of promises for improved social policy, but once voters experience improved social policies, it may well help parties get reelected. Thus it may take courage and vision for parties to "rock the boat" by pushing for implementation of effective social policies and for securing their financing, even in the absence of intense articulation of demands for such policies. This is easier to do for programmatic and disciplined left-of-center parties than for nonprogrammatic catchall parties. Donors, of course, can encourage incumbents to adopt certain kinds of social policy that then are likely to generate their own support constituencies.

Conclusion

On the basis of the lessons from advanced industrial democracies, as modified for Latin America (and other middle-income less developed countries with similar structural conditions and historical legacies), what would a politically sustainable, effective redistributive social policy regime look like? First, it bears reiterating that the median income earner in Latin America does not belong to the sociologically defined middle class. Rather, well over 60 percent of the population belongs to the urban and rural lower classes and the urban formal sector working class. If we include formal sector white-collar workers, the sociological lower and middle-middle classes (that is, excluding the upper-middle class of professionals and managerial employees), we arrive at 80 percent of the population. To include formal sector white-collar employees, benefits would have to be extended to the 80th percentile. Depending on the benefits, they could be extended in full or in a declining fashion. Including formal sector white-collar employees in the benefits would greatly strengthen the political support base because this category includes public sector employees, such as teachers and nurses, who tend to be well organized and vocal. One can easily identify a trade-off here between a more expensive social policy regime with an ironclad political support base made up of the lower and working classes with sectors of the middle class and a less expensive social policy regime with a 60 percent (or more) support base made up of the lower and working classes.

A politically sustainable, effective redistributive social policy regime, then, would consist of basic flat-rate family allowances paid to the lower 60 percent of income earners and slowly faded out between the 60th and 80th percentile. The allowances could be structured as CCTs, which are tied to compliance with school attendance and medical checkups for the children. Furthermore, they should be tied to job training for unemployed recipients and integration into public sector jobs. The policy regime would include basic flat-rate citizenship pensions for the same income categories (similar to the original Australian system), supplemented by a mandatory public earnings–related notional defined contribution system for the entire population. It further would include investment in public preschool and in free high-quality public primary and secondary education, as well as a unified public health care system with free access for the lowest three quintiles and an income-related fee structure for the other two quintiles. If all of this is financed by proportional taxation, it will be massively redistributive, as demonstrated by the case of Chile in appendix table 7A-1. This is true even if the benefits accruing to the second and third quintile are somewhat higher than those for the first quintile, and even if benefits reach into the fourth quintile on a declining basis.

Because such policies would unite the interests of the poor with those of the working class and the middle class of formal sector white-collar employees, the coalition supporting the maintenance of the programs would wield significant political power and stability. Still, the evidence we have presented in this chapter related to public opinion, vote choice, and policy formation suggests that creating such programs is not an easy task. Since it is unclear whether issues such as promises of social policy innovation influence electoral outcomes and whether factors such as campaign finance, the media, and interest groups strongly shape the behavior of politicians and parties, creating such programs can be extremely challenging. Our evidence suggests, however, that once policies such as a flat-rate family allowance, a citizenship pension, and inclusive systems of public education and health care are enacted, they will enjoy tremendous sustainability. The strong political support of *Bolsa Familia* in Brazil, Plan AUGE in Chile, and Uruguay's public preschool system is evidence of the strength of social policies that unite the bottom and middle of the income distribution. In the case of *Bolsa Familia,* the program is targeted at the poor and does not include the sociological middle class, but in some areas, the poor are so numerous that a ripple effect is being felt throughout their communities. In the cases of AUGE and Uruguay's preschool system, these benefits reach into the middle class.

At present, the upper two quintiles, that is, the upper and upper-middle classes (and even sectors of the middle and lower-middle classes) in most Latin American countries have opted out of the public education and health systems, so investment in these services will by necessity benefit the first three quintiles. In the longer run, however, if investment in public education and health services improves these services, it is reasonable to assume that at least the fourth quintile (60 to 80 percent) of income earners would return to the public systems. This then would further strengthen the political support base for high-quality public services, as white-collar workers would gain a stake in state-provided education and health. The key, then, is to build social programs that are effective at reaching the poor but that do not become "poor people's programs" because they entail basic rights to transfers and quality social services for lower, working, and lower-middle classes.

References

Bassett, William F, John P. Burkett, and Louis Putterman. 1999. "Income Distribution, Government Transfers, and the Problem of Unequal Influence." *European Journal of Political Economy* 15, no. 2: 207–28.

Bénabou, Roland. 2000. "Unequal Societies: Income Distribution and the Social Contract." *American Economic Review* 90, no. 1: 96–129.

Borge, Lars-Erik, and J. Jørn Rattsø. 2002. "Income Distribution and Tax Structure: Empirical Test of the Meltzer-Richard Hypothesis." *European Economic Review* 48, no. 4: 805–26.

Borzutzky, Silvia. 2002. *Vital Connections: Politics, Social Security, and Inequality in Chile.* University of Notre Dame Press.

Bradley, David, and others. 2003. "Distribution and Redistribution in Postindustrial Democracies." *World Politics* 55, no. 2: 193–228.

Carmines, Edward G., and James Stimson. 1986. "The Structure and Sequence of Issue Evolution." *American Political Science Review* 80, no. 3: 901–20.

Carsey, Thomas, and Geoffrey Layman. 1999. "A Dynamic Model of Political Change among Party Activists." *Political Behavior* 21, no. 1: 17–41.

Carter Center. n.d. "Political Finance in the Americas: Mapping the Media." Atlanta (www.cartercenter.org/documents/2291.pdf).

Castles, Francis G. 1985. *The Working Class and Welfare.* Sydney: Allen and Unwin.

Downs, Anthony. 1957. *An Economic Theory of Democracy.* New York: Harper and Row.

ECLAC (Economic Commission for Latin America and the Caribbean). 1998. *The Fiscal Covenant: Strengths, Weaknesses, Challenges.* Santiago: United Nations.

———. 1999. *Social Panorama of Latin America 1999–2000.* Santiago: United Nations.

———. 2001. *Social Panorama of Latin America 2000–2001.* Santiago: United Nations.

———. 2005. *Panorama Social de América Latina, 2005.* Santiago: United Nations.

Elster, Jon. 1985. *Making Sense of Marx.* Cambridge University Press.

Esping-Andersen, Gøsta. 1990. *The Three Worlds of Welfare Capitalism.* Princeton University Press.

Filgueira, Fernando. 1995. "A Century of Social Welfare in Uruguay: Growth to the Limit of the Batllista Social State." Public Policies for Social Justice Series 5. University of Notre Dame, Helen Kellogg Institute for International Studies.

Filgueira, Fernando, and others. 2006. "Universalismo básico: una alternativo possible y necesaria para mejorar las condiciones de vida." In *Universalismo básico. Una nueva política social para América Latina,* edited by Carlos Gerardo Molina. Washington: Inter-American Development Bank.

Gilens, Martin. 2005. "Inequality and Democratic Responsiveness." *Public Opinion Quarterly* 69, no. 5: 778–96.

Gómez-Sabaini, Juan Carlos. 2006. "Cohesión social, equidad y tributación. Análisis y perspectivas para América Latina." Serie Políticas Sociales 127. Santiago: United Nations Economic Commission for Latin America and the Caribbean.

Hacker, Jacob S., and Paul Pierson. 2007. "Winner-Take-All Politics: Organizations, Policy, and the New American Political Economy." Paper presented at the annual meeting of the American Political Science Association. Chicago, August 30–September 1.

Hicks, Alexander. 1999. *Social Democracy and Welfare Capitalism.* Cornell University Press.

Huber, Evelyne. 2006. "Un nuevo enfoque para la seguridad social en la region." In *Universalismo básico. Una nueva política social para América Latina,* edited by Carlos Gerardo Molina. Washington: Inter-American Development Bank.

Huber, Evelyne, Thomas Mustillo, and John D. Stephens. 2008. "Politics and Social Spending in Latin America." *Journal of Politics* 70, no. 2: 420–36.

Huber, Evelyne, and others. 2006. "Politics and Inequality in Latin America and the Caribbean." *American Sociological Review* 71, no. 6: 943–63.

Huber, Evelyne, and John D. Stephens. 2001. *Development and Crisis of the Welfare State: Parties and Policies in Global Markets.* University of Chicago Press.

———. 2007. "Successful Social Policy Regimes? Political Economy, Politics, and the Structure of Social Policy in Argentina, Chile, Uruguay, and Costa Rica." Paper presented at the meeting of the Latin American Studies Association. Montreal, Canada, September 6–8.

Huber, Evelyne, and others. 2008. "Social Policy in Latin America and the Caribbean Dataset 1960–2006." Chapel Hill: University of North Carolina, Department of Political Science (www.unc.edu/~jdsteph/common/data-common.html).

Hunter, Wendy, and Timothy J. Power. 2007. "Rewarding Lula: Executive Power, Social Policy, and the Brazilian Elections of 2006." *Latin American Politics and Society* 49, no. 1: 1–30.

Isuani, Ernesto Aldo. 1985. "Social Security and Public Assistance." In *The Crisis of Social Security and Health Care: Latin American Experiences and Lessons,* edited by Carmelo Mesa-Lago. Latin American Monograph and Document Series 9. University of Pittsburgh, Center for Latin American Studies.

———. 2006. "Importancia y posibilidades del ingreso ciudadano." In *Universalismo básico. Una nueva política social para América Latina,* edited by Carlos Gerardo Molina. Washington: Inter-American Development Bank.

Kangas, Olli, and Joakim Palme. 1993. "Statism Eroded? Labor-Market Benefits and Challenges to the Scandinavian Welfare States." In *Welfare Trends in the Scandinavian Countries,* edited by Erik Jørgen Hansen and others. Armonk, N.Y.: M. E. Sharpe.

Korpi, Walter. 1983. *The Democratic Class Struggle.* London: Routledge and Kegan Paul.

Korpi, Walter, and Joakim Palme. 1998. "The Strategy of Equality and the Paradox of Redistribution." *American Sociological Review* 63, no. 5: 661–87.

Lindert, Kathy, Emmanuel Skoufias, and Joseph Shapiro. 2006. *Redistributing Income to the Poor and the Rich: Public Transfers in Latin America and the Caribbean.* Washington: World Bank.

MacDonald, Stuart, and George Rabinowitz. 1989. "A Directional Theory of Issue Voting." *American Political Science Review* 83, no. 1: 93–121.

Mahler, Vincent, and David Jesuit. 2005. "Fiscal Redistribution in Developed Countries." Working Paper. Luxembourg Income Study.

Medici, André. 2006. "Políticas y acceso universal a servicios de salud." In *Universalismo básico. Una nueva política social para América Latina,* edited by Carlos Gerardo Molina. Washington: Inter-American Development Bank.

Mehrtens, F. John. 2004. "Three Worlds of Public Opinion? Values, Variation, and the Effect on Social Policy." *International Journal of Public Opinion Research* 16, no. 2: 115–43.

Meltzer, Allan H., and Scott F. Richard. 1981. "A Rational Theory of the Size of Government." *Journal of Political Economy* 89, no. 5: 914–27.

———. 1983. "Test of a Rational Theory of the Size of Government." *Public Choice* 41, no. 3: 403–18.

Mesa-Lago, Carmelo. 1994. *Changing Social Security in Latin America: Toward Alleviating the Social Costs of Economic Reform.* Boulder, Colo.: Lynne Rienner Publishers.

Moller, Stephanie, and others. 2003. "Determinants of Relative Poverty in Advanced Capitalist Democracies." *American Sociological Review* 68, no. 1: 22–51.

Papadópoulos, Jorge. 1992. *Seguridad social y política en el Uruguay.* Montevideo: Centro de Informaciones y Estudios del Uruguay.

Perotti, Roberto. 1996. "Growth, Income Distribution, and Democracy: What the Data Say." *Journal of Economic Growth* 1, no. 2: 149–87.

Persson, Mats. 1995. "Why Are Taxes So High in Egalitarian Societies?" *Scandinavian Journal of Economics* 97, no. 4: 569–80.

Pierson, Paul. 1996. "The New Politics of the Welfare State." *World Politics* 48, no. 2: 143–79.

Portes, Alejandro, and Kelly Hoffman. 2003. "Latin American Class Structures: Their Composition and Change during the Neoliberal Era." *Latin American Research Review* 38, no. 1: 41–82.

Pribble, Jennifer, Evelyne Huber, and John D. Stephens. Forthcoming. "The Politics of Poverty in Latin America." *Comparative Politics.*

Rosenberg, Mark. 1979. "Social Security Policymaking in Costa Rica: A Research Report." *Latin American Research Review* 15, no. 1: 116–33.

Sémbler, Camilo R. 2006. "Estratificación social y clases sociales. Una revisión analítica de los sectores medios." Serie Políticas Sociales 125. Santiago: United Nations Economic Commission for Latin America and the Caribbean.

Speck, Bruno Wilhelm. 2004. "Campaign Finance Reform: Is Latin America on the Road to Transparency?" In *Global Corruption Report 2004,* pp. 32–35. Berlin: Transparency International (www.transparency.org/publications/gcr/download_gcr/download_gcr_ 2004).

Stephens, John D. 1979. *The Transition from Capitalism to Socialism.* London: Macmillan.

Stimson, James. 2007. "Assessing Issue Impact on Election Outcomes." Memo. Chapel Hill: University of North Carolina, Department of Political Science.

Teichman, Judith. 2001. *The Politics of Freeing Markets in Latin America.* University of North Carolina Press.

Uthoff, Andras. 2006. "Brecha del Estado de Bienestar y reformas a los sistemas de pensiones en América Latina y el Caribe." Serie Políticas Sociales 117. Santiago: United Nations Economic Commission for Latin America and the Caribbean.

Van Kersbergen, Kees. 1995. *Social Capitalism.* London: Routledge.

Villatoro, Pablo S. 2004. "Programas de reducción de la pobreza en América Latina. Un análisis de cinco experiencias." Serie Políticas Sociales 87. Santiago: United Nations Economic Commission for Latin America and the Caribbean.

Table 7A-1. *Actual Income Distribution in Chile in 2000*

	Percent	
Top quintile	60.5	
Fourth quintile	17.7	
Third quintile	10.9	
Second quintile	7.0	
First quintile	3.7	
Assume a proportional tax of 20 percent		
Top quintile	12.10	(0.2×60.5)
Fourth quintile	3.54	(0.2×17.7)
Third quintile	2.18	(0.2×10.9)
Second quintile	1.40	(0.2×7.0)
First quintile	0.74	(0.2×3.7)
Add a flat rate benefit (transfers and services) to after-tax income		
Top quintile	52.40	$60.5 - 12.1 = 48.4 + 4$
Fourth quintile	18.16	$17.7 - 3.54 = 14.16 + 4$
Third quintile	12.72	$10.9 - 2.18 = 8.72 + 4$
Second quintile	9.60	$7.0 - 1.4 = 5.6 + 4$
First quintile	6.96	$3.7 - 0.74 = 2.96 + 4$
Assume that the bottom three deciles receive all of the benefits		
Top quintile	48.40	$60.5 - 12.1 = 48.4 + 0$
Fourth quintile	14.16	$17.7 - 3.54 = 14.16 + 0$
Third quintile	15.42	$10.9 - 2.18 = 8.72 + 6.7$
Second quintile	12.30	$7.0 - 1.4 = 5.6 + 6.7$
First quintile	9.66	$3.7 - 0.74 = 2.96 + 6.7$
Assume that the bottom quintile uses some services, such as secondary education, less than the next quintiles, and that some benefits accrue to the fourth quintile		
Top quintile	48.40	$60.5 - 12.1 = 48.4 + 0$
Fourth quintile	17.16	$17.7 - 3.54 = 14.16 + 3$
Third quintile	14.72	$10.9 - 2.18 = 8.72 + 6$
Second quintile	11.60	$7.0 - 1.4 = 5.6 + 6$
First quintile	7.96	$3.7 - 0.74 = 2.96 + 5$

Contributors

MAURIZIO BUSSOLO is a senior economist at the World Bank. He works on quantitative analyses of economic policy, trade policy, development, and growth. His recent research includes macroeconomic modeling of the evolution of global income distribution.

JAMES DAVIES is a professor in the Department of Economics at the University of Western Ontario. His research focuses on the global distribution of personal wealth, the design of tax policies, the distributional effects of tax policies, and inequality measurement.

ANTONIO ESTACHE holds the Bernard Van Ommeslaghe chair in the Economics Department of the Université Libre de Bruxelles (ULB). He is also a member of ECARES (European Center for Advanced Research in Economics and Statistics) at ULB. His current research focuses on fiscal incidence analysis, regulation, procurement policy, and impact evaluation.

RAFAEL E. DE HOYOS is currently the chief of advisers to the under-minister of education in Mexico. Before joining the Mexican government, Rafael was a researcher at the World Bank's Development Prospects Group and a fellow at the Judge Business School at the University of Cambridge.

MARKUS GOLDSTEIN is a senior economist at the World Bank. He has taught at the University of Ghana, the London School of Economics, and Georgetown University. He works on the delivery and financing of social services.

CAROL GRAHAM is senior fellow and Charles Robinson Chair at the Brookings Institution and College Park Professor at the University of Maryland at College Park. She works on market reforms, poverty, and happiness economics.

EVELYNE HUBER is Morehead Alumni Professor and chair of the Department of Political Science at the University of North Carolina at Chapel Hill. She has worked on a wide range of political economy issues, including in-depth analysis of welfare systems.

DANNY LEIPZIGER is vice president of the Poverty Reduction and Economic Management Network of the World Bank and vice chair of the Commission on Growth and Development. His research has focused on a wide range of public policy issues including development, finance, and infrastructure and industrial policies. He is a frequent commentator on global economic issues.

DENIS MEDVEDEV is an economist with the World Bank. He works on general equilibrium and microsimulation modeling tools to inform and motivate policy discussions with governments, notably in sub-Saharan Africa.

JENNIFER PRIBBLE is an assistant professor of political science at the University of Richmond. Her research focuses on Latin American political economy, social policy reform, and gender-related welfare policies.

ANDRÉS SOLIMANO is regional advisor at the United Nations Economic Commission for Latin America and the Caribbean. His research covers a wide range of policy issues including inequality, labor market reforms, international migration and remittances, the political economy of reform, key growth and stabilization policies, and globalization.

JOHN D. STEPHENS is Gerhard E. Lenski, Jr., Distinguished Professor of Political Science and Sociology and director of the Center for European Studies at the University of North Carolina at Chapel Hill. His main research interests are comparative politics and political economy, with a focus on Europe and the Caribbean.

Index

HJ 192.5 .S78 2009

Stuck in the middle

DATE DUE
